This is number one hundred and seventy-one
in the second numbered series
of the Miegunyah Volumes
made possible by the Miegunyah Fund
established by bequests under the wills of
Sir Russell and Lady Grimwade.

'Miegunyah' was the home of
Mab and Russell Grimwade
from 1911 to 1955.

Mark McKenna is one of Australia's leading historians. His most recent book, *An Eye for Eternity: The life of Manning Clark* (MUP) won five national awards. He is also the author of *Looking for Blackfellas' Point: An Australian History of Place* (UNSW Press), which won the Book of the Year and the Douglas Stewart Prize for Non-Fiction in the 2003 NSW Premier's Literary Awards. McKenna's essays, reviews and political commentary have appeared in *The Monthly, Meanjin, ABR, The Sydney Morning Herald, The Age* and *The Australian*.

—————————————

'McKenna's telling of early frontier stories captures the multiplicity of perspectives and meanings present in our continent's complex past. His story is anchored in the landscape and brought alive through a rich sense of place. The account that unfolds is one of invasion and conflict, but also of reconciliation; it is a rediscovery of history which offers possibilities of national understanding and rebirth.'

Noel Pearson

'With characteristic brilliance Mark McKenna wrenches neglected or unknown histories from the edges of our continent and our consciousness to create entirely new national landscapes. McKenna transmutes these forgotten stories into the purest gold. This is a book that will haunt your memory and ignite your dreams of what Australia once was and might yet become.'

Iain McCalman

FROM THE EDGE

Australia's Lost Histories

MARK McKENNA

THE
MIEGUNYAH
PRESS

THE MIEGUNYAH PRESS
An imprint of Melbourne University Publishing Limited
Level 1, 715 Swanston Street, Carlton, Victoria 3053, Australia
mup-info@unimelb.edu.au
www.mup.com.au

First published 2016
Text and photographs unless stated © Mark McKenna, 2016
Design and typography © Melbourne University Publishing Limited, 2016

Aboriginal and Torres Strait Islander people are respectfully advised that
photographs of deceased people appear in this book and may cause distress.

Every attempt has been made to locate the copyright holders for material
quoted in this book. Any person or organisation that may have been
overlooked or misattributed may contact the publisher.

Cover design by John Canty Design
Typeset in Bembo 11.5/15pt by Cannon Typesetting
Printed in China by 1010 Printing International Ltd

National Library of Australia Cataloguing-in-Publication entry

McKenna, Mark, 1959– author.

From the edge: Australia's lost histories/Mark McKenna.

9780522862591 (paperback)
9780522862607 (ebook)
First contact of aboriginal peoples with Westerners—Australia.
Shipwreck survival—Australia—History.
Aboriginal Australians—First contact with Europeans.
Australia—History

994.02

Australian Government

Australian Research Council

This research was supported under Australian Research Council's Future
Fellowships Scheme.

For Fiona, Siobhan and Claire McKenna

Contents

'No single story can ever explain itself: this enigma at the heart of story is itself a story. Stories produce offspring, genetic splinters of themselves, hapless embodiments of their original inability to tell the whole tale.'

James Wood
The Nearest Thing to Life

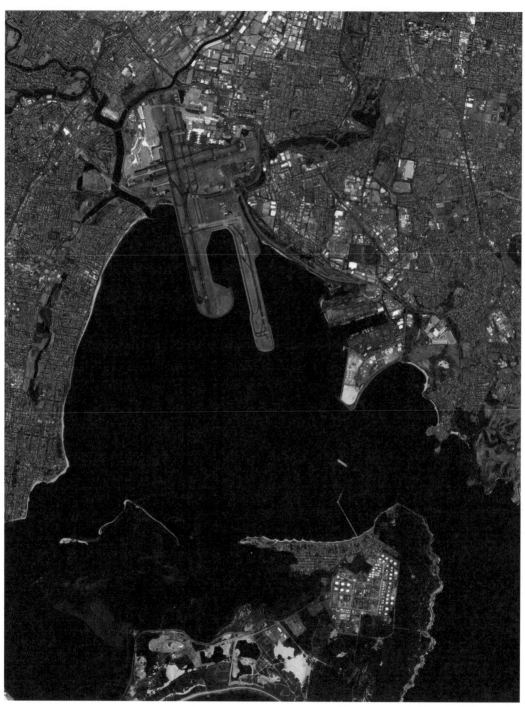

Satellite image of Botany Bay, New South Wales, 2004, Jesse Allen, Digital Globe

Eyeing the Country

THE VIEW THROUGH the departure lounge windows at Sydney Airport looks across the docking bays to runways in the near distance. The flat expanse of the tarmac shimmers in the heat. Bare and uncluttered, placeless and free, this wide-open road seems to stretch all the way to the horizon.

Airports do not give up their history easily. Like the 40 million people who passed through Sydney Airport in 2015, we move quickly through these limbos of arrival and departure on our way to the places that matter with little thought for what was there before the sea of asphalt was laid down. The past is buried beneath a landscape that has been reshaped so dramatically, it bears little resemblance to its original state in the late eighteenth century; in the case of Sydney Airport—a stream dammed, a river diverted, a harbour dredged and land reclaimed—wetlands have become runways.

Interred beneath the runways and the sea are the sites of some of the first encounters between Indigenous Australians and British marines and convicts; places where they approached one another with 'emotions of pleasure, astonishment, curiosity & timidity'—exchanging gifts and gestures of introduction, touching hair, skin and clothes—each searching tentatively for proof of the other's humanity. As the planes take off to the south, they climb over Kamay, otherwise known as Botany Bay. Here, in April 1770, Joseph Banks, naturalist on board James Cook's *Endeavour*, marvelled at the night-time vista on the water, when the bay was illuminated by the 'moving lights' of the tiny cooking fires burning on flat stones in the bellies of the Gweagal women's bark canoes.[1]

Entering Botany Bay on an almost windless, blue-sky day, Banks and Cook noticed a thin column of smoke rising into the air. From the deck of the *Endeavour*, they directed their 'glasses' towards the southern shore where they saw 'about 10 people' who left their fires as the ship approached and 'retired' to a more elevated point to observe their visitors from a safer distance. Cook soon hoisted the boats out with the intention of landing. As the *Endeavour* stood offshore, Banks lifted his telescope to observe the country and its people at closer quarters. Since he had left England almost two years earlier, 'perhaps for Ever', this had always been his first way of seeing the places and people he encountered: the telescopic eye. Standing on deck, little more than a kilometre offshore, Banks spied a group of Gweagal men gathered 'on the rocks opposite the ship, threatening and menacing with their pikes and swords'. With a telescope that provided magnification fifteen to twenty times greater than the naked eye, he could easily make out the 'broad strokes' of white paint that covered their bodies. The bold patterns over their 'breasts and backs' reminded him of soldiers' 'cross belts'. He could see them 'distinctly': they were naked, their faces dusted over with the same white paint, the white tips of their spears glistening in the sun. Later, two men disputed the visitors' right to land, 'waving' them 'to be gone', before several rounds of musket fire and the wounding of at least one Gweagal man finally forced them to retreat.[2]

From the moment Banks first saw Aboriginal people through his telescope a few days earlier at Murramarang Point, some three hundred kilometres south of present-day Sydney, he doubted the truth of what his 'glasses' revealed to him. Struck as he was by the remarkable clarity of the air and light in 'this southern hemisphere', he discerned five 'people' on the beach who appeared through his 'glasses ... to be enormously black'. He wondered if William Dampier's adverse description of the 'Indians' whom he had met on Australia's west coast almost a century earlier had influenced what he now believed he saw through his telescope. 'So far did the prejudices which we had built on Dampier's account influence us that we fancied we could see their

Colour when we could scarce distinguish whether or not they were men'.[3] When he finally came ashore on the southern shores of Botany Bay, Banks spat on his finger and rubbed the dirt-covered skin of one Gweagal man to see whether his blackness could not be washed away.[4]

The telescope was 'the first instrument to extend one of the human senses'. The main scientific objective of Cook's first Pacific voyage—observing the transit of Venus in 1769—was carried out with the aid of a mounted, reflecting telescope. Five years before the *Endeavour* set sail from England, the development of a new hand-held, achromatic telescope, which used three glass elements instead of two, reduced the distortion associated with earlier designs. The result was a portable device with far greater resolution, one that produced an image that was no longer blurred by a coloured fringe.[5] 'Spyglasses', 'opera glasses' and telescopes of all kinds were all the rage in late eighteenth-century London, enabling a way of seeing that allowed both intimacy and distance.[6]

When Banks and Cook came ashore at Botany Bay the watchers became the watched. Walking through the bush and coming upon the campsites of Aboriginal people, Banks was surprised to find them deserted. Little did he realise that they were scrutinising his party's every move. Nor could he understand how they perceived him. Aboriginal oral history of Cook's landing, told originally by Kurnell woman Biddy Coolman in the 1840s and recorded in 1905, remembered the violence of the encounter. 'They all run away: two fellows stand; Cook shot them in the legs; and they run away too!' When Aboriginal people first saw the sailors climbing 'up the masts' of the *Endeavour* they thought they were possums. The ship appeared to them like a 'floating island'. Believing as they did in a power greater than themselves—'something over them'—they saw the white men as 'the devil', a malevolent ancestor returned from the dead.[7] All of these things were naturally lost to those on board the *Endeavour*. Their view was radically different.

As Banks looked through his telescope at Botany Bay, the faces and bodies of Aboriginal men and women filled the frame, like museum exhibits in a glass case. The country was scanned and quickly assessed for its utility. The gaze was at once authoritative and acquisitive, empirical and scientific, one that placed itself above both 'natives' and nature. The telescope allowed Banks to spy the personal features of the Gweagal on shore without any obligation of human contact on his part, and to survey the land without setting foot on it. The same technology that had allowed him to see the soprano's facial expressions at the opera he attended in London shortly before his departure from Plymouth in August 1768, now allowed him to see Aboriginal people on the beaches of 'New Holland'.[8]

In 1790, when Governor Arthur Phillip had established a settlement of marines and convicts at Sydney Cove after quickly deciding to abandon Botany Bay in 1788, British telescopes were turned in the opposite direction. Desperate for the arrival of further supplies and craving 'intercourse with civilized society', Lieutenant Colonel Watkin Tench described an observation post that was constructed on South Head at Port Jackson. There, 'on the summit of the hill, every morning from daylight until the sun sunk', they lifted their telescopes, searching every speck on the waves of the 'vast' Pacific Ocean in the hope of sighting a ship from England. The telescopes that the British had turned initially on the land of their 'discovery' soon became instruments of longing: their most trusted means of disproving the mirages of both land and sea in a country that so often deceived their senses.[9]

In late 2014, I visited Kamay Botany Bay National Park. Standing close to the spot where Cook's party forced their way ashore at Kurnell, I looked north across the water towards the airport, watching as the planes took off in quick succession above me. Below them a parade of massive container ships were being towed out to sea. At that moment I thought of Banks out on the bay—one eye closed, his other flush against the eyepiece as he searched the shoreline—and I saw for the first time how his telescopic eye was the precursor to our contemporary way of seeing the country. The telescope, much like the camera and Google Earth, zooms in and isolates the object of vision. It allows us to see in fine detail what is within the frame, at the same time as it disconnects that detail from its surroundings and cuts off our peripheral vision.

As Banks's telescopic eye saw the land and its people as objects of scientific study, so our satellite eye further shatters the boundaries of time and place and allows us to command places into view without soiling our feet. We can see everything without going anywhere. And we compartmentalise places: some for leisure, some for conservation, some for plundering and profit, some for nation-making and some simply to tick off as 'done'. Like Joseph Banks's 'glasses', our all-seeing satellite eye can 'deceive us in many things'.[10]

'We saw, indeed, only the sea coast', reflected Banks, 'what the immense tract of inland country may produce is to us totally unknown'.[11] As soon as the *Endeavour* was anchored in Botany Bay in April 1770, the Australian continent was linked to Europe and the British imperial world. Like the destinations of the planes banking above me at Kurnell, those links were global but also highly selective. In linking our coastal fringe with the wider world, we have skirted around the edge or flown over much of the continent, establishing connections with some places and completely ignoring others. Our global networks and economies throw a vast shadow over the places, people and histories that do not concern them. Our view is at once all encompassing and blinkered. Too often, we fail to ask: what lies outside the frame? What places and histories lie beyond our angle of vision?

Australians think they know their history. But the truth is that much of it remains unknown. Our colonial perspective is just beginning to recede. We have only recently discovered the richness and mystery of our Indigenous histories and cultures and the extraordinary regional diversity that so much of our nation-making and popular history making has unintentionally worked to disguise. Since the demise in the 1960s of the idea of Australia as a 'British' society, we have tried, sometimes desperately, to agree on an alternative national narrative. Eternally preoccupied with questions of national identity and formation—Where and when was the nation born? How has the nation performed on the 'world stage'? What is uniquely Australian?— we have failed to embed our national story in the histories on our own soil. This is nothing less than a failure of our historical imagination.

Delivering a public lecture in London in 2013, novelist Tim Winton lamented the extent to which 'Australia the place is constantly overshadowed by Australia the national idea, Australia the economic enterprise'. In our rush to anchor the nation with a binding national history, whether that be Anzac Day, Federation, immigration or economic prosperity, we have lost sight of the 'specifics of place', of the geographical, cultural and historical diversity that constitute Australia 'the place'.[12]

Only when we shift our gaze beyond the Sydney–Melbourne–Canberra axis to the north, centre and far west of the continent, to the 'out there', the 'middle of nowhere', the back country and the Indigenous heartland, do we begin to understand the truly distinctive nature of our histories and patterns of belonging over time. Our view needs to be at once broader and more intimate. Imagine a map of Australia without state and territory borders, one that revealed the different 'countries' within the nation—Arnhem Land, Kakadu, the Kimberley, the Pilbara, the Mallee, the Monaro, Central Australia, and so the list goes on—one that was a meeting point between our Indigenous 'Countries' and the overlay of regional associations that have come in the wake of European settlement: a map of shared country. To understand place is to understand perspective, a particular way of seeing and being in the world, uniquely shaped by geography, climate, economy, culture and nature. Perhaps we would understand Australia differently—its craving for a foundational history that will inspire and unify the nation, its alienated federal democracy, its boom and bust economy and its hardline attitude to asylum seekers—if we started from the ground up, from the local and the regional perspective.[13]

Few of us today will live and die in one place. We move from one suburb, town or city to another, sometimes several times in our lives. Our attachment to place—refracted through personal experience and shards of memory—is individual, varied and multi-layered. A street corner, a city park, a backyard, the memory of a childhood home, the once-glimpsed view from a hill overlooking Florence, a farm paddock or a desert drive; all of these memories of place can imprint themselves indelibly on our hearts and minds. We belong where we feel at home. Yet in our ever-increasing mobility, there is a patent dilemma. 'One of modernity's most distinctive tensions', writes Robert Macfarlane, is 'between mobility and displacement on the one hand, and dwelling and belonging on the other—with the former becoming ubiquitous and the latter becoming lost (if ever it had been possible) and reconfigured as nostalgia'.[14] While we travel to seek the culturally authentic and the different, the economic forces that drive globalisation simultaneously work to break these differences down. The cities of Sydney and Melbourne have more in common with London and New York than they do with Broome, Alice Springs or Darwin. Yet in the face of the irrepressible forces of globalisation, the survival of cultural difference and the particular inflections of place take on even greater importance. Place and, more specifically, the *qualities* of place, are not merely villages, towns and cities, they are also paths and roads, deserts and forests, rivers and oceans, light and colour, sound and space as well as the fictive and intangible—places that are invented, remembered, sometimes not even visited save in our imaginations.

xvii

Imagine the country from the outside. For many visitors from overseas, the 'real' Australia is not the suburbs and cities. It is where the points of difference from the rest of the industrialised world can still be found: the 'outback' and the bush, those places that bear little or no resemblance to urban environments the world over. As the British novelist Will Self told an Australian audience in 2015, it is the 'physical reality' of the country that astonishes him, its Indigenous cultures and 'the tyranny of distance that white Australian culture is always trying to defeat'.[15] Leaving Australia to live overseas, as I have done on several occasions, the 'physical reality' of Australia slowly rises to the surface—the sensory dimensions of place that can sometimes only be fully understood by leaving the country behind—the overwhelming intensity of light and colour and the vast, resounding spaces of an island continent that can momentarily still homesickness when felt and remembered from far away.

At the heart of Australian history is an ongoing drama of epic proportions; the encounter between the cultures of one of the world's most ancient people and the cultures of Britain and post-industrial

Europe, and the millions of migrants from over 140 nations who have followed in their wake. An encounter that began with mutual fascination and curiosity and quickly turned to suspicion, animosity and open warfare in the nineteenth and early twentieth centuries, before Aboriginal people miraculously survived state and federal government policies designed to ensure their cultural annihilation, and finally established their human and cultural rights. Australia has only recently freed itself from the shackles of racism (the White Australia Policy was not dismantled until the 1960s and then only in piecemeal fashion), just as it has only recently begun to incorporate Indigenous knowledge of 'Country'—a term that expresses both the human and the natural worlds, livelihood, culture, belonging and spirituality— into the national imagination. One of the great, unknown questions of Australia's future is whether Australia's Indigenous and non-Indigenous cultures will ever come together in a shared, profound understanding of the continent. The encounter that began in 1770 at Botany Bay is still being worked through. But at least one thing is clear: it is impossible to conceive of any place that is not embedded with Indigenous story. There are no empty places in Australia.

'Of all the systems that are expressions of who a people are, the sharpest and clearest is their historical consciousness', wrote the late historian Greg Dening.[16] Historical consciousness—the remembering of the past and its resonance in Australia today—lies at the heart of this book. The Indigenous history that was destined for extinction at the time of Federation in 1901 ultimately came to unsettle the moral legitimacy of the Commonwealth. The gradual surfacing of the very history that had allegedly been 'vanquished' would come to represent the most significant shift in historical consciousness in twentieth-century Australia. For non-Indigenous Australians, this would prove to be a slow and traumatic realisation. As two generations of historians have shown, there was no history of Australia that was non-Indigenous.[17] From the moment of first contact, settler history became part of Indigenous history and Indigenous history became part of settler history. 'The songlines of the women of central Australia', as Indigenous leader Noel Pearson so eloquently expressed, 'are also the heritage of non-Aboriginal Australians. It is this culture that is the Iliad and Odyssey of Australia. It is these mythic stories that are Australia's Book of Genesis'.[18] In recent years, Australia has seen the history of relations between Indigenous and non-Indigenous people through the prism of mourning, shame and atonement. There has been an understandable need to 'acknowledge' the injustices and mistreatment of the past, and 'move on'. If there is a danger, it is that in seeking to 'move on' from stories of violent dispossession and decimation of culture we will once again turn away from our colonial past. 'Moving on' should not be code for forgetting. As I try to show in the pages that follow, it is only by returning to this history and grounding it in 'the specifics of place' that we can reveal the true depth, richness and complexity of Australia's foundation.[19]

From the Edge begins with the story of the walk of seventeen men along the coast of south-east Australia in the late eighteenth century. Although I have known about this story for nearly twenty years, I have long wanted to write the story at walking pace; to slow down the action and understand the true nature of the epic journey that these men undertook. While their ordeal has been presented in potted form and memorialised locally, it has never been told with close attention to the landscape through which they moved, nor to the Aboriginal people and cultures they encountered along the way. They walked 700 kilometres through territory unexplored by Europeans long before the nation was imagined, a time when Australia was already *founded* as a complex mosaic of Indigenous Countries. Remarkably, one of Australia's greatest survival stories and cross-cultural encounters has remained largely untold since 1797.

Founding stories from the littoral edge of the Australian frontier— Port Essington on the Cobourg Peninsula in West Arnhem Land, the Burrup Peninsula in the Pilbara and Cooktown in far north Queensland—are the focus of the chapters that follow. Like the story of the walk along the coast, I was drawn to these places in particular because I slowly came to see that their histories had profound national resonance. Yet like so many other places across the Australian continent, their histories—both on the edge of the continent and on the edge of national consciousness—have yet to seep into our national mythology. Port Essington, the site of a short-lived 'new Singapore' in the mid-nineteenth century and yet another failed attempt to establish a British presence in Australia's north, is one of Australia's most revealing examples of how the frontier encounter changed Europeans as much, perhaps even more, as it changed Aboriginal people. On the Burrup Peninsula, home to both Australia's largest development project (the North West Shelf Gas Project) and the world's most significant and ancient collection of rock art, the region's Indigenous history and rich cultural heritage has been largely obscured by the rush to extract every last ounce of profit from the land and sea. At Cooktown—where James Cook stayed for seven weeks in 1770 while repairing the *Endeavour*, and a brief gold rush 100 years later resulted in one of the most sudden, intense and violent clashes on the Australian frontier—Aboriginal elders and local historians have transformed the town's history through their shared telling of the meeting between James Cook and the Guugu Yimithirr in 1770. In different ways, each of these histories of place positions the encounter between Aboriginal and non-Aboriginal Australians—each irrevocably altered by the other—at the heart of the nation's creation.

Before I began this odyssey, I thought I knew Australia. But researching and writing this book I have discovered how much I still have to learn. To know the intricacies of any place—its flora and fauna, its soil and geology, its rivers and oceans, its topography and climate, its ways and stories—takes more than a lifetime. Indigenous knowledge of the continent has been built incrementally over thousands of generations. Intimate knowledge of place comes not from 'seeing' but from the steady accrual of knowledge and stories over time. The myriad places and histories of Australia are inexhaustible. The country that we long perceived as a 'land without history' is one of the most deeply storied countries on earth. This book seeks out four of those stories in the familiar and forgotten places of Australia. It begins by way of walking. The year is 1797.

CHAPTER ONE

Walking the Edge:
South-East Australia, 1797

T HE WILDNESS IS ancient and humbling. Seen from offshore, the island barely rises above sea level, a lonely outcrop of monumental granite and low-lying, windswept scrub that lies in a treacherous body of water off Australia's south-east coast. On a clear day, when the white shallows appear beneath a translucent sea, it's possible to imagine Preservation Island and the entire Furneaux Archipelago for what it is: the remains of the land bridge that once joined Tasmania to the Australian mainland some ten thousand years ago.

Preservation Island,
Bass Strait, 2013

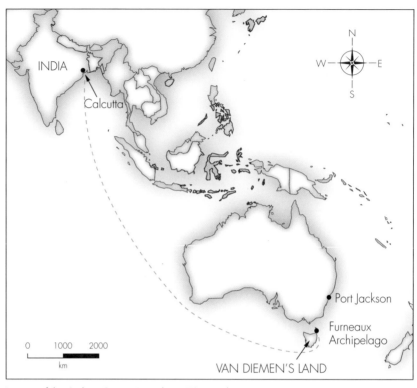

Journey of the *Sydney Cove*, November 1796 – February 1797

In November 2013, I came to this remote island off Tasmania's north-east coast in search of a remarkable story of human endurance. After the wreck of the merchant ship the *Sydney Cove* in February 1797, this tiny island in Bass Strait—little more than three kilometres long and one kilometre wide—became the site of the first European settlement south of Sydney. Few Australians are aware of the story that unfolded from Preservation Island and even fewer are aware of its true significance.[1]

The first overlanders in Australia to pass through extensive stretches of Aboriginal Country have been largely forgotten. These men experienced the most sustained contact with Aboriginal people in the early colonial period beyond Sydney. Between March and May 1797, they traversed 700 kilometres of Australia's south-east coastline, meeting and sometimes camping with Aboriginal people from at least eight distinct language groups between northern Victoria and Sydney.

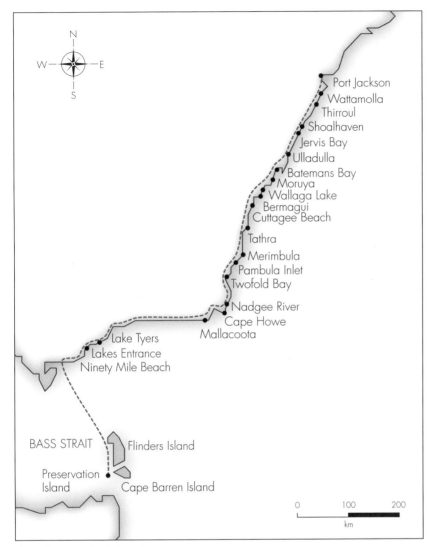

The walk north, March–May 1797

Although the progress of their journey was recorded, sometimes in graphic detail, they were not funded by the state or charged with the duty of scientific discovery. In fact, most of them were not even European. The great majority of them were Bengali seamen, otherwise known at the time as 'Lascars'.[2]

For sixty-two days, five British seamen and twelve Lascars walked through what they saw as a nameless landscape.[3] Aside from the sprinkling of place names bestowed by James Cook from the deck of the *Endeavour* in 1770—Point Hicks, Cape Howe, Mount Dromedary, Batemans Bay, Pigeon House, Botany Bay and Port Jackson—they had no other signposts to guide them. Indeed, many of the places they left behind them remained unnamed by Europeans until figures such as George Bass and Matthew Flinders followed in their wake. In any case, they had no authority to name. They were not explorers. They moved through the landscape not to discover but to escape, not for adventure but because of misadventure. And although they walked further on Australian soil than any non-Aboriginal person had walked before them, they remain today much as they appeared to the Aboriginal people they encountered along the way—apparitions, wayfarers who have yet to walk into history.[4]

William Clark was twenty-seven when he left his hometown of Campbeltown in the Scottish highlands for Calcutta in 1796. Born into a merchant family, he quickly learnt that the sea was his escape route from this secluded port on the southern end of the Kintyre Peninsula. In the mid- to late eighteenth century, Campbeltown's prosperity rested largely on its herring industry, blazing malt whisky and mediocre coal. In little less than fifty years it had expanded from an insignificant fishing town into a thriving port with a population of over five thousand. Nestled at the head of the loch and surrounded by the nearby islands of Arran, Islay and Jura, the crescent-shaped town that circled the bay owed its livelihood to shipowners and merchants such as Clark, Campbell & Co. who had traded there from at least the early 1790s. The merchants' ships plied the west coasts of England and Scotland and the north-east coast of Ireland only 19 kilometres away, but they also sailed further afield to Scandinavia, Germany, France, Holland, the Americas and the West Indies. As the ever-expanding trade networks of the British Empire opened up new markets in British North America and large parts of Asia, the Scottish economy boomed and its diaspora intensified. By the late eighteenth century, Campbeltown had benefited enormously from this swelling global traffic and became a popular disembarkation point for emigrants from the Scottish Highlands to North America. There were days when well over a hundred ships stood in Campbeltown's harbour, the din of their creaking timbers, the gulls' cries, and a thousand sailors' voices echoing around the bay.

For the merchant, life at sea could easily promise more than life on the land. Poverty was still rife in the highlands in the late eighteenth century and life for most people was frugal and brutally short. Life expectancy was less than forty years. William Clark's merchant father, William Clark senior, died in 1778 when he was in his mid-thirties. His mother, Margaret, lived only a little longer into her early forties. She had given birth to thirteen children in all, eight to William Clark senior, only three of whom survived to adulthood, and five to her second husband, of whom only two survived her death in 1788. By the time William was nineteen he had lost several brothers and sisters and both parents. Already working in his father's shipping company, he was destined for life as a merchant. Not long after his mother's death, William's elder brother, John, left to trade with Robert and John Campbell in Calcutta. Encouraged by his brother's success and lured like so many Scots before him by the flourishing opportunities abroad, William quickly followed in John's footsteps. If his future were secure in Campbeltown, it would prove to be far more fragile abroad. With the prospect of greater wealth came greater risk. But risk was calculated differently in the 1790s. Life was a more tenuous and uncertain proposition. In their restless search for knowledge, adventure and profit, generations of British emigrants left their homeland for years at a time, never certain that they would see their families again. Leaving his sister Anna and two half-sisters behind him in Campbeltown, William had no inkling that within little more than twelve months he would be sailing to the infant British penal colony at Port Jackson (Sydney) more than sixteen thousand kilometres away.[5]

When William arrived in Calcutta in 1796, the imperial city was on the cusp of a period of rapid expansion that would begin in earnest in 1798 with the appointment of the extravagant Marquess Wellesley as Governor-General. A centre of trade since the late seventeenth century when it was little more than a collection of mud huts, Calcutta had quickly taken on a grand appearance even before it became the capital of British India in 1772. The Dutch and the Danes also maintained their settlements at Chinsurah and Serampore only a few kilometres away from the British settlement at Fort William, which stood in 'the middle of the town, on the river's edge'. Fuelled by the enormous profits made by the East India Company's monopoly trade in textiles, salt and opium, much of the city's development was unplanned and haphazard. In the eyes of one new English resident entering the city at the time, it appeared 'as if all the buildings had been thrown up in the air and stood now as they had fallen to the ground'. After sailing more than one hundred and sixty kilometres along the Hooghly River towards Calcutta, a breathtaking scene greeted Clark as he approached the British settlement that spread for 5 kilometres around the fort. As the river widened and turned 'suddenly to the north', a 'stately forest of masts, vessels [and the] immense bustle of commercial business' came into view. The banks of the river were 'studded with elegant mansions'. Esplanade Row, which fronted the fort, appeared dream-like, 'composed almost entirely of palaces'. These magnificent, 'lofty, detached flat-roofed mansions', with their elegant 'flights of steps leading up to the entrance[s] and colonnades', formed the heart of the 'White Town', the bastion of neoclassical splendour and British privilege, which stood in stark contrast to the 'Black Town' where the Bengalis lived in 'low, small', hastily erected one-storey, thatch-roofed bamboo huts crowded into 'narrow and crooked' streets. Into this mesmerising city of wealth, squalor and poverty built on the exploitation of the local population, Clark had come to join the growing band of private traders and profiteers that had proliferated since the partial breakup of the East India Company's monopoly and the British government's assumption of responsibility for the colony in 1784. Like his brother John, he had come to Calcutta to make his fortune.[6]

Disembarking, William made his way from Fort William along 'the Course', the wide dust-ridden promenade where almost everyone in Calcutta walked in late afternoons to seek relief from the suffocating humidity that engulfed the city during the height of the wet season, before working his way down to Theatre Street, where European plays had been staged for over twenty years in the theatre built by Governor Hastings in 1775. Situated directly behind the fort, not far from Park Street Cemetery, the agency offices of Campbell & Clark in Theatre Street were established in 1790 in the very heart of the White Town. Robert Campbell and his older brother John were in partnership with John Clark when William arrived. Despite the intensely competitive market that existed in British India, these two families of typically industrious, educated Scots, already connected through their families' business associations at home, did not take long to display their commercial acumen. Not content with a shipping agency and their wharves and warehouses near the fort, they also owned a 6-acre rum distillery site, which by the time of William's arrival was producing close to 10000 gallons of spirits every month. Imported wine, beer and spirits were the agency's stock-in-trade. There was high demand for alcoholic beverages from East India Company associates and employees in India and they found markets in the Dutch East Indies, China, Manila and Brunei, often trading spirits for tea, spices, sandalwood and textiles. Typically, an advertisement for their firm appeared in the *Calcutta Gazette* on 27 October 1796, not long after William's arrival: 'Messrs [Robert] Campbell and [William] Clark, [Merchants of Theatre St, Calcutta] Selling Madeira Wine, English Claret, Old red Port, Coniac [sic] Brandy, Jamaica Rum, Holland's Gin and Pale Ale'.[7]

Campbell and Clark were country traders—independent merchants under licence, operating separately from the British East India Company—and they were constantly on the lookout for new markets, particularly in the Pacific and South China seas. In May 1796, an opportunity arose that would ultimately change the course of both William Clark and Robert Campbell's lives. One of the agency's clients, Captain James Storey, who had just returned from New South Wales with the *Sovereign*, informed them of the enormous potential for trade with the penal colony at Port Jackson. Storey no doubt explained the illicit rum trade fostered by the New South Wales Corps and the colony's desperate need for goods and supplies, one that could obviously be satisfied much more quickly from India than from England. Despite the initial intention of the Colonial Office that the convict colony would not trade with the East India

Company's settlements, the advantages of a trade nexus with India and China were recognised almost from the colony's inception and the restrictions were relaxed. By May 1792, the East India Company was providing convict transports as part of its trade between Britain, India and China, while several ships in the 1790s had already left from Bengal and Bombay to supply Port Jackson. Robert Campbell, who was by far the most experienced of the agency's partners, having traded in Calcutta since 1787, immediately seized on Storey's intelligence and began his search for a ship and crew that could sail for Sydney. This was not so much a trade venture as a sales opportunity. Sydney in 1796 was hardly in a position to fill Campbell and Clark's ship on its return voyage with goods in exchange. Nor was there any explicit request from the colony. In the long term, however, if they could make this first venture a success, the prospects for future trade with the fast-growing colony were promising. Eager to capitalise on the opportunity, they wasted little time.[8]

Within a few months, Robert Campbell and William Clark had found a suitable vessel, the *Begun Shaw*, a recently repaired, 30-metre, 'two-decked, three masted' country trader captained by another intrepid Scot, Gavin Hamilton. Expecting this would be the first of many voyages to Sydney, they decided to re-christen the ship *Sydney Cove*. Hamilton was born on the small island of Arran, barely twenty kilometres across the water from William and John Clark in Campbeltown, and had moved to Glasgow as a young man to make his career at sea. In his late thirties, he was already an experienced commander, having sailed trading vessels from port to port in India and west to the Persian Gulf for nearly a decade. The *Sydney Cove* venture was very much a family affair: three Scottish highlanders who had joined forces in Calcutta with the expectation of making a handsome profit by establishing a permanent trade connection with the colony at Port Jackson.[9]

By November 1796, Hamilton, Campbell and Clark had appointed the ship's crew and assembled its heady cargo: including well over one hundred casks of rum, 'Pipes' of Madeira wine and cases of beer, champagne, gin and brandy; barrels of tar, chests of Chinese porcelain, textiles, tea, tobacco, soap, vinegar, candles, bags of rice and sugar, several horses and cattle, one buggy and one organ. It was a ship-ment guaranteed to deliver sweet music to the marines and convicts at Sydney Cove. At twenty-seven, William Clark was entrusted with the position of 'supercargo'. Assisted by his Bengali 'man-servant', he was responsible for all the goods on board. Hamilton chose Hugh Thompson as his first mate together with second mate Leisham, seamen John Bennet and two other Europeans, several of whom had probably served under his command before. The bulk of the crew comprised forty-four Lascars, who were given 'blankets' in preparation for their first experience in southern oceans. Both Muslim and Hindu, Lascars were often recruited from Sylhet, a region in the north-east of Bengal, and contracted through a middleman who then appointed an overseer to manage them for the duration of the voyage. Perceived as compliant and 'industrious', they received less than half the wage of European sailors, an inequality sanctioned by the British government. Barefoot, and wearing their 'loose drawers made of white cotton, a white frock or jacket, and ... turbans', they were the backbone of British trade in India, 'Burma, China, the Malay archipelago and East Africa, as well as Britain'.

On 10 November 1796, with their Lascar underlings in tow, Gavin Hamilton and William Clark set sail from Calcutta bound for Sydney. After negotiating the notorious sandbanks and fast-rising tides along the Hooghly River, their ark of alcoholic delights and assorted luxuries would have to sail 12000 kilometres to its namesake, Sydney Cove.[10]

Although Hamilton was an experienced navigator, he had never overseen such a long-distance journey before, and the *Sydney Cove* was far from freshly minted. With a pocket marine chronometer to calculate his longitude, a sextant to indicate his latitude, and a logline and sand-glass to tell his speed, Hamilton would have to rely on Dutch maps and Cook's chart of the east coast of Australia. Because 'square-rigged ships' like the *Sydney Cove* sailed 'best with the wind behind them', he needed to look for the most 'favourable routes'. Hamilton left Calcutta in the north-east monsoon season, sailing south with the prevailing winds, down the Bay of Bengal and across the equator, until he hit the roaring forties and turned east, then crossing the Indian Ocean towards the south-west coast of Australia. He would round the south-west corner of the continent and cross the Great Australian Bight, sailing east until he reached the west coast of Tasmania, which his maps indicated was still attached to the mainland. Finally, after rounding Tasmania's southern coast, he could head north along the east coast to Sydney. Hamilton would need all his experience, the full cooperation of his crew and a fair share of luck.[11]

Four weeks out from Calcutta, already well south of the equator on the eastern fringe of the Indian Ocean, yet still more than a thousand kilometres from the west coast of Australia, Hamilton encountered the first of several setbacks. A 'severe' south-easterly gale and a 'tremendous sea' saw the ship 'labour so much as to make water at the rate of six Inches per hour'. For the next four days, leaking from the starboard bow, the ship struggled under its storm sails against the sea's fury. Forced to use both pumps to remove the water that he could hear pouring in yet was unable to reach because the leak was behind a large 'timber', Hamilton tried in vain to stem the water's flow. 'Strong gales and heavy seas' continued to batter the *Sydney Cove* until 30 December. When they finally eased, he attempted to use the sail he had prepared for 'fothering the ship'. This desperate measure involved stuffing the hole with a sail sewn together with other materials, then positioning it with great difficulty over the starboard bow and hoping that the water pressure would then force the sail into the hole and if not stop the leak, at least moderate it to a manageable level. Somehow, they succeeded in getting this makeshift cork into position but that same night, it was 'torn to pieces by the heavy pitching of the ship'. Still 'making six inches of water per hour' the crew managed to drag the remains of the sail back on board. Two weeks later, on 16 January 1797, Hamilton finally succeeded in plugging the hole, 'which reduced the leak to four inches of water per hour'. By this time many of the Lascars were already close to exhaustion.

The *Sydney Cove* rounded the south-west coast of Australia on 25 January and met 'a perfect hurricane' from the south-west. Taken by surprise, Hamilton immediately 'handed the top sails in'. Leisham was the unlucky man chosen for the task. In a raging storm, while four others assisted him on the yard, he climbed up the rigging and out along the yardarm with his feet on the ratlines and his body bent over the timber yard as he tried to pull up the sail and bunch it against the yardarm. His job was to tie the sail off, thereby reducing the area exposed to wind and decreasing the sail's propensity to heel the ship over and cause it to broach. As the ship rolled and pitched in the gale, the motion was magnified several times over for Leisham high above. His hands numb from the freezing wind, his eyes barely focusing in the dark, he struggled with the stiff canvas sail, which was wet, heavy and flapping violently. In one terrifying moment, as the *Sydney Cove* plummeted yet again in the huge seas, Leisham lost his grip and fell from the 'Main Top Sail Yard Arm'. Hamilton was so preoccupied with saving the ship that he was unable to rescue him. Leisham drowned within minutes.

Still, the tempest showed no sign of abating. With the sea 'running dreadfully high', the topsail 'in rags', and the 'mizzen top sail' and driver 'blown to pieces', the leak continued to worsen. Hamilton ordered the Lascars to man the pumps on deck but they had reached the limits of their exertion. 'The weather was intensely cold with hard rain which so frightened the Lascars that they absolutely refused to touch the pumps'. Hamilton tried to convince them of the urgency of the situation to no avail. He resorted to 'force' but still they refused. He could see that they were 'benumbed and frightened'. So he ordered all but the sick on deck and 'secured the hatches'. There was now over a metre of water in the pump well and Hamilton was forced to compromise. He insisted they bail the water out directly from the well below, which at least meant they were sheltered from the worst of the weather. They agreed and with 'much good will', bailed throughout the night, managing to keep the water level below the point of no return. The next morning, the 'gale still blowing with the utmost fury', the ship was under intense strain. Hamilton was forced to keep all hands bailing and pumping into the second night. But within the space of the next five hours, he lost five of his crew. In their 'sick and weakly state', battered by the 'severity of the weather', they had 'drop't down Dead at the Pumps'. With no time for formalities, their bodies were thrown overboard. The gale subsided the following morning just in time to allow Hamilton to get 'a new Fore Sail Bent' and put the ship 'in a little better order'. He sailed on, the westerly winds pushing him along the bight towards Tasmania. Yet after all they had endured, their final ordeal was still to come.

On 27 January, Hamilton succeeded in placing a new 'piece of canvas over the starboard bow where the leak was' but still the water came in at the rate of 'eight inches per hour' with a 'constant heavy sea running' until the *Sydney Cove* 'rounded Van Diemen's Land' five days later. By 4 February, they had passed Maria Island, which had been marked on Tobias Furneaux's chart of Tasmania's east coast during Cook's second journey in 1773. These waters could be treacherous in normal conditions, let alone in gale-force winds with a leaking ship manned by an ailing crew. After sailing under great difficulty for thousands of kilometres, Hamilton was now only a few hundred kilometres from his destination. But at 3 p.m. on 8 February, approximately one hundred and fifty kilometres east of Cape Barren Island, tossed again in heavy seas, the ship sprang such a serious leak that Hamilton, after consulting his carpenter and his chief mate, Thompson, was left with only one alternative. Their pumps could not keep pace with the inrushing water. If they were to 'save the lives of the crew' then he had to 'bear up for the Land' and manoeuvre the ship into a sheltered position before he could have any hope of fixing the leak.

Forty kilometres to the west of Cape Barren Island, with all men, both 'sick and well', either 'employed at the pumps or bailing', Thompson urged Hamilton to throw their bags of sugar and heavy bales and boxes overboard, but the water continued to pour in at such a rate that by 8 p.m. there was over one and a half metres of water in the well. Pushed in by roaring south-easterlies, the ship was foundering fast. At midnight the water had reached the 'lower deck hatches' and Hamilton finally sighted land at 'two miles distance'. In the darkness, he could make out the 'high perpendicular rocks' with the 'heavy surf breaking upon them'. To avoid 'instant destruction' he hove the ship to until morning, re-positioning the sails as the ship performed yet another lumbering dance until it finally ceased sailing, further stressing the hull and making the leak even worse. By daybreak the *Sydney Cove* was lying on its side. Spotting 'an opening in the land', Hamilton did his best to bring her 'head around' and made all the sail he could towards a 'small island' but the ship would hardly respond because she was almost completely waterlogged. The horses in between decks were up to their knees in water. Aware the ship was about to go down, Hamilton sent the longboat on shore with rice, ammunition and firearms. Only a matter of minutes after the longboat left, the ship struck a sandbar in 6 metres of water. As soon as the longboat returned he landed the sickly part of the crew while others followed the next day. The *Sydney Cove* had reached its final resting place nearly five hundred nautical miles from Sydney. Hamilton, Clark, Thompson and their exhausted crew found themselves standing on the uninhabited, isolated patch of earth that would later be named in memory of their experience—Preservation Island—the damaged longboat or a passing ship their only hope of salvation.[12]

On the morning of 9 February 1797, Hamilton and Clark surveyed the scene. They had passed through a narrow channel and were stranded on the edge of the Furneaux Archipelago. The east coast of Tasmania was less than forty kilometres away. Standing on a small beach on the southern side of Preservation Island and looking out on the jagged peaks of the nearby islands, they could have been forgiven for thinking that by some miracle they had landed on the west coast of Scotland. The landscape was strangely reminiscent of their homeland. Every piece of land was prey to the sea; there was a fierce, untamed majesty in these islands that demanded respect. Yet before they had time to even contemplate their surroundings there were more pressing matters to attend to. Hamilton noted that 'not a drop' of water could be 'got from the wreck' and they had only torn sails from which to erect makeshift tents. Many members of the crew were so exhausted they were unable to move. The ship was a few hundred metres offshore, slowly sinking into its watery grave, and Hamilton had only a short time to salvage what he could from the wreck. After combing the island in search of water, he eventually dug a well of 2 metres depth and found brackish water that 'answered the purpose'. He then landed the horses and stock and led them to the water. Many years later, some historians would make much of the fact that these animals were 'the first cow and the first horse to be brought ashore in Van Diemen's Land'.[13]

The next morning, Hamilton sent all his able hands, hungry and tired, their clothes still damp, to retrieve and dry the 'wet rice out of the wreck' while others erected tents and brought back whatever cargo they managed to drag in from the ship. In the maelstrom of the wreck the longboat had been severely damaged. Hamilton knew that he had only a few months before 'the winter set in' and given the weak state of so many of the survivors, they would surely perish in such exposed conditions. He had to repair the longboat quickly, send it to Sydney, request assistance and 'save the crew and cargo'. For the next two weeks, 'the carpenter and a gang of hands' attempted to raise a 'strake' on the longboat—adding another piece of timber so as to raise the hull's sides in preparation for the arduous voyage ahead—while 'all the others who could work' hoisted 'spirit casks out of the ship'. As supercargo, Clark was determined to assist Hamilton in retrieving as much of the ship's merchandise as possible. No effort was spared. As the spirits and wines were hauled ashore, many of the crew found the temptation too great, breaking open the barrels and indulging in drunken reveries that Hamilton found 'very improper'. The warmth of the alcohol at least deadened their cold and pain and allowed them to momentarily forget the dire situation they were in. But Hamilton could see his precious cargo being drunk before it reached the auction room floor. He commanded that the wine and spirits be 'saved to a small adjacent island' which could only be reached by boat except during very low tides when the reef that linked the two islands was almost dry. There were now two island prisons: one for the survivors of the wreck and one for the rum. When I walked the northern shoreline of 'Rum Island' in 2013, it was still possible to find the rusted iron castings from the *Sydney Cove*'s rum barrels lying in the sand.

One of the most difficult transitions for Hamilton was to ensure the transfer of his command from the sea to land. No longer bound by the rituals and constraints of the ship's world, the hierarchy that existed at sea was much harder to maintain on the island. Although he probably rang the bells each morning, marked each day off the calendar and held a meeting to allot the tasks for the day ahead, he could not monitor his crew's every move as he could at sea. At the same time, while it was his duty to protect his cargo, he also had to be careful not to exacerbate the emotional and physical distress of the survivors. Well-liked and respected by nearly all who recorded their impressions of him, Hamilton appeared to be the ideal person for the challenge that lay ahead of him. Despite the hellish 3-month voyage of the *Sydney Cove*, he had lost only a handful of men. It was a remarkable feat of seamanship to have got them this far. But this knowledge was tempered by their extreme isolation. By the end of their second week on the island, the survivors could see their ship offshore lying 'much on one side'. The wreck was 'almost covered very high'. Only at low tide was there any chance of retrieving any more cargo. The sight of their listing ship sinking slowly into the sand only reinforced their utter desolation.

View from Rum Island, Preservation Island in mid-foreground, 2013

The longboat was now their best hope of rescue. By Sunday 26 February, after two weeks' work, the repairs were complete and the boat was in 'good order'. Hamilton placed the vessel under the command of his chief mate, Hugh Thompson, assisted by William Clark. The *Sydney Cove's* carpenter, seaman John Bennet, one other British seaman and twelve of the strongest Lascars made up the rest of the boat's crew. A gathering was probably held that Sunday to pray for their safe passage to Sydney. They would sail the next day. Seventeen in all, they were crammed into a tiny vessel no bigger than a surfboat, equipped with oars and rigged with a single small sail. There was little room for much besides their essential gear and the meagre provisions they'd managed to procure from the wreck. The longboat was entirely exposed to the elements but they were well primed: they had already endured many days of exposure for the last two months. Knowing that they were sailing for Sydney and the ultimate hope of rescue steeled them for the journey ahead. Before they departed, Hamilton handed Thompson a letter he had written to Governor Hunter in Sydney, in which he explained their ordeal, informed him of their valuable cargo and asked for a merchant or government vessel to render him assistance and 'get the crew to Port Jackson'. Clark carried a pencil and journal or ship's manifest with him that contained an inventory of the ship's cargo and would enable him to record their progress. He turned twenty-eight that day. That night, together with Hamilton and the others, Clark organised the final plans and agreed on particular courses of action depending on what happened. They were well aware how dangerous the voyage would be.

―――――――

The following morning, Monday 27 February, the *Sydney Cove* survivors gathered on a small beach on the south-western end of Preservation Island, standing among the sculpted granite boulders at the water's edge. The necessary moment of separation had come, and with it mixed emotions of anticipation and fear. The scene on the beach is not hard to imagine—the raised arms of those on shore as they waved their companions farewell, and their shouts and cries

Beach at Preservation Island, Rum Island in the distance, 2013

as they wished them a safe voyage; a call and response of defiance and hope from shore to sea. Clark and Thompson knew that their chances of survival now rested on the success of the longboat's voyage to Sydney. The weight of responsibility was palpable. As the longboat pushed away from the shore, Hamilton knew that he had done all he could. The challenge now was to dig in and survive until help arrived.

Until the longboat's departure, Hamilton's command had guided the crew from the moment they left Calcutta. Now, as they sailed the longboat north along the coast of Flinders Island, it was Thompson and Clark who were called upon to make decisions. Much would depend upon their leadership and navigational skills. Hamilton had equipped them with a sextant to enable them to calculate their latitude. Little did they realise that crossing Bass Strait in a longboat would be a voyage that the most experienced of sailors would not wish upon themselves even two centuries later. If there was an advantage to the longboat it was the fact that without a deep keel it would have been able to put in to various stops along the way. Even if the weather were kind, the journey would have taken them nearly two weeks, more than enough time spent in a small boat in the open sea. They had a little rice but needed to replenish their provisions and water as they headed north.[14]

The first two days of their journey went largely to plan. Leaving behind the northern tip of Flinders Island, they managed to cross the strait and by the morning of 1 March had sighted the mainland. Heading north along the Victorian coastline that same evening, the wind picked up from the south-east and within a few hours it had reached gale proportions. In a matter of minutes the storm became so intense that the longboat was in 'great danger of foundering'. As they were not far from shore, Thompson and Clark immediately looked to put in but they could see the surf breaking 'with such violence' they decided that it wasn't worth the risk. At that moment, as the heavy seas filled their boat with water, they might well have thought that it was their destiny to die at sea. Unable to land, and with the waves crashing over the boat, they 'came to with both anchors'—'the only chance of preservation'. If they could sit out the storm, perhaps by daylight they could manage to put in, then recover and sail on the following day. But all through the night the sea continued to break over them and the longboat filled with water again and again. It was back to bailing. At daybreak, 'they cut both cables and set the foresail' and decided to head for shore. But as the longboat crashed through the surf, the boat was totally flooded. Somehow they managed to get close enough in to allow the crew to reach the shore before the boat went down. All seventeen men swam or floundered their way through the last few waves to the beach. They'd had little time to think of gathering their belongings. Standing on the sand only minutes afterwards, they looked out to sea and watched as their longboat 'went to pieces' in the surf.

They were wrecked on the middle of Ninety Mile Beach in north-east Victoria. The longboat was irreparably damaged. Their possessions were either lost at the bottom of the sea or, for the lucky ones, washed up on shore. The shock and despair they felt was exacerbated by the realisation that Hamilton and thirty or more of their fellow crew were still stranded to the south while the British colony at Sydney was more than seven hundred kilometres to the north. They had survived their latest ordeal, but for how long? From here, there were only two options: build cairns and signal fires in a hope that a passing ship would see them—there were next to none passing in 1797—or set out to walk to Sydney. But in the state they were in that morning, they could think of little beyond the obvious necessities of survival.

For the next three days they repeated a similar task of retrieval to the one they had performed only weeks earlier off Preservation Island, collecting whatever things they could find from the wreck. Combing the beach, they were fortunate to find a few bags of rice and a handful of other provisions and belongings. They had landed approximately forty to fifty kilometres south-west of Lakes Entrance, in the territory of the Gunai Kurnai. Although there is no evidence that they met the Kurnai during the two weeks they spent recovering here, it is difficult to believe that the Kurnai did not see them. Behind the narrow stretch of beach that faced Bass Strait was a series of marshy lakes protected by steep dunes and coastal heath. The lakes and the eucalypt and banksia woodland beyond them were abundant in wildlife: black swans, pelicans, grebes, ducks and cormorants, dingoes, wombats, eastern grey kangaroos, black wallabies and echidnas. Clark noted that they had in their possession 'one gun, two pistols, and two small swords', more than enough weaponry with which to hunt game. Although after total immersion in salt water during the wreck, it's possible that some of their firearms were useless. When they had collected all that could be found on the beach, they sheltered behind the dunes, took stock of their provisions and regathered their strength as Clark and Thompson slowly came to terms with their situation. Mindful of their companions waiting expectantly on Preservation Island and their own isolation, they decided that they would walk to Sydney.[15]

From this point, any semblance of the world they had left behind in Scotland and Calcutta fell away. They had lost the last thread of that connection when their longboat broke to pieces on the beach. Now

19

they found themselves setting out to walk further than any Europeans had ever walked in Australia, through swathes of coastal country unknown to anyone except its Indigenous owners. Everything would be for the first time. They had no idea of what lay before them, of how they would find their way over headlands, along ridgelines and across major rivers. They knew only that they had to head north until they reached Sydney, never allowing the coast out of sight or earshot lest they be lost in the interior. They knew they would encounter 'the natives' but had no prior knowledge of them, nor of the infinite sources of sustenance the environment could provide. As for provisions, they had only a small amount of rice per day to sustain them. They needed to find food and water every day to supplement their supplies. They were drastically unprepared to undertake such a journey with one significant exception: they were tough and hardened by the adversity they had already overcome. In many ways, they were more likely survivors than castaways attempting to undertake a similar journey today.

They began their walk with next to nothing. Clark, Thompson, Bennet and their two British companions wore caps or hats that they had salvaged from the longboat, while their shoes were the goatskin 'straights' made in India, designed for use on either foot. At best, this sleek, thin-skinned footwear would have lasted little more than a week. A few days' walking through thick scrub and over rocky headlands would have cut them to shreds.[16] The majority of the Lascars were probably barefooted. As well as firearms and swords, Clark and his party carried axes, a handful of knives and tools, cooking pots, water containers and calico, either on their person or in shoulder bags. Although they set out during the first weeks of autumn when the temperatures were mild (most days hovering between 17 and 25 degrees) and the ocean currents relatively warm, on certain days the sun was still hot enough to burn them severely. Exposure to extreme heat, wind and rain, countless bites from sandflies, mosquitoes, ticks and march flies, as well as badly scratched legs, arms and faces from occasional bush bashing were all guaranteed irritants. As for potentially lethal snakes—red-bellied blacks, browns, tigers and death adders—ignorance was bliss. Hamilton had sent only the youngest and fittest of the survivors. Five British men between the ages of twenty and forty, their clothes ragged and torn, their faces bearded, their hair long, walking with twelve Lascars in much the same bedraggled state. One Lascar was Clark's 'man-servant' yet he remains a shadowy figure. In fact all the Lascars are unnamed, silent and ghostlike, as almost nothing about them was recorded. Even Hugh Thompson, John Bennet and the mysterious 'carpenter' exist as names at best. William Clark's journal of the walk uses only the first-person plural ('we'). Walking together with one object in mind, the shipwrecked party merged into one body.

On Wednesday 15 March 1797, Clark wrote the first words in his journal: 'We began our journey for Port Jackson'. The first 25 'miles' along the narrow strip of sand that constituted Ninety Mile Beach was relatively easy going. Just before Lakes Entrance, they reached a river 'so large that [they] were obliged to construct a raft to cross it'. After sailing from the other end of the world, the masters of the world's oceans were brought to their knees at every river crossing. Every time they reached a large river mouth, they were forced to halt and build a raft, sometimes for up to three days. Not all of them could swim. Ignorant of the density and moisture content of freshly cut Australian hardwoods, their first rafts sank. Leaving the raft behind them once they had crossed the first river, they soon reached yet another river crossing, only to set to work on the next raft. Through 'miserable experience' they soon learnt to use dry timber. Although the Kurnai no doubt observed them from the beginning of their trek, it was not until the fourth day, 18 March, that Clark wrote of their first encounter with Aboriginal people. Somewhere between Lakes Entrance and Lake Tyers, fourteen Aboriginal men approached them. Clark vividly described the Kurnai's amazement at what was clearly their first meeting with Europeans.

They were struck with astonishment at our appearance, and were very anxious to examine every part of our clothes and body, in which we readily indulged them. They viewed us most attentively. They opened our clothes, examined our feet, hands, nails, etc; frequently expressing their surprise by laughing and loud shoutings. From their gestures during this awkward review it was easy to perceive that they considered our clothes and bodies as inseparably joined.[17]

The astonishment was felt on both sides. The Kurnai's laughter and shouting was accompanied by Clark's wonder at their appearance: 'strong and muscular, with heads rather large in proportion to their bodies. The flat nose, the broad thick lips … their hair long and straight … fish-bones or kangaroo-teeth fastened with gum or glue to the hair of the temples and on the forehead. A piece of reed or bone is also worn through the septum, or cartilage of the nose, which is pierced for the admission of this ornament'. The clinical detail of the description belied the drama of the encounter between the two groups as Clark and his party stood like mannequins for inspection. If the Kurnai men were amused, Clark was perplexed, repelled by the 'rancid' fish oil that covered their hair and bodies. His initial impression of them was predictable: 'they present', he wrote, 'the most hideous and disgusting figures that savage life can possibly afford'. His views would soon change. Forced to stop at each river crossing for days at a time, fatigued by the daily exertion of the walk and with their rations dwindling, it soon became clear that they could not survive without the assistance of the local Aboriginal people. As each day blurred into the next, they would become more dependent on the 'savages' who moved effortlessly through the same country.

William Clark's journal was 'compiled partly from recollection, and partly from the assistance of memoranda written with a pencil' at the time of the walk. The introductory passage to the journal states baldly that 'they began their march' to Port Jackson, as if their bodies were steeled in military-like defence against the environment and they had little interest in the country through which they were moving. Yet as Clark's later entries would reveal, what was about to unfold was no 'march'. As they moved north along the coast, they walked not like soldiers but vagrants, lost in a country for which they possessed no deep well of ancestral memory or songlines of their own. North was their only lodestar. And yet despite their forlorn situation, they marvelled at the beauty and wildness of the landscape before them.

Five days out, after climbing over very 'high bluffs and sharp rocks' and finding a 'few shell fish' on the way, they made another raft and successfully crossed Wingan Inlet, just south of Mallacoota. As he floated across the river, its 'delightful' banks with 'tall and majestic trees' overwhelmed Clark. The country had a 'dignity' all of its own. Walking on towards Mallacoota, he remarked again on the 'beautiful scenery' that 'opened' to their 'view'. Looking inland from the beaches he saw the 'high hills' of the Howe Range in the distance, 'covered to their summit with lofty trees'. Even his apprehension of the Aboriginal people he now knew were watching his party's every move, and his ever-present fear that they might never reach their destination, could not blind him to the magnificence of the country.

Coastline near Mallacoota, Victoria, 2013

Remarkably, much of the coast they traversed from Ninety Mile Beach, through Croajingolong to Mallacoota and on to Cape Howe, looks much the same today—wild and largely unspoilt—except that many of the river mouths have since narrowed considerably due to siltation caused by land-clearing upstream. Some rivers that Clark was forced to cross with a raft can now be waded across at low tide. At Mallacoota, the party moved inland about 'three or four miles' to find a narrow stretch of an 'immense river' where they spent three long days building a raft before they could walk on towards Cape Howe near today's New South Wales – Victorian border. Here, the high, windswept, ever-shifting dunes reach right to the water's edge. 'Fatigued' by climbing the 'hills of sand', they passed by scores of Aboriginal middens accumulated over thousands of years, evidence of the abundance of seafood potentially available to them. By 29 March, after two weeks' walking and rafting, they had traversed nearly two hundred kilometres without loss of life. Preoccupied as Clark and Thompson were with their own struggle for survival, they spurred one another on with the thought of Hamilton and the others marooned back on Preservation Island. By late March they had been underway five weeks from Preservation Island, yet Sydney was still more than five hundred kilometres away.

Retracing Clark's steps in 2013, I saw my fellow walkers from a distance as they made their way along the coast: a line of solitary figures on the sand, their presence dwarfed by the vastness of the space surrounding them and the cavernous skies above. When I saw the country with my own eyes, I understood for the first time why Clark had been so moved to describe its 'delightful verdure'. At certain points where the melaleucas cling to the headlands and hills above the shoreline, their luminous green canopies, constantly flattened by the onshore winds, appear from a distance like the grass fields of Scotland or Wales. Only on close inspection is the illusion broken. The further I walked, the more I could understand their isolation. Clark and his British companions had never experienced an environment like this before.

On the edge of
Nadgee Lake, New
South Wales, 2013

They were accustomed to the closely settled towns and villages of
their homeland or the British East Indies, which were always within
relatively easy reach. The Lascars too were unfamiliar with such
remoteness. A life at sea involved many moments of extreme isolation,
but the ship was a tightly enclosed remnant of the world they had
left behind, their one floating link to 'civilisation'. On the beaches
of New South Wales in 1797, Bengal and Britain were phantoms of
the imagination.

25

From Cape Howe, Clark and Thompson headed north through
Nadgee Nature Reserve, an area that contains some of the most
untamed coastline in south-east Australia. Along the red-rock shoreline and headlands, white-bellied sea eagles circle constantly above,
their massive wingspans visible from far away. After walking along
the northern edge of Nadgee Lake, they followed ancient Aboriginal
paths through banksia and hakea heathland towards Nadgee River,
ground parrots and bristle birds their constant company. The heath
seemed to stretch all the way to the eastern horizon, hiding the stone
ceremonial circles that Aboriginal people had built not far away on
the Devonian mudstone cliffs that faced the sea. When they reached
Nadgee River, approximately forty kilometres south of Eden, they fell
in with a group of Aboriginal people who would transform the next
stages of their journey.

Nadgee River, New South Wales, 2013

As the party attempted to wade across the river, one Aboriginal man 'threatened to dispute' their landing. But Clark and Thompson led them across nonetheless and succeeded in establishing 'reconciliation' with 'the natives' after giving away 'a few strips of cloth'. They were now in the territory of the Thaua, which stretched northwards beyond Eden and Twofold Bay. Until this point they had seen only Aboriginal men. Standing on the northern bank of the river, Clark watched, surprised, as Thaua women and children came out from 'behind the rocks' to 'show themselves'. 'They were the first women we had seen', and 'from their cries and laughing', he reflected, 'it is evident they were greatly astonished at our appearance'. Again, Clark was torn between fascination and disgust, describing the Thaua women in what was probably a journalistic postscript, as 'the most wretched objects [he] had ever seen—equally filthy as the men … so devoid of delicacy … that they seem to have nothing even human about them but the form'. Little did he realise that the willingness of the Thaua men to allow their women and children to be seen was a sure sign of the friendship to come.

The next morning, 30 March, they followed a well-worn Aboriginal path through the heath, the ground carpeted in fallen leaves that cushioned their bare feet. Upon reaching a large river at Wonboyn 'too deep to ford', they stopped to build yet another raft, when to Clark's delight 'three of our native friends, from whom we parted yesterday re-joined us and assisted us over'. He was overwhelmed by their generosity—'for the act was really kind, as they knew we had this river to cross and appear to have followed us purposely to lend their assistance'. From now on, they were frequently helped across rivers and shown the way north along traditional paths. Because they were passers-by, moving through Country rather than seeking to occupy and settle the land, they presented less threat to the Aboriginal people who invariably saw them as the ghosts of their departed ancestors 'jumped up white'. Travelling further north to Twofold Bay and Pambula, through patches of country strewn with 'a variety of flowers', they were followed by their 'old friends' most of

27

Heathland, Nadgee
Nature Reserve, New
South Wales, 2013

the way. Nearly fifty years later, an old Thaua man who was in his late teens when Clark's party passed through Twofold Bay in 1797, told the story of the first white men who came through his Country, and how his people retreated to the hills, 'appalled by the horrid colour of the newcomers'.[18]

North of Twofold Bay at Pambula Inlet, the Thaua received them in 'a very amicable manner', even providing them with a meal of shellfish, which allowed them to regain their strength and walk on another '6 miles'. As they continued through Merimbula and Tathra and entered Djirringanj Country, they looked to Aboriginal people for food and water. The terrain was becoming more difficult, and they again found themselves the next day walking over 'very high bluffs, sharp rocks ... and very thick brushwood', which so 'bruised and wounded their feet' that some of the weaker members of the party 'remained lame for sometime afterwards'. They crawled for the last '10 miles', losing two of their companions who failed to reappear until midday the following day. It was the first serious indication that some members of the party were beginning to weaken. Despite the looming prospect of failure, Clark persisted with his journal writing at the end of every day. He could still find it within himself to enjoy the pleasures of the country through which they were moving. On 5 April, three weeks underway, he savoured the delights of some 'skate' and a shark 'about 4 feet long' they had managed to catch near Tathra. After crossing 'a delightful plain' and traversing 'hills and valleys' the following two days, he reclined on a riverbank that evening, listening to the distant 'roaring of the surf on the seashore'. Unbeknown to him, the beauty that he found in the landscape was also reflected in Djirringanj place names such as Merimbula—'beautiful place of plenty, paradise'. At moments like these his trek appeared idyllic. But entering the second half of their journey, Sydney would begin to appear beyond their reach. With their rice finally at an end, a diet of fish alone was not sufficient to sustain them, especially as they were still seeking to average 25 kilometres a day. Drawn increasingly into the world of the Aboriginal people they were meeting along the way—their rituals and protocols, especially those associated with territorial incursion—Clark and Thompson discovered that they were slowly being enveloped in cultural practices that bewildered them. Compared to the encounters between the British and the Eora at Sydney Cove, they were meeting Aboriginal people on far more vulnerable terms: weakened by fatigue, with limited arms, without shelter and transport, and with no means of demonstrating their 'authority'. As they continued their passage along the coast, disagreements began to break out over how to best deal with 'the natives'.

After crossing Murrah River, 'about fifty armed natives' confronted them. This was the largest body of Aboriginal people they had seen to date. Clark was determined 'to betray no symptoms of fear'. Together with Thompson, he advanced towards them, 'and after some preliminary signs and gestures on both sides' and satisfying their demand for longer pieces of calico, he managed to come to 'some understanding'. These tentative gestures—raised hands or outstretched arms with open palms to indicate peaceful intentions—were made amid the crossfire of Clark's Scottish brogue knocking up against the voices of Aboriginal men; a barrage of salutations, reassurances, warnings and declarations that were uttered instinctively even though they could only be understood when acted out. The two groups parted, Clark admitting that he was 'glad' to be 'rid of them'. But as soon as they set out the next morning, heading north towards Bermagui, the same group of Djirringanj men appeared before them at Cuttagee Beach, making 'dreadful shoutings' and raising their spears 'ready to discharge'. This time, Clark and Thompson singled out the men they 'supposed to be their chiefs', and after 'making them some small presents', were again allowed to proceed. It was much the same the following morning on a sandy reach beside the Bermagui River. 'Overtaken' by some of the same Aboriginal men they recognised from the previous two days, they determined to make a show of strength. There they stood as one on the sand, a huddled group of frightened interlopers, brandishing their crude clubs, 'one gun, two pistols and two small swords'. The display worked magnificently. They managed to exchange a piece of cloth for a 'large kangaroo's tail' from which they made a nourishing soup. It was one of their few meals of red meat since they left Preservation Island and it gave them the strength to walk on another 30 kilometres 'over a number of rugged and disagreeable heights'.

Cuttagee Beach, 7 kilometres south of Bermagui, New South Wales, 2013

By the time they reached Wallaga Lake on 11 April, Clark was beginning to discern the differences between the Aboriginal groups they were meeting along the way. They had now entered the Country of the Walbanga, which stretched all the way from Wallaga towards Ulladulla. In the centre of the lake was Merriman's Island, its outline the shape of the black duck—'Umbarra'—the Walbanga's totem. Immediately, Clark noted their friendly disposition. 'As far as we could understand these natives were of a different tribe from those we had seen, and were then at war with them. They possessed a liberality to which the others were strangers, and freely gave us a part of the little they had'. Treated to a meal of mussels, Clark was surprised when the Walbanga invited the party to 'remain with them for the night'. They accepted gladly, following the Aboriginal men through the bush until they reached the camp by the lakeside. Here, sitting on the ground, they participated in an evening's entertainment. Women and children were brought out to 'see' them, and they sat patiently while they were inspected in close detail. They had learnt by now how to play the subjects of mirth and curiosity. Before the entire tribe, Clark and Thompson mimed the fierce and intimidating demeanour of the Djirringanj men who had caused them so much trouble during the previous days. They mimicked their shouting, their raised spears and their rude behaviour. It was a bravura performance. Both the 'old and the young' in the audience rushed to give them more of their shellfish in appreciation. For the Aboriginal people at Wallaga Lake, this theatre by firelight was the first time they had seen Europeans at such close quarters. Clark's intense dislike of their warring neighbours no doubt endeared his party to the Walbanga. News of the British settlement north of Sydney had certainly travelled north and south along the coast. Whether the Walbanga saw Clark as being somehow connected to the strangers residing to the north is difficult to know. But the mere fact that Clark explained to the Walbanga his party's need to continue northwards may well have been understood as attempting to reach Sydney. For Clark and the others, now more than a month underway from Preservation Island, and embedded in Aboriginal culture and Country as they were, Hamilton and the survivors were no doubt slipping more and more from view. When Clark departed in the longboat, his mission was to request help from Governor Hunter in Sydney. Yet here he was requesting help from 'the natives', without whose assistance he knew they surely would have perished. He had discovered one thing: outside of the tiny settlement at Port Jackson, there was nothing British about the continent of New Holland. Having already traversed more of the country than any other European before him, Clark was beginning to appreciate the intricate web of Indigenous Countries imprinted on the land. He was the nomad, the ghostly visitor passing through one occupied territory after the next, each with its own language, system of law, songlines and unique cultural protocols.[19]

For the next five days, as they pressed on towards Jervis Bay, Clark and Thompson were fed and assisted all the way by Walbanga men. They followed the party and helped them across three 'large rivers' in their canoes—at Narooma, Tuross and Moruya. These crossings gave the Walbanga much amusement because so few of Clark's party knew how to sit properly in their canoes. Every time they pushed out from the bank they would soon capsize, or as Clark politely explained, their crossings were accompanied by 'several duckings'. He watched with some embarrassment as his men fell out of the canoes while 'the natives' managed to put three or four passengers in their 'rude little vehicles formed of bark, tied at both ends with twigs, and not exceeding 8 feet in length, by 2 in breadth' and 'paddle about in them with the greatest facility and security'. Clark wondered if their generosity was spontaneous or 'that perceiving we should find it difficult they had come to our assistance'. But there was little doubt that the Walbanga men had intentionally followed Clark's every step, informing their countrymen ahead to assist the walkers in an effort to speed their progress northwards. They alone knew where the shallow crossing points were at every river mouth. They knew how to save the walkers time, 'avoid several high points and cut off a great deal of ground'. And of course, they knew where to find food and water. At one point, Clark actually used the word 'guide' to refer to one Aboriginal man who showed them the best path to take and also instructed a group of his people ahead to give the ailing party 'a plentiful supply of fish'. Originally wary of meeting Aboriginal people when they set out, they were now looking for them every step of their journey—'we now often stopt some time with the natives when we found them kind to us'. Yet despite the generous assistance they had received to date, in the space of a few days only eight members of the party would be strong enough to continue.

At Moruya River, on the morning of 16 April, Clark and Thompson were forced to leave nine of their men behind, all of them Lascars. They could walk no farther. While Clark hoped that they might catch up 'in a day or two', he knew they were farewelling them for the last time. The Lascars were never seen or heard of again, although given the hospitality of Aboriginal people throughout this stage of their walk, the chances that the stronger among them were adopted by the Walbanga, and survived, seem high. The remaining members of the party—Clark, his Lascar man-servant, Thompson, Bennet, the 'carpenter' and three Lascars—were reluctant to leave the nine behind at Moruya, but they were now in a position in which every day lost further decreased their chances of reaching Sydney.

The following day, at Tomakin, after searching upstream for shallow water, they found an 'old canoe on the bank' of 'a narrow but deep river'. Thinking they were safe, Clark and three others crossed over. Thompson, however, 'who could not swim … was left struggling in the water by the canoe sinking under him'. The tidal currents were dangerously strong. As Clark later described the scene, 'this was witnessed by four Bengal blacks, who, though they were adept at swimming, stood unmoved spectators. I instantly jumped in and flew to his relief, although very much fatigued and very cold. I seized him by the hair and drew him to the shore motionless … placed him over a rock with his head downwards, pressing him at the same time on the back, by which means he discharged much seawater by the mouth, and in a little time recovered'. Clearly angered by the Lascars' refusal to help Thompson, Clark offered no clue as to why they remained 'unmoved'. Yet it seems possible that they were angered by Thompson and Clark's decision to leave their compatriots behind at Moruya. They had not wanted to continue without them.

Severely weakened by his near drowning, Thompson slowed the party's progress. They could only walk 13 kilometres the following day. Clark decided that he would walk with Thompson while the others went ahead to the next river crossing. Two days later, he finally caught up with them. On 20 April, they were fortunately shown the way by their Aboriginal guide beyond Batemans Bay, through an 'immense wood, the plain of which was covered with long grass'. So dependent had they become on Aboriginal people, Clark complained as they left Ulladulla that they had 'walked 10 or 12 miles each day without meeting with any natives, and being wholly without nourishment almost perished for want'. As they approached Jervis Bay, now little more than two hundred kilometres from Sydney, they would encounter the greatest test they had faced so far.

At 9 a.m. on the morning of 26 April, Clark's party reached Wreck Bay near Sussex Inlet, the Country of the Wandandian, which extended north to Nowra. There, they 'observed several natives on the top of a high bluff'. At first Clark thought they appeared friendly.

When they 'made signs' that they were hungry, they were immediately brought 'plenty of fish'. But as they carried on they were soon confronted by a hundred 'strong natives … shouting and [howling] in a most hideous manner'. Two more Lascars had already dropped behind, and Clark knew they were alarmingly outnumbered: 'we were only six opposed to such a multitude … [and had] only one musket unloaded and two pistols out of repair'. Until now, they had managed to avoid violence but on this occasion, either because they had unknowingly failed to pay due respect to cultural protocols regarding their presence in Wandandian territory, or because some of their 'signs' were misread, a handful of Aboriginal men 'began throwing their spears'. As Clark raised his arms, pleading with the men to 'desist', he was speared 'through both hands'. In the same moment, his man-servant and Thompson were also wounded. The spearheads had probably broken the bones in Clark's hands and he was forced to pull them out. They were now completely at the mercy of the Aboriginal men. Yet just when they thought death was imminent the men began to walk away, and within minutes the hundred-strong group had retreated into the bush. Walking in 'considerable pain' for another '8 miles' until they came to Bundarwa, the north arm of Jervis Bay, they were overtaken by the same group of Aboriginal men.[20] This time, Clark was convinced 'they intended to murder [them]'. Yet if this had really been the Wandandian's intention, they surely would have killed them earlier. The superficial wounds they had inflicted on the party were most likely ritual markings brought on by their unlawful activities in Country. The closer they came to Sydney, the closer the party came to entering the territories of Aboriginal people who had received regular news of the deaths of so many of the Eora at Port Jackson from disease and violence, their lands taken by the British without their consent. Yet Clark's fears proved totally unfounded. No spears were thrown. They were led to the Wandandian's campsite and obliged to spend the night there, as would have occurred if they were Indigenous visitors. 'Welcome to Country' was not a handshake; ceremonies could often last several days. But Clark and Thompson knew none of this. Still fearful that they would be speared again, and with their wounds causing them distress, they were unable to sleep.

Lying awake around the campfire that night, they wondered if this would be where their journey would end.

When light broke the next morning, they left the campsite unimpeded, walking around the white-sand horseshoe arms of Jervis Bay. Although they were followed initially, by 9 a.m. they were finally on their own, their daily progress now significantly reduced by their injuries and debilitating fatigue. Because he had recorded how far they had walked each day in his journal, Clark knew they were now within striking distance of Sydney. If they could average roughly the same rate of progress or even slightly less from here on, they would reach Sydney in less than two weeks. Famished, they ate 'wild plants' as they had done for most of the latter part of the journey. While they were often shown the edible bush tucker by their Aboriginal friends, when alone, they could have inadvertently picked 'herbs', fruits and flowers that were either poisonous or only meant to be consumed after sufficient preparation. Too exhausted to search far for drinking water, they drank 'brackish water', which only worsened their condition. Yet they staggered on, somehow managing to reach the massive banks of the Shoalhaven River on 30 April where, that evening, six Aboriginal men assisted them across in canoes.

The party was now reduced to five: Clark and his Lascar man-servant, Thompson, Bennet and the carpenter. Thompson had still not fully recovered from the incident at Tomakin, and his spear wounds only exacerbated his situation. The carpenter, frustrated by his inability to extract more food from the Aborigines, became increasingly agitated in his dealings with them. In their severely weakened state, the party could only walk a few kilometres each day. Day after day, beach after beach, the sound of the surf washed over them, each step harder than the next. The effort to continue each morning became greater, the delirium into which they were slowly being lulled making the temptation to halt almost irresistible. From here on, with his hands causing him too much pain to write more than a few words, Clark's journal entries dropped off. Yet all five men walked on from Shoalhaven through Tharawal Country for 'fifteen days'. The final journal entry seems almost uninterested, stating retrospectively that these days 'were much the same' as the rest. Perhaps the scale of the country through which they walked had finally overwhelmed him. After walking for two months—the stigmata on his palms a burning reminder of his passage through Aboriginal Australia—Clark cared only for deliverance.[21]

For the next two weeks, as the night temperatures began to fall with the approach of winter, they managed to walk 100 kilometres. Given the state they were in, an average distance of 12 kilometres per day was a heroic rate of progress. On 15 May, shortly after they left Thirroul, Clark was surprised to find a small beach strewn with large chunks of coal. That night, they used it to make a roaring fire, its sustaining warmth sending them into a deep sleep and tempting them to rest for another day. Under extreme stress, the divisions between them had started to widen. The carpenter, 'churlish and avaricious, and without sense or foresight', often 'seized [the Aborigines'] fish', yet gave them 'nothing in return'. On many occasions, his selfishness and insolence deeply 'offended' the Aboriginal people and foolishly placed all their lives at risk.[22] Until now, Clark and Thompson had been able to keep the carpenter's base instincts in check. But the weaker and more desperate they became, the will required to override his impatience and greed was harder to muster. The next day, as they entered what is now Royal National Park, south of Sydney, Thompson could go no farther. Aware that they were now less than three or four days' walk from their destination, Clark reluctantly decided to leave him behind, telling him that they would send for help once they got to Sydney. The carpenter, also in a poor state, volunteered to remain with Thompson and 'keep him company'. For Clark, the wrench of leaving the 'amiable man' he was so very 'fond of', and with whom he had journeyed for the last seven months, was excruciating. He did not trust the carpenter but nor could he bring himself to leave Thompson alone. Together with his loyal Lascar man-servant and seaman John Bennet, he continued on to Sydney clutching his journal and the letter that Hamilton had given Thompson two months earlier.[23]

The following day the three men reached Wattamolla ('place near running water'), a small cove barely forty kilometres south of Sydney. They were now so exhausted they were reduced to 'crawling' on the sand. Nearly every day of their epic journey, Clark had dreamt of the moment when a passing ship would see the crooked line of walkers on the shore and end their ordeal in shouts of joy. Looking out to sea, there were surely many times when he had imagined a ship on the horizon, his eyes frequently deceiving him. But on this occasion the long-anticipated moment was not an illusion.

Clark spotted a small fishing boat not far offshore. The mere sight of it returned all his energy at once. Feverish with excitement, the three men scampered 'along the rocky shore', frantically 'waving' and shouting to the boat, the sound of the sea drowning their cries. At first the fishermen didn't notice them. But when one man finally saw them, the boat turned and came in. Barely able to comprehend the forsaken figures on the beach, the fishermen 'picked up [the] three men, in a most wretched and worne out condition'. Clark's moment of salvation had finally arrived.[24]

On 17 May 1797, William Clark, his Lascar servant and John Bennet were once again at sea. 'Scarcely alive', they gazed out from their tiny fishing boat onto the massive, vertical sandstone cliffs that skirt Sydney's coastline, the large boulders strewn at their feet like the remains of an ancient fortress. Whether or not they had the strength to tell their story to the fishermen who saved them, these few precious hours would remain with them forever. Six months after leaving Calcutta, they were finally arriving at their destination.[25]

Their astonishment and relief was tinged with despair and anxiety. They had lost twelve of their fellow walkers, while the fate of Thompson and the carpenter, as with Hamilton and the survivors on Preservation Island, was still unknown. As they entered Sydney Harbour and sailed past the lonely signal mast that stood on South Head, the satellite of British civilisation that had lured them half-way round the world in search of wealth slowly came into view. Rounding Bennelong Point and anchoring in Sydney Cove, the scene that greeted them was more like a makeshift English village than the capital of a southern empire: small fenced allotments creeping above the shoreline, a wattle and daub church with thatched roof and earthen floor, rudimentary convict cottages spreading over The Rocks, a 'wooden bridge' across an already polluted Tank Stream, and a solitary windmill standing on what would later become Observatory Hill. As soon as they stepped ashore, they were led immediately to Government House, the most prominent and impressive building in the colony, which stood little more than a hundred metres from the

Sandstone coast, south of Sydney, 2013

quay, close to where the corner of Bridge and Phillip streets stands today. There, 'they were received [by Governor Hunter] with that humanity which their unparalleled sufferings could not but inspire'.[26]

The arrival of the three castaways in Sydney created a minor sensation. It was not only Hunter who wanted to hear of their ordeal, but also anyone who was interested in the country beyond the colony's boundaries. Within a matter of weeks, Clark had told his harrowing story to Hunter, Lieutenant Colonel David Collins, and the maritime explorers George Bass and Matthew Flinders. The insignificant settlement at 'the extremity of the globe' was effectively an island surrounded by hundreds of Aboriginal Countries, of which the bulk of the settler population was largely ignorant. For colonists who had little idea of what Collins nonchalantly termed the 'unsettled part of New Holland', the news that Clark and his party had walked through more than seven hundred kilometres of unknown country was staggering. Everyone in Sydney wanted to know the answer to one question: what was out there? Critical of Hunter's failure to explore the surrounding country, the Scottish Martyr and Unitarian Minister Reverend Thomas Palmer, who was transported to the colony in 1794, could barely contain his excitement at the news of Clark's arrival. 'Of this wonderful country', reflected Palmer, 'we have little or no knowledge, except a small portion of the seacoast of a corner of it. With two armed ships and a schooner on purpose for the use of the colony, no discovery has been attempted. Such things are never thought of; and if a private adventurer undertakes them, he is discouraged. Chance however has done something'. Palmer, who craved intellectual stimulation and the trappings of society, felt the exile of life in Sydney keenly. For a cultured man who lamented that he had read 'over and over' his 'little stock of books' and who was intensely curious about both Aboriginal people and the country around him, Clark's story confirmed his sanguine view of New Holland. Like Hunter, Palmer was excited by Clark's assessment that the strong tidal currents to the north of the (Furneaux) 'archipelago' indicated the existence of a 'navigable passage' between the mainland and Van Diemen's Land. If this were true, he wrote, 'the passage to India would be very considerably shortened'. But most of all, he was struck by Clark's glowing description of the country through which he had travelled.

> The country is described as totally different from this, very rich and fertile, abounding in pines and firs, of which there is not one here. In all the intercourse of whites with the uncorrupted natives of this country, they have found them most kind, humane and generous. Where the mate and supercargo were wrecked, no civilized Europeans could exceed them in kindness. They supplied them in abundance, and successive parties of fresh natives, equally kind, shewed them the way.[27]

Only weeks after Clark's arrival, the tale of his journey was already being adjusted around the edges to reflect the storyteller's prejudices. Whereas Palmer spoke enthusiastically of the kindness of Aboriginal people, Hunter condemned the 'savage barbarity of the natives', while Matthew Flinders faithfully relayed Clark's experience of 'friendly' Aborigines and 'the hostility of others', as did Collins, who described them as 'frequently very kind, and at other times extremely savage'. Very quickly, the survivors' story became an allegory for the colonists' hopes and anxieties regarding the expansion of settlement. The telling of Clark's ordeal could be used both to confirm the benign intentions of the 'natives' and to establish their 'barbarity'. Unlike Palmer, Hunter insisted that all fourteen walkers who failed to reach Sydney had been 'much annoy'd and wounded' by Aboriginal people, despite the fact that he had no direct evidence to support the claim. The day after Clark arrived, Hunter sent one of the fishermen who had rescued the three survivors in a small whaleboat to search for Thompson and the carpenter. When the fisherman returned, he reported that 'nothing could be discovered of those helpless people except a few trifling things they had with them, part of which being covered with blood, gave us reason to suppose they had been destroyed by the natives'. At least in the case of Thompson and the carpenter (as Clark told Collins), there was every chance that they had met their end due to the 'morose, unfeeling disposition of the carpenter', who insisted that because the Aborigines 'were black fellows', it was right to take their food 'by force'. Clark was convinced that the carpenter's arrogance and bloody-mindedness had cost both men's lives. Rather than blame Aboriginal people, for whom he now held deep respect, he preferred to blame one of his own. Three months later, when Hunter sent George Bass and Clark in search of the coal that Clark had discovered during the final days of his journey, a Tharawal man led them through the bush to what he claimed were the skeletons of the two men. One skull was 'much fractured', from which Hunter hastily concluded that the men were 'no doubt murdered by the natives'. However they met their death, for Clark to see Thompson's skeleton was a gruesome reminder of how close he had come to meeting the same fate. Of the nine Lascars left behind at Moruya and the three others who had been unable to continue, nothing was heard again. No matter how many times Clark, his Lascar man-servant and Bennet told their story, they would always remain to some extent alone with their experience. For many of the colonists at Sydney Cove, the walkers' journey was both beyond the bounds of settlement and beyond the bounds of comprehension.[28]

While Clark and his Lascar servant recuperated, Hunter busied himself arranging the despatch of two vessels to sail down to Preservation Island. John Bennet, who had already recovered, decided that he would join the rescue mission. On 30 May, the schooner *Francis* and the 'decked longboat' *Eliza* departed from Sydney.

If Thompson and Clark had struggled to sustain the physical effort of walking more than twenty kilometres every day, Hamilton had fought tenaciously to shield his crew and passengers from the elements. After the departure of the longboat from Preservation Island in February, the weather turned extremely 'cold with almost constant gales and heavy rain'. In trying conditions yet again, Hamilton did his best to keep the remaining crew employed salvaging the last casks of rum from the *Sydney Cove* and 'washing cargo cloths at the well'. Suffering from exposure, many of his men were unable to work. Hamilton's sick list quickly increased to thirteen. Even the healthy Lascars were prevented from working more than two to three hours 'in the middle of the day' due to the severity of the weather. Hamilton's provisions were also running low. Within a few weeks he was not able to 'allow more than One Tea Cup of Rice per Diem for each Man'.[29]

On 23 April, the weather 'blew a perfect hurricane from the south, with much thunder, lightning, rain and extreme cold', and continued unabated until 1 May. The survivors' tents 'were by this time in tatters' and 'every Lascar' was 'sick'. Unable to even keep a fire burning to 'cook their pittance of rice', Hamilton's crew were dropping fast. Many complained of swelling all over their bodies, especially at their feet, likely symptoms of scurvy. That week, Hamilton buried three Lascars and one European passenger. The gale had finally finished off the *Sydney Cove*. The ship's bottom was now 'totally gone', with the main and mizzenmasts 'gone thro' her'. Not one person was strong enough to attempt salvaging more cargo from the wreck. Instead, Hamilton gave the few Lascars who could still 'move about' the Sisyphean task of 'rolling the spirit casks on logs of wood' so as to prevent the 'salt sand' from 'eating into the iron hoops'. 'When that was done', they dried the 'cargo cloths' and rice, and began building a rudimentary 'house large enough to contain all hands in bad weather'. Building suggested permanence, but Hamilton had no choice. If they were struck by another storm of equal intensity, he knew that 'inevitable death' awaited them. Unlike Clark and Thompson, he had no Aboriginal guardian angels to rely on.[30]

By the time Hunter had despatched the rescue vessels, Hamilton and his remaining crew had been waiting for assistance for nearly four months. The captain of the *Sydney Cove* was now the last European on the island, his Lascar crew having remained loyal to the end. There was no descent into *Batavia*-like carnage. Despite his increasing despair as winter arrived, every day dawned with the hope of rescue. Hamilton built at least one signal cairn and posted men on 'Lookout Rock'. Every morning, he pondered the fate of Clark and Thompson and scanned the horizon with his telescope for the slightest sign of a ship out to sea. On clear days, when the cold air from the Antarctic brought a razor-sharp light, he could see the columns of smoke rising from the Aboriginal campfires on the Tasmanian mainland and even the snow-capped hills around Launceston. In his tiny, '4 oared' jollyboat, he fought the strong east-west tides and explored Cape Barren and the neighbouring islands, identifying the safe sea lanes and charting the immediate area—making him the first person to suspect that 'there is a strait through this part of the coast & that Van Diemen's Land is an island'.[31]

With the last of the cargo salvaged, Hamilton turned his mind to building a shelter and fully exploiting the island's rich array of food sources. The longer they spent on the island, the less dependence they came to have on their rations of rice, which were becoming all but depleted. Fortunately, as time passed, the abundance of choice revealed itself: wallabies and wombats, fish and shellfish, snakes and frogs, Cape Barren geese, quail and ducks (at least, when the soaks on the island were full), limpets that clung to the brilliant orange, black

The rocky landscape of Preservation Island, close to where Hamilton set up the survivors' campsite, 2013

and yellow lichen-covered rocks, supplemented by salt that could be scraped off the granite after the water had dried, and perhaps even succulents and saltbush. But the survivors' most accessible food source was right in front of them, fighting for the same patch of ground on which they pitched their tents—the thick, oily smell from the rookery filling the air and the incessant din of the birds' squawking keeping them awake at night. Every September on the equinox, more than eighteen million 'mutton-birds' (or short-tailed shearwaters) descend on Tasmania. They populate Preservation Island in their thousands, burrowing in the ground 'like rabbits' to make their nests, laying their eggs in late November (which hatch in mid-January) and leaving the island by the end of April. Each night, 'a little after sunset', the sky above the survivors' tents turned 'dark lead' as the birds returned to their nests. Every step they took on the island filled in another of the birds' burrows. Hamilton, who surely had knowledge of the migratory habits of shearwaters in Scotland, would have known that the birds would not be with them indefinitely. He needed to kill as many birds as possible before they departed, smoke them and store them in the shelter for the winter ahead. In the colourful words of a later visitor to the island, mutton-birds made 'a nourishing sort of food when eaten with potatoes, to such constitutions as those who are inured to a life of hardiness'. By May, Hamilton had managed to erect a basic 'hut', with his 'two hens' and a handful of pigeons penned close by. The Lascars, having busied themselves killing and smoking the birds over the previous weeks, had amassed a reasonable supply of meat. With this vaguely agricultural set-up and his one remaining cow, Hamilton was modestly prepared for winter. But nothing could nullify the aching loneliness of waiting for assistance. As he intimated later to Hunter, there were many times when 'he held no hope of being rescued'.[32]

———————

On the morning of 8 June, everything changed. Hamilton sighted 'a longboat to the west of the island' and 'immediately launched [his] jollyboat' in pursuit. But to his 'sorrow', before he could approach the boat it had sailed completely 'out of sight'. Undeterred, he returned to the island, 'showed English colours' and built a massive fire. Within a matter of hours he saw a schooner off the eastern shore but the sea was by then dangerously high and he could not risk taking the jollyboat out. Two days later, when the longboat again appeared 'in sight' he finally managed to reach her. As he hoisted himself aboard and greeted Captain Archibald Armstrong, Hamilton's relief was overcome by his pressing need to know what had happened to Clark and Thompson and the rest of his longboat's crew. There on the deck of the *Eliza*, in a few breathless minutes, Armstrong told Hamilton of the men's 3-month ordeal, of how they had been 'stranded in a violent Gale' and forced to proceed 'to the Colony by Land', and how the 'remainder of the boat's crew had been left in the Woods unable to come further', some of them 'perishing for want' and 'some of them wounded by the Natives among which number was Mr. Clark having received a wound by a Spear thro' both hands' from which he was still recovering

A 'soak', close to Hamilton's campsite, Preservation Island, 2013

in Sydney. As Hamilton tried to digest the news that fourteen of the men he had sent to Sydney had died, Armstrong explained that the schooner he had sighted two days earlier was indeed the *Francis*, sent by Hunter to rescue him and to retrieve the cargo from the *Sydney Cove*. When the *Francis* arrived off Preservation Island the following morning, Hamilton was reunited with walk survivor John Bennet. Over the next two weeks, as the crew from the *Francis* and the *Eliza* assisted the able-bodied Lascars in loading as much of the salvaged cargo as possible, Hamilton listened to Bennet's story of the longboat's wreck and the crew's 700-kilometre trek north along the coast. Measured against this experience, the story of Hamilton's travails on the island paled by comparison. While they had moved through stretches of unknown country on foot, he had merely dug in. His last days and nights on Preservation Island were spent trying to reconcile his elation and disappointment. He was alive and much of the cargo had been retrieved. But he had lost his ship, his first mate, and more than twenty men, and still he had not reached Sydney.[33]

Fearing that Hamilton and some of the survivors he had left on Preservation Island in February might not be alive when the *Francis* arrived, Clark had suggested to Hunter that he send six men (possibly former convicts) who would remain on the island to protect the cargo that could not be loaded onto the rescue vessels. But Hamilton took one look at this motley band of recruits and rejected the idea, finding them 'very improper to be left in charge of spirits'. He then turned to Bennet and five of his fittest Lascars and asked them to remain on the island until he could return in another vessel from Sydney and retrieve them with the last of the cargo. Bennet and the Lascars did not need to be ordered; they 'volunteered'. Bennet had only had a few weeks to recuperate in Sydney before he sailed back to the island on the *Francis*. Now he found himself marooned there a second time, issued with an official certificate by Hamilton that placed him 'in charge of the Cargo saved from the Wreck of the Ship *Sydney Cove* on and for Account of the Underwriters on the said Ship'. That Hamilton went so far as to formally declare Bennet's role on paper said much about the necessity and power of the written word in the late eighteenth century. Even on this remote island in the southern seas, two weeks' sail from the nearest settlement, Hamilton's proclamation carried authority. They had sailed from Calcutta to sell Campbell and Clark's cargo at Port Jackson, and this objective was always uppermost in Hamilton's mind. Despite all they had been through, he remained determined to save 'as much of the cargo as possible'.[34]

On 23 June, nearly six months after they were shipwrecked, Hamilton and the remaining Lascars finally left Preservation on board the schooner *Francis* and the 'sloop' *Eliza*. Sailing through 'dreadful weather', the two ships were separated in 'a violent storm'. The *Francis* arrived safely in Sydney on 3 July and Hamilton 'immediately landed the Goods ... and deposited them in his Majesty's Store' and waited for the *Eliza* to arrive. The following morning he met Judge Advocate Richard Atkins, and 'gave notice' that he would lodge a legal 'protest' which would explain how he had lost the *Sydney Cove* in violent 'winds and weather'. Days and weeks passed and there was still no sign of the *Eliza*. On 17 July, Sydney was struck by gale-force south-easterly winds, which tore down 'trees' and 'chimneys' and 'two of the vanes of the windmill', while the torrential rain was so heavy that some of the ships in Sydney Cove 'brought their anchors home'. As David Collins feared, the violence of the storm seemed ominous. It 'increased the apprehensions of everyone for the safety of the long-boat'. Captain Armstrong and the *Eliza*'s small crew, including the 'seven or eight lascars' they had rescued from Preservation Island, never arrived in Sydney. Hunter lamented that 'three infant orphan children' survived Armstrong, the man who had kindly offered his assistance when he had needed another vessel to accompany the *Francis* to Preservation Island, while the Lascars, after surviving one shipwreck and months of privation, lost their lives on the very vessel that rescued them. Of the fifty or so people who had left Calcutta in November 1796 on board the *Sydney Cove*, less than half were still alive.[35]

Reunited in Sydney, Hamilton and Clark finally had time to tell one another their stories. Each man had his tale of perseverance and woe, lightened now by the divine taste of the food and wine they shared at Hunter's table and elsewhere in town. While Hamilton knew that his 'duty' was to 'remain [there] for some time' in order to secure another vessel, retrieve the last of the cargo and, as 'agent for the underwriters', oversee its sale, he was also eager for Clark to return to Calcutta and inform Robert Campbell of his ship's fate. Due to the shortage of available vessels in Sydney, Hamilton would have to wait until December before departing for Preservation Island. Meanwhile, Clark looked for passage on the first available ship leaving Sydney. By late July he had fully recovered, although the scars on his palms would remain with him for life. If he wrote home to Scotland from Sydney, as he almost certainly did, his first words would probably have expressed the difficulty of holding a pen or of grasping any object in his hands.

After accompanying Bass down the coast to retrieve the coal in early August, he quickly secured a berth on board the *Britannia* bound for England via Canton. As the ship sailed through The Heads with Clark, his servant and several of the Lascars who had accompanied Hamilton from Preservation Island on board, it carried various accounts of their epic journey: Hunter's dispatches to the Colonial Office and his letter to Sir Joseph Banks, Thomas Palmer's letter which spoke enticingly of 'the finest country [he] ever saw', the correspondence Hamilton and Clark sent to their families in Scotland, and the battered, blood-stained journal that Clark had kept on his walk. Also on board the *Britannia* were the specimens of coal that Clark and Bass had broken from the face of the cliffs at 'Coalcliff' several days earlier. Hunter had placed them in a box especially for Joseph Banks's perusal: 'In short, Sir Joseph, it appears that this part of the country abounds with coal & probably other useful matter'. Leaving Sydney, Clark knew like few others the vastness and magnificence of the country that lay beyond the colony. He had met Aboriginal people as few others had met them—as a temporary visitor to their lands—before the rapid loss of so much of the cultural knowledge they had accumulated over millennia. Yet his experience would be largely remembered in the future for his 'discovery' of coal. As Hunter told Banks, he wanted to go and see this 'coal country' for himself. Usefulness of country was what mattered.[36]

With Clark bound for Calcutta via China, Hamilton settled in to a more comfortable life in Sydney and discussed the sale of the spirits with Hunter. Long convinced of the 'ruinous' effects of the 'excess in the use of spirits' on the convict colony, and reluctant to fuel an alcohol trade with British India that he would otherwise have discouraged, Hunter ultimately had little choice but to purchase the alcohol in order to control its sale and distribution. While he bemoaned the large numbers of convicts who had been 'launched into eternity' after their enthusiastic participation in numerous bacchanalian festivals, the news that hundreds of barrels of rum were languishing south of Sydney spread like wildfire around the town. In September, Hunter had the spur he required to purchase the spirits, when rum fever led fourteen convicts to hatch a harebrained scheme to escape, sail to the wreck of the *Sydney Cove* and attempt to claim the rum for themselves. After thieving a boat on Parramatta River they sailed down the coast with the intention of floating the ship, or at the very least raiding it of all its cargo and selling the proceeds overseas. Miraculously, this ill-prepared band of Irish marauders managed to reach as far as Wilson's Promontory. There, on a small offshore island, seven of the convicts stole out to sea one evening while their fellow escapees were asleep, effectively leaving the others for dead. The betrayers reached the Hawkesbury before eventually turning themselves in. Two were later put to death for escaping from Sydney. For the seven convicts who woke to find themselves stranded, they remained for weeks on the island before George Bass spotted them while he was exploring the coast in early January 1798.[37]

At first, when Bass saw the smoke from their fire he thought that they were Aboriginal. But when he went ashore to speak with them he realised that they were white 'and had some clothing on'. Two convicts swam off as soon as they saw him, more fearful of capture and execution than of losing their lives slowly from starvation. Bass, who was eager to prove the existence of the strait between the mainland and Van Diemen's Land, gave them some provisions and told them he would return to help them on his way back to Sydney. But it was precisely lack of provisions that forced Bass at Westernport to turn back for Sydney without crossing the strait. When he reached the convicts again in early February, he could only manage to fit two of the most ill on his small boat. He then took the other five across to the mainland, gave them his pocket compass, a musket and ammunition, some fishing gear and the few clothes he could spare, before telling them the news they did not want to hear: they would have to walk to Sydney. As Bass later told Hunter, this moment of separation was wrenching both for him and the convicts—'when they parted ... some tears were shed on both sides'. All of the men knew that fourteen of Clark's party had lost their lives attempting the same journey twelve months earlier. They began their walk far less equipped to survive their ordeal, while the Aboriginal people who again saw a line of weary walkers making their way north along the beaches of their Country surely wondered if this procession of ghosts would continue indefinitely. All seven convicts failed to reach Sydney and no trace of them was ever found. How far did they walk? As far as Moruya, where they could possibly have met a few of the Lascars who had been taken in by local Aboriginal people in 1797, or as far as Jervis Bay? In March 1801, while exploring the coast south of Sydney, Lieutenant James Grant reported the discovery of human bones near an Aboriginal campsite. One of his crew 'picked up part of a human skull ... with the cavities of the eyes and part of the bones of the nose still attached to it ... he also found a piece of the upper jaw ... [and] the vertebrae of the back with evident marks of fire on it'. Yeranabie, the Aboriginal man who accompanied Grant on his voyage, allegedly 'interpreted' that the bones were the remains of 'a white man [who] ... had come from some ship which ... had broke down—been lost to the southward'—and that the Aborigines had eaten him. Grant took the bones on board and later sent them to the surgeon and anatomist WL Thomas in London asking him to examine them in order to prove the 'colour of the person'. Not surprisingly, Thomas was unable to enlighten him. By the early 1800s, some of the first settler oral histories of cross-cultural encounters outside Sydney were laced with these bizarre tales of 'native savagery' and cannibalism, stories of lost white men wandering half-starved through Aboriginal coastal lands seeking redemption.[38]

By the time Bass was making his way back to Sydney in February 1798, Hamilton had already sailed down to Preservation Island and returned with Bennet, four Lascars (one having died) and nearly all the remaining cargo, including his mare. The wreck of the *Sydney Cove* was now 'entirely washed away'. Hamilton listened to Bennet's distressingly familiar tales of their six long months on the island, battling gales and storms and living on smoked mutton-birds and the kangaroos they had killed on nearby islands. After more than one year spent either marooned on the island or walking the coast, Bennet had finally been liberated but his subsequent fate remains a mystery. Most likely he returned to Calcutta or England, another refugee from the wilds of New South Wales.

A few weeks before Hamilton and Bennet returned to Sydney, Clark arrived back in Calcutta where he and Robert Campbell were immediately 'admitted partners in … the firm of Campbell and Clark', which included Clark's brother, John. They were not deterred in the slightest by their experience with the *Sydney Cove*. Instead, Clark's news of the colony's dearth of supplies only increased their determination to fill another ship with saleable Indian goods and sail as quickly as possible for Sydney, this time with Robert Campbell aboard as 'agent and underwriter'. Days after his arrival in Calcutta, Clark, perhaps with Campbell's and his brother's encouragement, had also made contact with a journalist and discussed the publication of excerpts from his journal. He was well aware that his story could make his name, especially back in Britain, where firsthand accounts of similar adventures with the 'natives' in the far-flung corners of the Empire were eagerly consumed by the reading public. He had carried his pencilled journal with him ever since the morning he had left in the longboat from Preservation Island. In late December 1797 and early January 1798, a 6000-word 'abstract' from his journal appeared in Calcutta's *Asiatic Mirror* and was immediately syndicated to a number of other newspapers, including many in England and Scotland. It was written up with the assistance of the journalist who he entrusted with the story. As a result, its introductory passages are replete with the standard tropes of European contempt for Indigenous cultures. Clark is forced to cross 'unfrequented deserts' inhabited by 'barbarous hordes'. Whoever assisted him certainly felt free to inject his own words into the narrative, yet strangely, Clark's true voice—more descriptive and restrained, and less given to melodrama and hyperbole—is always apparent. How much material he left unpublished is difficult to estimate because the original journal has never been found. But the British journalist certainly gave his abstract the full romantic treatment, converting Clark's experience into the predestined triumph of brave British men who overcame the 'natives' and unimaginable horrors on the 'inhospitable shores' of New South Wales'. Eventually, the story Clark published in Calcutta found its way back to Sydney and later appeared in Historical Records of New South Wales, thus slipping into history.[39]

In February 1798, as Robert Campbell prepared to sail for Sydney aboard the *Hunter* (an ingenious example of flattery, which was designed to win the Governor over to the agency's future trading plans), Hamilton was making his second and final voyage back to Preservation Island on the *Francis* with Matthew Flinders, who had happily agreed to Hunter's request to survey as much of the area as possible. During their 4-day stay on the island, Hamilton watched over the loading of the last of the *Sydney Cove*'s cargo. Broken up by the westerly winds, the ship's beams and timbers were now scattered along the shorelines of the neighbouring islands, the flotsam of speculative commerce. Flinders busied himself charting the islands and acquainting himself with the local wildlife. 'I levelled my gun at [a large seal], which was sitting on top of a rock with his nose extended up towards the sun, and struck him with three musket balls. He rolled over, and plunged over into the water; but in less than half an hour had taken his former station and attitude. On firing again, a stream of blood spouted forth from his breast to some yards distance, and he fell back, senseless. On examination, the six balls were found lodged in his breast; and one, which occasioned his death, had pierced his heart: his weight was equal to that of a common ox'. Mapping and shooting went hand in hand. Everything that moved had to be tasted: wombats (like 'lean mutton'), echidnas ('somewhat aromatic') and penguins ('strong and fishy'), their skin making excellent waterproof caps. Flinders's crew killed 'as many large [seals] as there was time to skin whilst taking the bearings', as well as capturing a wombat, which he took back with him to Sydney where Hunter, after failing to keep the animal alive, 'preserved it in spirits' and shipped it to 'the Literary & Philosophical Society ... at Newcastle upon Tyne' where it remains today in Newcastle's Great North Museum, a stuffed specimen standing ridiculously on its back haunches like a gigantic squirrel.[40]

Flinders, who had been unable to accompany Hamilton on his first journey to Preservation Island six months earlier, left the question of the strait undecided as the *Francis* sailed quickly back to Sydney as soon as the cargo was loaded, although later that year he returned with George Bass and proved the existence of the strait that Hamilton had all but confirmed. Like Collins and Hunter, Flinders recorded Clark and Hamilton's stories of the wreck, and the traces of his astonishment at their survival are visible in his brief but vivid account. When he arrived in Sydney with Hamilton, their bounty of sealskins created a frenzy of interest. Before the year was out, a ship had set up base on the south coast of Cape Barren Island. This enterprise would result in the successful sale of over nine thousand skins to a Canton merchant. In the years ahead, many other firms and speculators would follow them, including none other than Campbell & Co. Well before the first British settlement in Tasmania at Risdon Cove in September 1803, there were over two hundred sealers living on the islands of Bass Strait. Stories were later told of these men building 'double ended boats' from the 'timbers' of the *Sydney Cove*, as they went from island to island 'clubbing seals'. In 1802, the crew of Nicolas Baudin's *Naturaliste* noted the large numbers of seals on the islands and saw the remains of the *Sydney Cove*'s 'sternpost'. Hamilton's hut on Preservation Island quickly became a halfway house for bands of sealers and the Aboriginal women they 'traded' or stole from the mainland.[41]

With all the salvaged cargo now safely unloaded in Sydney, Hamilton immediately arranged for its sale on Campbell's behalf. Although Hunter had already agreed that the government would purchase the spirits, no other collection of goods had been as much discussed in the colony's short history. With little competition, the cargo fetched 'enormous prices'. Collins looked on with dismay, complaining that the money that should have been spent on improving farms was 'lavishly thrown away'. For Hamilton, the huge profits were at least some compensation for all he had endured. He had fulfilled his responsibilities beyond all expectations. Yet when he was finally relieved of his duty, he fell ill.

Few details are known about Hamilton's life in Sydney between July 1797 and mid-1798. Robert Campbell was already on his way from Calcutta to Sydney when the cargo was sold in March. When he arrived in the *Hunter* on 10 June, Hamilton was gravely ill. He had little more than a week to live. Time enough though to tell Campbell his story and to inform him of the successful retrieval and sale of the cargo. It was eighteen months since they last spoke in Calcutta. Unfortunately, no report of their conversation exists, nor of Hamilton's logbook from the *Sydney Cove*, which was most likely lost in the wreck. Hamilton died in the third week of June 1798 aged thirty-eight, almost as if he had waited until the moment he could personally account for the ship's fate in the presence of its owner. Collins, who reported Hamilton's death, indicated that his health had been poor since he was rescued from Preservation Island: 'Captain Hamilton, the commander of the *Sydney Cove*, survived the arrival of the *Hunter* but a few days. He never recovered from the distresses and hardships which he suffered on the loss of his ship, and died exceedingly regretted by all who had the pleasure of his acquaintance'. Hamilton's funeral was held at St Phillip's Church, the wattle and daub structure that would be burnt down only three months later by convicts angered at Hunter's decree that attendance at church services was compulsory. He was buried in the cemetery in George St near the site of today's Sydney Town Hall. Robert Campbell wrote the initial inscription on his gravestone: 'Here lieth the body of Captain Gavin Hamilton, Commander of the ship *Sydney Cove*, who departed this life June 20 1798, Aged 38 years'.[42]

Campbell returned to Calcutta shortly after Hamilton's death, having sold most of the *Hunter*'s shipment for a handsome profit and purchasing harbour-frontage in preparation for his return as a merchant on a more permanent basis. In Calcutta, from late 1798 until August 1799, he continued to trade in 'wines and goods of every description' with William and John Clark. Before Campbell returned permanently to Sydney, the Clarks entered a new partnership with another Scot, Allan Maclean, a firm that was still trading when Campbell left Calcutta for his new life in Australia in early 1800. Two months later, William Clark's death was reported in the Calcutta press: '30 April, William Clark, died in Calcutta, aged 32, buried in the South Park Burial Ground', today one of the oldest cemeteries in the city.[43]

Whether Clark died from one of the countless tropical diseases that killed thousands of Europeans in late-eighteenth-century Calcutta or from some other cause long related to his ordeal in Australia is difficult to know. During these years it was not uncommon for European residents of the city to 'gather together in the cold season just to congratulate each other on having survived'.[44] Perhaps Clark had decided that he would never again return to New South Wales. Perhaps he walked himself not only to Sydney but also out of the entire country forever. Like Hamilton, yet unlike every other person who died as a result of the *Sydney Cove*'s misadventure, Clark died under the weight of his memories and still bearing the physical scars from his trial in the wilderness, the last of the ship's leading men to fall.

William Clark never published any further account of his experience in New South Wales. His brother John probably inherited his precious journal, which likely remained with William until his death, along with his other possessions. In 1802, John Clark returned to England and filed his will before travelling north to his birthplace in Campbeltown where he died a wealthy man on 21 June 1804. He left a substantial inheritance to his 'nephew' William Clark, whom he encouraged to sail to Calcutta as soon as he turned eighteen, and there establish himself as a merchant as his uncles had done before him. In the days after John Clark's death his relatives searched his house looking for his will. They claimed to have found it in a 'small travelling portmanteau which had arrived with the deceased but a very few days before from London and in which he frequently kept his papers of moment and consignment'. He had apparently crossed out several sections of his will, which they testified had indeed been made in his hand and not in one of their own. Regardless of their intentions, the 'Bengal merchant' John Clark had accumulated enough riches to keep most of his extended family members financially secure for the rest of their lives.[45]

When I visited Campbeltown in late 2014, I held a faint hope that the contents of John Clark's portmanteau (including the Holy Grail—William Clark's journal) might be found somewhere in a local archive or in a forgotten trunk of family memorabilia kept by one of his descendants. I combed local libraries, museums and historical societies and the state archives in Glasgow. I published the story of the wreck in local newspapers to alert as many people as possible to my search. Silence. But I did come away with the unforgettable memory of Clark's homeland: the bare, windswept, impossibly green hills of Kintyre and Arran and their run of tight-knit towns huddled on the north-east edge of the Atlantic. Of the world that existed in the late eighteenth century, little remained save the simple, elegantly carved, medieval Celtic cross that stood in the town's main street. I left Scotland mindful of the courage and sheer gumption displayed by Clark and Hamilton in journeying so far from their homeland. The steps they took to advance their wealth and knowledge, and the cultural differences they encountered, were far greater than anything we could possibly experience today. Theirs was truly a journey into the unknown.

In years of searching, my most remarkable find was not in Scotland but in the Mitchell Library in Sydney, when on little more than a hunch, I requested a box entitled 'collection of pamphlets consisting mainly of Australian biographies'. Apparently, somewhere in this collection there was a cutting relating to Captain Gavin Hamilton. It proved to be far more than a mere biographical reference. In the very bottom of the box I found a large envelope with the handwritten title: 'Captain Gavan Hamilton and the Campbell's of the Wharf and Duntroon'. Inside was a batch of correspondence from the first decade of the twentieth century that brought me closer to Hamilton than I had ever expected to come.

The most surprising document in the collection was a letter written on 18 April 1910 by John Hamilton of 'The Pound', Heathcote, Victoria to Captain JH Watson, vice-president of the Australian Historical Society. Responding to Watson's article in a Sydney newspaper on the wreck of the *Sydney Cove* and the burial of Gavin Hamilton, John Hamilton offered a rare glimpse into his family history. His father was 'Captain Peter Hamilton, mariner and shipowner at Port Glasgow 1840', who was born in '1796' on the 'Isle of Arran'. Peter was Gavin Hamilton's nephew. With his parents and young family, nine in all, he left Scotland in October 1841 bound for Port Phillip on the barque *Welcome,* captained by the 19-year-old Henry Morris. He had promised the ship's owner that he would watch over Morris and be sure that 'everything was right on the way'. Everything did go smoothly until the ship tried to enter Port Phillip Bay on 13 February 1842 but was forced back due to strong northerly winds. When the *Welcome* finally managed to reach The Heads on 22 February, the ship was buffeted by gale-force winds and storms off Cape Nelson. Moments after Peter Hamilton left instructions with two men at the wheel and walked forward along the deck, a large wave 'smashed 16 feet of the bulwarks' and swept him overboard. He was never seen again. The waters of Bass Strait had claimed two members of the Hamilton family. Peter lost his life only a few days' sail from where his uncle was shipwrecked forty-four years earlier. After relating the tragic tale of his father's death, John Hamilton then turned to the story of the *Sydney Cove*, offering a remarkable summary of the correspondence his ancestors in Arran had received from his great-uncle Gavin Hamilton in the 1790s:

This statement I am going to give you about Gavin Hamilton is what I heard from my mother & eldest brother who are both dead now. My mother was born in 1806 & died in her 94th year … The last letter my Grandfather received from Gavan was from India saying you need not expect me home for some years yet as I am about to sail with a full cargo to a new & distant land but he did not say where the land was. He had been away for 6 years then trading somewhere. The next word we had from India was that Gavan & his ship had never reached the port of destination, she had become a total wreck & all hands lost, it did not say where she was lost. As my grandfather heard he had some property out at Bengal he wrote out to see about it. The word he got [from] home was that his papers had all been lost in the wreck & they could not do anything about it …[46]

These few words of family oral history conjured another world, one in which lands still remained 'unknown' and in which time, distance and communication were imagined on a completely different scale. A world where Gavin Hamilton could think of sailing to an unnamed 'distant land' and write Shackleton-like to his family: 'do not expect me home for some years'. Robert Campbell or William Clark undoubtedly wrote from Calcutta with news of the loss of the ship although it is possible that Hamilton had also written to his family from Sydney. In a later letter to Watson, penned in 1910, John Hamilton implied that such correspondence existed: 'My sister wrote home to our cousins at Arran to see if their mother (my aunt who died a few years ago aged 86) must have destroyed all the letters. I also think the same as you do that we shall not learn anything further'.[47] Old letters—the stuff of history—consume too much space for the living. But Gavin Hamilton's story lived on in another way. When the old Sydney Burial Ground on George Street was closed in the late 1860s, Hamilton's was the only 'legible headstone' left standing. The graverobbers and stray pigs that had disturbed so many other graves in the cemetery over the years appeared to have accorded him unusual respect. In the same envelope in which I found John Hamilton's letter was another letter to Watson from F Campbell of Yarralumla, the grandson of Robert Campbell. Written in June 1910, it told the story of how Hamilton's grave was moved to Rookwood.

[Hamilton's gravestone] was placed there by the late Hon. John Campbell of Campbell's Wharf (Campbell & Co.) some fifty years or more ago, who also took care the bones were conveyed carefully from the site of the present Town Hall to the necropolis at Rookwood. In regard to the possible existence of any authentic diary of these heroic sailors sufferings, I should under the circumstances have very grave doubts.[48]

After his return to Sydney in 1800, Robert Campbell established himself as one of the colony's most successful merchants and squatters. As part compensation for the loss of one of his ships, he eventually received an extremely generous grant of over four thousand acres (1600 hectares) of land near Queanbeyan, which he named Duntroon. Throughout his later life, Campbell told the story of the wreck of the *Sydney Cove* to his family and friends on countless occasions. Long after he died, the details of the story in the oral history of the family blurred. Hamilton became Clark. He was both captain of the ship and the man who led the surviving walkers to Sydney where he died a hero's death, 'laid up by his sufferings'. But the depth of the Campbell family's debt to Hamilton was amply illustrated by the poignant story of Robert's eldest son, John, who had listened to his father tell the story so many times as he grew up, personally accompanying Hamilton's remains for reburial in Rookwood Cemetery. In both families the saga of the *Sydney Cove* became an origin story that explained their presence in Australia. In 1997, the bicentenary of the wreck of the *Sydney Cove*, Hamilton's descendants gathered on Preservation Island to commemorate the event. The survival of the story in national memory was another matter.[49]

The names that were eternally marked on the map of the Furneaux Islands after the wreck of the *Sydney Cove*—Clarke Island, Preservation Island, Hamilton's Road, Armstrong's Channel and Rum Island—were not eligible to be the names of the nation's discoverers. From the moment George Bass returned in the *Reliance* after establishing the existence of Bass Strait, his tiny vessel was 'consecrated' by the colonists in Sydney. As the French naturalist and historian Francois Peron astutely observed after his time in the colony, Bass's vessel was 'preserved in [Sydney] harbour, with a sort of religious veneration: some snuff boxes have been made out of its keel, of which the possessors are both proud and jealous; and the governor himself thought he could not make a more acceptable present to our chief than a piece of the wood of this sloop, encased in a large silver tooth-pick box; round which were engraved the principle particulars of the discovery of [Bass] straits'. In a convict colony desperate to establish respectability and a more honourable founding history than the one thrown ashore by the miscreants of Great Britain, the story of the *Sydney Cove* was of little use save as an accidental usher to far more worthy events. Yet if Bass and Flinders knew the country at all, it was largely from the deck of their ships as they mapped the periphery of an unknown land. They only made the occasional foray inland and their judgement of what they saw was swift. As Hunter said of Bass's journey in early 1798, he made 'several excursions into the interior of the country' on his way back to Port Jackson, and 'found in general a barren, unpromising country, with very few exceptions, and were it even better, the want of harbours would render it less valuable'. Clark knew the coastal lands of southern New South Wales far more intimately than Bass and Flinders. The land they found bare, he found fertile. Every inch of the coastal country they had surveyed through the eyes of a telescope, he had traversed on foot. The country was indelibly imprinted on his soul.[50]

Throughout the nineteenth and twentieth centuries, the wreck of the *Sydney Cove* and William Clark's epic trek appeared briefly in general histories of maritime exploration and occasionally in the Australian and British press. The Lascars were almost always reduced to minor bit players or denigrated for their lack of 'initiative', while the 'Aborigines' appeared more often than not as sources of hindrance rather than help.[51] At other times, they were maligned for having 'either harried the exhausted men or carelessly [thrown] them the remains of [their] savage meals'.[52] These heroic renditions often involved what appear in retrospect as diversionary spats over the 'first white [man] to set foot on the soil of Victoria', 'the first to set foot on Bass Strait soil' or mistaken claims that the *Sydney Cove* was the 'first wreck of a British vessel in Australian waters'.[53]

In the early twentieth century, one newspaper account suggested that the shipwreck survivors did not qualify as true discoverers. Clark's party apparently did little more than test the ground for more worthy characters such as George Bass, who was really 'the first white man to tread the shores of the Southern Province'.[54] In 1947, a memorial was erected at Coalcliff to mark the 150th anniversary of Clark's discovery of coal, and another in 1997 at Tathra on the New South Wales south coast, to commemorate the bicentenary of '17 brave sailors' 'desperate walk to safety'.[55] In a futile attempt to invest the walkers with nobility, the maverick historian Isaac Selby wrote a 5-act play in 1956 entitled *The Pilgrims of New Holland*. Fortunately, Selby's wooden script was never performed.[56] No matter how hard they tried, whether by harping on the first white man theme, the beginning of the sealing industry, the discovery of Bass Strait or returning again to the discovery of coal, the tellers could not deny that the story had passed 'utterly out of the memory of men'.[57] Not until January 1977, when a team of Launceston divers found the remains of the *Sydney Cove* at the very moment interest in Australian history was booming, was the wreck and surrounding area legislated as an 'historic site'. Diver Ken Atherton found the ship 'sitting in a sand bar in about 6 metres of water ... all that was showing was two or three planks of wood, the rudder and the rudder stock'.[58] After delicate excavations of the wreck in the 1990s, which eventually resulted in artefacts from the *Sydney Cove* forming the basis of a permanent exhibition at Launceston's Queen Victoria Museum, excavations of land sites on Preservation Island in the 2000s, and the ongoing research and publications of maritime archaeologist Mike Nash over more than two decades, the story of the *Sydney Cove* was finally lifted from relative obscurity to greater prominence.[59] The Scout Associations of Victoria and New South Wales staged a re-enactment of the walk for its bicentenary in 1997. When they reached Sydney they placed artefacts from the wreck of the *Sydney Cove* with the remains of Gavin Hamilton in Rookwood Cemetery.[60] And in 2012, Sydney Harbour Foreshore Authority sponsored a creative 'Bollywood' interpretation of the ship's voyage 'as told though the eyes of an 11-year-old Indian-Australian girl'.[61] The story was gaining greater traction in local communities and slowly becoming more inclusive. Yet the most difficult part of the story to grasp—the exchanges between Clark's party and the Aboriginal people they met during their long walk north—remains the source of its greatest significance and mystery.

Relics from the *Sydney Cove* in storage, Queen Victoria Museum, Launceston, Tasmania, 2013

Contemplating the artefacts from the *Sydney Cove* that rest behind glass in the Queen Victoria Museum at Launceston—Indian leather shoes, clay pipes, an hourglass, the broken mouthpiece of a flute, exquisite Chinese porcelain, stray pieces of the ship's timbers smoothed and sculpted into corporeal stillness after two centuries lying on the ocean floor, bottles of 'pale ale' with the Campbell & Clark imprint still visible on their wax seals—each object painstakingly labelled, numbered, catalogued and memorialised, it is possible to see how we create history through material remains far more readily than we do through the telling of stories alone.

To exhume the great drama at the heart of the story of the wreck of the *Sydney Cove* is to grapple with the central, elusive drama of Australian history itself: the encounter between Aboriginal people and the strangers who came across the seas to claim their lands. Through the eyes of William Clark we glimpse the different coastal territories and cultures of Aboriginal people to the south of Sydney, and through the Lascars, shadows though they may be on the pages of Clark's journal, we witness how 'subject' peoples were forcibly swept up by the British Empire's relentless pursuit of knowledge and wealth. And in the months-long struggle between Clark, Thompson and the carpenter over how to 'handle' Aboriginal people, we find the embodiment of the ongoing dilemma of British colonisation: how should 'we' deal with 'them'? Should we try and understand Aboriginal people? Should we recognise and respect their cultural difference, or should we ask them to speak, work, pray and think like 'us'?

The story of Clark's walk along the coast is one of strangers who pass through vast areas of the country and leave Aboriginal cultures intact. Nearly all the party's contact with Aboriginal people was peaceful. If not for the generosity of those they met along the way, all seventeen walkers would have perished long before they reached Sydney. There was in fact very little conflict. It is overwhelmingly a story of cooperation and hope. Perhaps now, after more than two centuries, we finally have the eyes for what took place on the beaches of New South Wales in 1797.

63

CHAPTER TWO

'World's End': Port Essington, Cobourg Peninsula, West Arnhem Land

Their first thought was of England. The sight of the chalk-white cliffs reminded them of home: visions of Dover in the Arafura Sea. But any trace of familiarity would soon be shattered. Even for those among them who knew New South Wales, this was another country. From here, Sydney, more than four thousand kilometres to the south, seemed as far away as London. The place they would dub 'World's End' had its own suffocating rhythms: the air thick and heavy, the sea warm to touch, the mangroves putrid and impenetrable, the

The white cliffs of 'home', Port Essington, 2014

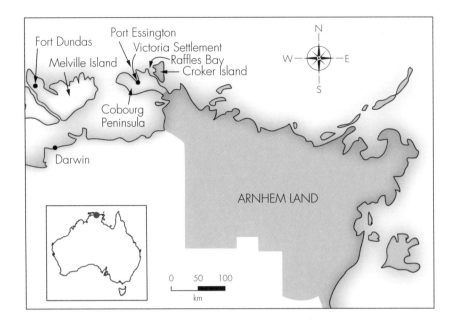

heat oppressive, the mosquitoes and white ants voracious. They were always under attack.[1]

In the dry season, from April to late August, the south-easterlies provided some relief. But from the end of September when the winds eased, a stifling stillness and humidity descended. The isolation they experienced was not only one of distance. Everything was out of alignment: the seasons, the climate and every element of the natural world. Even their bodies seemed ill adjusted—the perspiration that poured daily from their skin, the inevitable rashes and fevers, the languorous days and the long, sleepless nights. As white men and women in Australia's tropical north, they felt and lived *out of place*.

Here, at Port Essington, on the tip of the Cobourg Peninsula in West Arnhem Land between 1838 and 1849, a small band of British officials and marines attempted to found a garrison in the far north of the continent. They were trying for the third time. Spurred on by fears that the Dutch or the French would settle Australia's northern coastline, two earlier attempts by Britain to 'check-mate' their imperial rivals—at Fort Dundas on Melville Island (1824–29), and Raffles Bay on the north-eastern end of the Cobourg Peninsula (1827–29)—had failed miserably. The question of whether foreign powers could take possession of points on the coast of Australia was 'much debated at the time'. In 1824, uncertain of its sovereignty over northern Australia, the British government sent the 38-year-old Captain James Gordon Bremer of the Royal Navy, a veteran of the Battle of Trafalgar, to take possession at Port Essington. Bremer sailed up the east coast of Australia from Sydney, passing through the Torres Strait before heading along the north coast, his crew amazed by the 'immense body of light' that emanated from the 'natives' burning of Country, the evening glow so bright that it made everything 'perfectly visible' for miles around.[2]

When Bremer arrived at Port Essington on 20 September, he took possession through the customary rituals, which, in the proud words of his ship's purser, Henry Ennis, saw vast swathes of foreign territories 'turned, as it were by magic, into … British settlement[s]'. Marines were landed on shore, a tall, 'conspicuous tree' was 'cleaned round for the occasion', a 'new' Union Jack was nailed to it and the proclamation read loudly. Bremer took possession of 'the north coast of New Holland, or Australia … between the meridian of 129 [degrees] and 135 [degrees] east of Greenwich, with all the bays, rivers, harbours, creeks, &c. in, and all the islands laying off … in the name and in the right of His Most Excellent Majesty George the Fourth, King of the United Kingdom of Great Britain and Ireland'. 'Three volleys' were fired, the 'colours saluted', and 'three hearty cheers' roared, before Bremer's ship, the *Tamar*, replied with a royal salute of twenty-one guns.[3]

Such was the manner in which pieces of Australia were gradually spirited away under British law. Hundreds of thousands of square kilometres of Aboriginal lands—Bremer effectively extended the western border of New South Wales to the current border between Western Australia and the Northern Territory—became the property of the Crown through exuberant incantation. It was miraculous. Possession of Country occurred without knowledge of Country and without any need to negotiate with its Indigenous owners. By sending Bremer to the north coast of the continent, Britain was effectively admitting that in order to successfully ward off rival European powers, its possession of the country needed to be asserted anew in different parts of the continent. Australia was not founded in one moment;

rather, it was possessed in an ad hoc, piecemeal fashion, the arms of British law seizing the continent gradually over several decades.

Unable to find sufficient water at Port Essington, Bremer sailed on to establish Fort Dundas on Melville Island, where he hoisted the colours on 21 October, the anniversary of the Battle of Trafalgar, and 'gave dinner on board for eighteen', washed down with 'bumpers of claret'. Before he departed from Port Essington, his lieutenant, John Septimus Roe, who had accompanied Phillip Parker King in the *Mermaid* in April 1818 and later became the first Surveyor-General of Western Australia, buried a bottle 'containing a parchment with an account of our having taken possession of that part of the country for the British Crown'. Deep in the same hole and around the fireplace they had used, Roe left coins 'to show [they] had been there' before giving 'Ilamarryi'—the narrow strip of land that divided the inner and outer harbours—the somewhat prosaic name of 'Point Record'. They believed the country was now theirs. But taking legal possession was one thing, conquering territory quite another. On the shores of Port Essington in 1824, Bremer's possession of the country existed on paper only.[4]

During the handful of days Bremer's party spent at Port Essington in September 1824, they saw no 'Aborigines', only countless 'birds of a beautiful plumage'. Yet there seems little doubt that from elevated positions across the water, not far from where Bremer would ultimately establish Victoria Settlement in 1838, Aboriginal people watched the movements of his ship and crew with hushed curiosity, just as they had observed King's *Mermaid* six years earlier. Then, when King had tried to explore 'an opening in the mangroves', they had screamed 'loudly in angry threatening voices' and showered his men with spears and stones. The sight of Bremer's ship anchored offshore was not unprecedented. From the early seventeenth century they had heard reports of Dutch ships passing along the coast, one of which, *Nieuw Holland*, entered Port Essington in 1705. Bremer's *Tamar* was merely another white bird that would appear for a few days and be gone, perhaps returning generations into the future.[5]

Fourteen years later, in late August 1838, as Bremer's four ships— *Britomart*, *Orontes*, *Alligator* and the chartered schooner *Essington*—

67

stood in Sydney Harbour loading their equipment and stores in preparation for founding the garrison at Port Essington, the captain and his crew were addressed by the city's leading merchants, among them Robert Campbell, former owner of the *Sydney Cove* and esteemed member of the New South Wales Legislative Council. On the deck of the *Alligator*, Campbell and his colleagues told Bremer of their hopes for the settlement 'in the wilds of Australia' and how it would surely become a booming port for 'trade with the Islands of the Eastern Archipelago', no doubt filling their pockets with rivers of cash for years to come. For now, they refrained from investment until settlers were granted access to land. Newspaper editorials imagined a port that would become 'one of the most important centres of civilization and Christianisation in the known world', and a 'half-way house for future steam boats from Sydney to Calcutta'. Bremer had the good sense to remind them of the 'difficulties and privations' that were 'inseparable' from a position such as Port Essington. Well prepared, he carried a ready-made settlement in the holds of his ships—cows, sheep, pigs, poultry, 'giant kangaroo dogs' and several prefabricated buildings that could be erected quickly on arrival—although things did not begin well when, ominously, a punt ferrying the building materials for the church sunk in the harbour, delaying his departure by several days.[6]

When Bremer finally arrived for the second time on the shores of Port Essington in October 1838 with thirty-six Royal Marines, he carried the expectations not only of the British Admiralty but also of Sydney's political class, many of whom saw him as the founder of a new Singapore—a thriving 'emporium' that would one day become the capital of northern Australia. They believed that the garrison would flourish as lands in the interior were gradually opened up to thousands of free settlers. It would also serve as a safe haven for ships passing through the Coral Sea and Torres Strait. In honour of his 'Virgin Queen', who had ascended to the throne little more than one year earlier, Bremer named the settlement Victoria. Along the shoreline of a harbour 'sufficiently spacious to contain all the ships in the world', he could see the tamarind trees that marked the campsites of Makassan fishermen, evidence of just some of the trade he hoped to cultivate in the years ahead. Yet within a matter of months it became clear that without a dramatic influx of free settlers, any suggestion of an expanding colony was little more than fantasy.[7]

For most Australians, the story of Victoria Settlement is largely unknown. Except for historians of Australia's north and those who reside in the Northern Territory, it occupies a minor footnote in the history of colonisation. Like the bottle buried in the sand by John Septimus Roe in 1824, it is yet to be discovered as a failed founding moment in Australia's historical imagination. Failure is certainly not the reason for forgetting. Australians have remembered and even celebrated failures, Gallipoli being the prime example. But the story of the 11-year-long struggle to establish Victoria Settlement is much more than an ill-conceived venture plagued by environmental disasters that was never given sufficient backing by the imperial government. More than two decades before Darwin was founded and at a time when the British settlements in Port Phillip, Adelaide and Perth were still in their infancy, the settlement at Port Essington carried the first wave of countless dreams of developing Australia's north, and it said much about the shifting strategies of British colonisation. The eyes of Bremer's garrison were turned outwards to Asia and the Pacific while the vast continent at its back remained an ocean of obscurity.

The British were the last to arrive at Port Essington. From the early eighteenth century, Aboriginal people had been accustomed to the annual visits of Makassan fishermen from Sulawesi as they exploited Australia's northern coastline for pearl and turtle shells and trepang (otherwise known as sea slug or bêche-de-mer), an exotic delicacy prized as an aphrodisiac in China. Long recognised as one of the most important trepang sites on the Australian coast, Port Essington usually received the Makassans in December. They often anchored at 'Point Record' and stayed until March or April, attracting Aboriginal people from up and down the coast and far inland. As well as items of trade such as textiles, rice, tobacco, Dutch gin, iron knives and tomahawks, they brought with them prefabricated 'hut panels of woven cane', which they used as living quarters and smoke houses. Eager to travel, Aboriginal men had long sailed with the Makassans to Indonesia and far beyond, sometimes living away from home for several years.

Languages, ideas, goods and blood—Dutch, Malay, Timorese and Papuan—had mingled with Indigenous cultures in the north for generations. This was a littoral world of cross-cultural contact and long established trade networks in which the British would largely remain outside observers—an intricate web of land and sea that was already founded and storied in deep time.[8]

The local land-owning Aboriginal group at Victoria was the Majurnbalmi clan, who spoke Garig as well as the languages of neighbouring Cobourg clans with whom they intermarried and collaborated, such as Iwaidja, Wurruku and Marrku. They also spoke Makassarese, pidgin Malay and pidgin English, which they had learnt during the brief British settlement at Raffles Bay. Long before Bremer arrived, the country around Victoria Settlement was multicultural and multilingual. Consequently, no single term accurately identifies the Aboriginal people who lived at Port Essington in 1838. Our instinctive need for one tidy tribal name falls short. The society was complex, its networks of association and cultural knowledge intricate and extensive, understood by only a handful of outsiders nearly two hundred years later.[9]

News of the Makassans and the lands to the north of the Arafura Sea travelled inland. In the rock shelters of the Arnhem Land escarpment, where the extraordinary galleries of Aboriginal art had existed for thousands of years, diamond designs and 'parallel, horizontal and vertical blocks' were inspired by the decorative patterns found in Indonesian textiles, while sketches of Dutch ships had graced the same walls centuries before Bremer arrived to found Victoria Settlement in 1838. The north coast of Australia, which the Makassans called 'Marege', was a vast tapestry of Indigenous Countries, each connected to the wider world and bearing its own distinctive cultural traditions and spirit of place. In Arnhem Land alone there were more than twenty different language groups when the British arrived, many of them already infiltrated by European and Makassan words. Over four hundred Indigenous place names on the Cobourg Peninsula bear testament to the intricate knowledge of Country honed, practised and maintained over millennia by its Aboriginal inhabitants whose languages today have largely fallen into disuse.[10]

From the ruins of Victoria Settlement, the remains of the jetty visible in the distance, 2014

Like William Clark's epic trek through the Indigenous territories of south-east Australia in 1797, the story at the heart of Victoria Settlement is the meeting between the Indigenous people of the Cobourg Peninsula and those who came to take possession of their land. Their contact was different from almost everywhere else in Australia. Because the British made no attempt to settle the inland and the garrison remained relatively small and vulnerable, Aboriginal people were largely free from the threat of losing their land. The relative absence of violence created an unusual laboratory of mutual fascination and cultural exchange. At its forefront was a diverse cast of European drop-ins: Royal Marines, scientists, carpenters, blacksmiths, surgeons, naturalists, artists, gardeners, linguists, buccaneers, explorers and missionaries. All of them were drawn to understand Indigenous language and culture, to gain even the smallest insight into another way of being in the world.

———

In the 'grey' light of the morning of 27 October 1838, the *Alligator* sailed into Port Essington harbour. The sense of anticipation coupled with the awareness that those on board were about to found a new British settlement silenced everyone. All hands stood on deck 'occupied with [their] own thoughts', looking 'anxiously' across the water to 'catch a glimpse of the spot' where Bremer would disgorge the contents of his Noah's Ark and pitch camp.

On the voyage north from Sydney, Bremer's 'draughtsman and linguist', 25-year-old George Augustus Earl, stayed out each night 'leaning over the hammock nettings', wondering if he would live to see Australia's northern shores 'occupied by a busy people'. Now, as the land 'clothed in open forest' came slowly into view, he noticed a group of Aboriginal people camped on the beach. But the scene before him was not what he had expected. They were 'dressed up in all sorts of fantastic finery which they had obtained from the crew' of the schooner *Essington* which had arrived ten days earlier. Wearing the clothes of English gentlemen was their reward for helping the *Essington*'s commander to off-load the frame of the church. In the deluded eyes of its chief sponsor, Bishop of Australia William Grant Broughton, the church would quickly become the epicentre of 'Christianity in the Arafura Sea'.[11]

As the *Alligator* came closer to shore, two Aboriginal men approached the ship in a canoe. On board, Earl watched as the elder man, 'Langari', delivered a 'long address, shedding many tears and frequently touching his shoulders with both hands in a sort of half embrace', while the younger man, 'Wanji-wanji', stood in 'a state of intense fright', his teeth chattering, his eyes 'rolling about in agony of alarm'. The two men had come from nearby Raffles Bay and had known Captain Collet Barker, the commandant of the short-lived settlement there in the late 1820s. Barker had established warm relations with the Aboriginal people after his predecessor, Captain Henry

Smyth, in a frenzied reprisal attack, had killed up to thirty men, women and children. In the few months before the settlement was abandoned, Barker camped with them and joined in performances of their songs and dance in an effort to regain their trust. It was no coincidence that Langari and Wanji-wanji, who believed Bremer to be Barker returned, wished to be dressed in European clothes as they had done on so many occasions when Barker lived among them nine years earlier. Because of the previous settlement at Raffles Bay, Aboriginal people at Port Essington had far more experience of the British than Bremer's marines had of them. They knew the brute force of British arms—at Raffles Bay, Smyth had fired an 18-pounder cannon at them—and they knew the pleasures of cross-cultural friendship and exchange. Most of Bremer's party, however, had joined the expedition in Plymouth and had only limited or second-hand knowledge of 'Aborigines'. In the months that followed, it was the new arrivals that would have the most to learn.[12]

Like Bremer, Earl was an irrepressible enthusiast for the future prospects of the settlement. Appointed as the government's official 'interpreter', his task was to familiarise himself with the 'native' languages and people at Port Essington. Young, curious, possessed of a razor-sharp intellect and a wry sense of humour, he was also keenly aware of the challenge of persuading others to his point of view. In a typically candid moment before leaving Sydney, he flippantly remarked that apart from Bremer, commander of the Royal Marines Captain John McArthur, himself and one or two others, 'not a soul among us appears to care much whether we succeed or not'. As they loaded the provisions and cargo, many men told him how much they feared the long periods of isolation ahead. For those accustomed to life in London or Sydney, the prospect of living indefinitely in a tiny community thousands of kilometres from the nearest British settlement filled them with dread. Now they were here, Earl immediately saw how the necessity of providing the basic means of survival—clearing trees, shooting game, planting seedlings and erecting buildings—helped to keep those fears at bay. Keeping busy was the answer to stress and anxiety, filling every waking hour with work until there was only one thing to do at the end of the day—collapse into an exhausted heap. And so it proved at Port Essington, at least initially.

After Bremer settled on the site of the settlement immediately north of the 'white cliffs', roads were cut, wells sunk, tents set up, the prefabricated frames were laid out on shore, while the land for the garden was 'enclosed' and made ready to receive the plants from 'Rio Janeiro' and Sydney. Earl, who was not labouring himself, was elated to see so much activity: 'the woods absolutely rang with the sound of the hammer and in every direction the white posts of the new buildings were seen gleaming through the trees'. So 'addictive' had this daily grind become, Earl noticed how the men now baulked at the suggestion of returning home, the urgent task of furnishing their 'daily existence' allowing them to put aside 'all worldly consideration'.[13]

Assisting the British in building every block of their new Singapore were Aboriginal people: showing them their paths through the forest, leading them to their best springs, procuring them seafood (for which they traded biscuits, tobacco and clothes), 'bringing in honey', dragging away the branches of felled trees, ferrying supplies ashore, carrying provisions to and fro, and engaging occasionally in what the British labelled property 'theft' but which to them was property rightfully theirs. Although the experience of Aboriginal people on the Cobourg Peninsula with the Dutch, the Makassans and the British indicated that no visitor was likely to be a permanent presence on their lands, the ability of men such as 'Langari', 'Yamaloo', 'Miro', 'One-Eye', 'Mingo' and others from Raffles Bay to understand at least basic English suggests that Bremer was able to communicate his intentions: they were here to stay. In any case, the frantic construction that took place from dawn till dusk left them in little doubt. Within three months, Bremer boasted to Sir John Barrow in London that he had 'a very admirable little town' laid out like an English village, with thatched cottages and garden plots surrounding a main square. The storehouse, officers' quarters, pier, church, hospital, cemetery and Government House—'neatly painted with Venetian blinds'—were all but complete. Earl was amused by the 'war-like appearance' of the settlement. On 'the edge of the white cliff', the '*Alligator*'s eighteen-pounders' commanded the entrance to the inner harbour, the ship's cannons—almost ludicrously stark against the white rock—waiting for an enemy that would never materialise.[14]

Although the portability and relatively quick erection of prefabricated buildings was testament to the extraordinary mobility and resourcefulness that had long characterised British imperial expansion, it also revealed a cavalier indifference to the site-specific requirements of design and construction. While local Aboriginal people sheltered under simple shade structures in the dry months and 'relatively complicated' reed domes in the wet season, the British seemed determined to reconstruct little England in the tropics. Government House, with its small eaves, tiny windows and complete lack of ventilation, was a furnace all year round. The few marines whose wives had accompanied them were eventually housed in the 'married quarters', a row of ironstone Cornish cottages backed by garden plots, their dark chimneys stacked at the southern end.

In stifling humidity, the women, clothed from head to toe, stood over open fires in sauna-like conditions, pools of dignified perspiration oozing from every pore of their skin. John McArthur's observation regarding gardening at Port Essington held for every aspect of their venture: it was a constant challenge to 'abandon preconceived notions and prejudices'.[15]

75

Remains of the 'Married Quarters' at Victoria Settlement, Port Essington, 2014

The shock of the new—crocodiles devouring Bremer's dog and tugging at men's blankets as they slept in their hammocks, white ants finding the legs of his sofa despite him moving it daily from one corner of his tent to the next, and the sheer luxuriance of the natural environment—ensured that there were more than enough distractions in the first few months at Victoria Settlement. As Earl observed, everything possessed 'the charm of novelty', including Portuguese Timor and nearby islands, which were less than two weeks' sail away and ideal for securing supplies and spreading word of the garrison that clung to the water's edge at Port Essington. When one marine did venture inland from the settlement he was overwhelmed by the abundance of wildlife: wetland pools 'with over 500 black swans', wide river banks covered in palms 15 metres high, scores of flying foxes, multitudes of brightly coloured 'parakeets', giant crabs lurking in the mangrove swamps and the most beautiful waterlilies growing in the rivers. The intensity of colour, the richness of the light and the wild cacophony of unfamiliar forest sounds were arresting. Yet all of this paled before the curiosity and wonder they felt when contemplating Aboriginal people's skilful exploitation of natural resources.[16]

From the moment Bremer's party arrived in the harbour, they had admired the grace and dexterity with which Aboriginal people moved on land and sea. Their largest canoes, modelled on the Makassans' and preferably hewn from the 'kapok' ('wirdil') tree, were capable of carrying up to twenty people. One of their methods for catching fish suggested magic of a kind. After they had dragged 'whole Pandanus trees' through the water for several minutes, possibly to disperse another plant ('mayak'), the fish floated to the surface 'stupefied' by the 'narcotic' effects of the mayak's poison. At other times, women waded out to collect shellfish while the men immersed themselves in the mud flats waiting silently for a water bird to land before grabbing it with their bare hands. They were equally ingenious in finding honey in the forest, identifying the branches of the appropriate tree by 'whistling … in a peculiar manner, and thus inducing the bees to hover over their treasure-trove'. Once the swarm gathered over the hive they climbed the tree with their tomahawks and cut the branch down. To the marines who first journeyed inland, their navigational skills were mystifying. Walking through 'thinly but beautifully wooded country' along 'impressive' ancient paths connected by bridges made from palm, Aboriginal people found their way to their destination with 'extraordinary precision', far better than the British 'could have done with the best compasses ever made'. Once beyond the narrow bounds of the settlement, the British were almost entirely dependent on Aboriginal bushcraft. When one of Bremer's sailors went missing for four days, he was found on 'the verge of death' and taken to an Aboriginal camp where he was fed, his slashed and crippled feet 'washed' and other 'charitable offices' performed on him, before he was eventually returned to the settlement. Their generosity, skill and knowledge of the country could not be doubted. But none of this could shift the fundamental belief of the British that Aboriginal people occupied a lower scale of humanity. Despite knowing that they were clearly present before the British arrived, even someone as perceptive as Earl had his blind spot: '[We are] the first occupants of a new country' he wrote triumphantly.[17]

77

Wetlands, Cobourg
Peninsula, 2014

In early 1839, it appeared that the decades-long fear of French imperial ambitions in Australia was about to be realised. The French naval explorer Jules Dumont d'Urville entered Port Essington harbour in the *Astrolabe* and anchored close to the settlement on 7 April. On a mission to claim the South Pole for France, d'Urville devoted several months of his voyage to exploring the Pacific. He was pleased with what he found when he came ashore: 'I came up alongside a fine jetty about 6 metres long, solidly constructed and furnished with steps to facilitate landing. On the jetty is a flagstaff from which was flying the flag of Great Britain … Government house, built entirely of wood at Port Jackson, and set on piles, offered every comfort. All the rooms were well arranged and convenient: drawing room, bedrooms, study, bathroom, lavatory, offices—all was provided'. It was clear to d'Urville that the settlement's existence was to ward off the French and 'mark' the fact that the British had taken 'possession' of the entire continent. At the same time, he had grave doubts about Victoria's future.

That evening, mutual suspicions were put aside when d'Urville and his officers were invited to 'Monsieur Bremer's table' for dinner. Grateful for the invitation, d'Urville was nonetheless sceptical of his host's ability to provide haute cuisine from the settlement's produce alone. The thought of that, he sniffed, would be 'woeful'. 'But, thanks to beautiful beef, superb turkey and excellent Timorese poultry, accompanied by vintage Sauternes and Bordeaux, we had a charming dinner'. For the visitors' entertainment, Bremer's eldest son, Edward, performed a 'burlesque', miming Aboriginal dances, singing their songs and mimicking their use of the 'woomera and spear'. One hundred and fifty years later, when the first archaeological excavations took place at Victoria Settlement, Jim Allen unearthed the Chateau Margaux seals from the bottles that were probably drunk that evening: 'one of only four wines to be assigned the ultimate Premier Cru (first growth) status'. Nearby, in an Aboriginal midden, he discovered another glass bottle seal belonging to 'John Alberty Bordeaux Vieux Cognac', bottled in 1815. More a bacchanalian feast than a congress of imperial rivals in the South Pacific, the *grand repas* at Port Essington helped to clarify matters. When the haze from the vintage wines and tobacco smoke cleared the next morning, Bremer was convinced that the French posed no threat, while the French were glad to leave the settlement to what they were certain would be the same fate as Raffles Bay. As one of their officers acidly remarked, 'you [British] must have a mania for colonies to drop one down in Port Essington'.[18]

After eight months, in June 1839, the settlement was all but established and Bremer and Earl decided to leave for Sydney, leaving Victoria under the charge of the commander of the Royal Marines, Captain John McArthur, a dogged, melancholy man who would ultimately remain in the position for the duration of the settlement. Bremer had returned to Sydney to ascertain whether the British government had finally authorised the colonisation of Port Essington. Disappointed to discover that no instructions had been issued, he persuaded New South Wales Governor George Gipps to allow 'persons of respectability' to occupy half-acre 'town allotments, within a half a mile of the settlement', and 'suburban allotments of five acres each', within five miles, at an annual rent of 5 shillings per half-acre, an extremely unattractive proposition to settlers who could find more permanent land offers much closer to Sydney. But Bremer would never return to Victoria to realise his plans. After taking troops to Norfolk Island to help Gipps put down a convict rebellion, he was called away by the Admiralty to take command of the East Indies station and sailed off to settle trading disputes in China. As it turned out, he was fortunate to leave.[19]

Any trace of hubris concerning the future of Victoria was obliterated on 25 November 1839. 'At midnight the wind drew round to the eastward, and blew a perfect hurricane, before which nearly everything gave way; the trees came down in every part of the settlement, the marines' houses were all blown down, the church only finished a week shared the same fate'. Two hours later, the wind shifted suddenly to the north with tremendous fury. The gardens were 'uprooted' and Government House was torn from its stone piers and 'blown away from them to a distance of nine feet'. As the sea rose to 'ten feet and a half', the jetty and storehouses on the beach were washed away. The naval sloop HMS *Pelorus* was ripped from her moorings and 'driven on shore', her starboard side 'buried nine feet in the mud, leaving the keel three feet clear of the ground'. Eight people were drowned. Only the hospital and officers' mess survived unscathed. Surveying the scene in disbelief the following morning, McArthur wrote despondently that the 'work of 12 months had been nullified in 12 hours'. Earl, returning months later, found the desolation gave the country 'the appearance of England in the depth of winter'. The settlement had been all but wiped out.[20]

In the enormous effort of rebuilding Victoria, the process of adaptation was painful and slow. McArthur learnt to use the local ironwood, which although harder to work, was more resistant to white ants. Buildings were raised off the ground on 2.5-metre piles to allow for termite inspection, as in colonial Asia and Africa. The hospital was built from brick and stone. Bark cladding proved far cheaper and easier to use than weatherboards, while steep pitched roofs were far more effective against the tropical downfalls. All of this they learnt from trial and error. But there were other things that could not be adjusted so easily. For the few men and women who lived at Victoria throughout the 1840s there was a constant struggle to overcome isolation, ennui, homesickness and the very real threat of an early death. Malaria and other diseases stalked the settlement at every turn. Lieutenant George Lambrick lost his wife and two children within eighteen months. Nothing could stem the high attrition rate. As John Mulvaney calculated, the stark fact is that 'more than 40 per cent of persons stationed [at Port Essington] either died or were invalided out'. Those who attended the regular burial services at the cemetery wondered if they would be next.[21]

McArthur's correspondence, with its frequent mention of 'great suffering', makes for difficult reading, as does his palpable frustration with the time taken to communicate with the British government. It was impossible to make swift decisions. In the corridors of the British Admiralty and the Colonial Office, Port Essington was a strategic *point* on a map, a military outpost that was either to be funded and supported or abandoned. Letters to England from Victoria could take well over six months to arrive and more than a year would pass before a reply was received. In August 1843, after losing many to malaria, the settlement's numbers were reduced to forty-six. McArthur wrote to London requesting that a relief party be sent immediately. Seventeen months later a party of fifty Royal Marines finally arrived from Dublin. The mere 'sight of a vessel' approaching the settlement created mixed feelings, the colour of the wax seal on the back of a long-awaited letter possibly indicating bad news from home. To break the seal and read the letter was to condense months of expectation into a rush of anticipation, 'joy and anxiety' before it was immediately re-read, the emotional response of the reader reaching out across distance and time to the moment when the letter was written, already more than a year gone.[22]

To lighten his men's boredom and the almost prison-like claustrophobia induced by the climate, McArthur organised games with 'bat and ball', 'stone gathering competitions', sprinting races and wrestling matches, sometimes between different ships' crews such as the *Beagle* and the *Britomart*. These tests of strength and athleticism suited the male-dominated society at Victoria, which prized physical prowess and survival skills above all else, qualities that bristled in a man such as the hunter Hutchings, a 'huge fellow, rough and ready', who would emerge from the forest 'hung round with game'—geese, ducks, kangaroos and 'handkerchiefs full of small birds'—'his face smeared with perspiration and blood'. One escape from brutish masculinity was theatre—the most celebrated example at Port Essington took place in 1843, when four ships happened to be visiting and Captain Owen Stanley staged the play *Cheap Living* (written by Frederick Reynolds and first performed at Drury Lane in 1797). The prologue to the published version of the 'farce' explained the play's cross-dressing: 'you must fancy a female is really a man; Not merely conceal'd in the manly array, But a man, bona-fide, throughout the whole play'. Stanley had found an ingenious way of bringing more women into the settlement, even if only for one evening. To stage the production he painted his scenery using what he called 'the earths of the country', emulating the Aboriginal use of local soils. The play was staged in a converted workshop named 'Victoria Theatre'. It was a riotous success.[23]

Turkey Bush in flower,
Cobourg Peninsula,
2014

There were also more serious distractions. Victoria was a highly contained and unusually fertile field of scientific observation and collection. As the only settlement in northern Australia at the time, it was visited by several naturalists and held a strong attraction for those such as John Gilbert, who lived there from 1840–41 and collected for John Gould. Some of the earliest and largest flora and fauna specimens from Australia's north came from Port Essington. The settlement was effectively Britain's window into Australia's tropical environment and was of 'outstanding importance' to Australian biology. The journals of the naturalists who visited, and many others including that of McArthur, contain valuable lists of birdlife, often with detailed descriptions of wingspan and plumage ('flycatcher? amber colour above the beak, long black white-tipped tail, white throat … speckled breast white belly'). When the collections of fauna and flora eventually left the settlement they immediately entered an international market. The birds and mammals collected by Gilbert were unwanted by Gould and eventually sold to museums and private collectors in Britain and Europe. Aboriginal artefacts and bodily remains such as skulls and bones also found their way into British collections, traded at Victoria for tobacco, food or alcohol, or simply pilfered from burial sites, the very process of collection reflecting British racial ideology that placed Aboriginal people on a lower scale of human development.[24]

Many of the journals that have survived from both residents and visitors to Victoria, some written at the time and unpublished, others undoubtedly embellished before later publication, display a similar pattern in their descriptions of Aboriginal people. The author—usually a naturalist, explorer or scientist—begins with predictable prejudice: he is offended by their nakedness and complains about their unreliable work habits. They walk too slowly through the forest. They have no interest in busyness. He views them condescendingly and is convinced they are 'savage', ugly and harmless, with no capacity for abstract ideas and reasoning. He is struck by the fact that they seemingly fail to grow things and appear to have no care for the future. Yet the longer the writer remains at Victoria, the more he is drawn into their culture—what begins as dismissiveness slowly gives way to fascination. In some cases, entire journals are turned over to describing Aboriginal culture. Word lists are provided. Cultural practices are meticulously documented, and all the while there is a constant tension between attraction and revulsion. The more deeply the author reflects on Aboriginal culture, the more potentially threatening the experience becomes. To truly understand and admire Aboriginal culture was also to risk undermining European cultural assumptions. The experience was both immensely rich and deeply unsettling for both parties.[25]

Indigenous body marking at Port Essington was a practice that excited the curiosity of the British. Some of the marines enjoyed being asked to daub the bodies of Aboriginal people with 'red paint'. Intrigued by the raised scars on the chests and shoulders of Aboriginal men, the Scottish surgeon Archibald Sibbald decided that he would try it for himself. He wrote:

> The natives of the N. Coast have a habit of raising large swellings on their bodies … To see how it was managed I got it done to my left shoulder. The manner of doing it is as follows; they take a lancet; a sharp shell in their native state & cut two perpendicular lines, the length [the marking] is to be, they cut with a scraping motion as is done in etching … then they take different coloured earths or chalks, for instance red & white, mixed on a leaf for a palette, & getting a small stick, bite the end to make it hold like a paint brush, this they paint over the scars alternately of different colours & ascending to the number of markings to be raised.

Sibbald's initial enthusiasm soon waned. 'This operation of painting goes on every day, till it is large enough; but whatever may [please them] would not similarly suit a European, so I put a stop to it on the 4th day.'[26]

83

Like Sibbald, the 19-year-old naval surveyor John Sweatman was immediately drawn to Aboriginal people, envying their lifestyle—'far happier than many who enjoy every comfort'—enjoying the sexual favours of Aboriginal women, and recognising his total dependence on Aboriginal guidance in the bush ('I don't know what we should have done without them'). Sweatman's keen visual eye, already attuned to 'wild and picturesque images of 'native life', was attracted to 'the rows of fires shining at a distance through the dark trees, with black naked figures flitting about among them'. Almost every evening during his stay at Victoria, Sweatman joined Aboriginal people around their campfires, 'the old women cooking their evening meals, the men smoking or talking and the younger people singing', accompanied by 'the bee-like buzzing of their bamboo instruments', which formed the ambient soundtrack to daily life at the settlement. Sweatman's friendship with Aboriginal people reflected the deepening bonds between the two cultures at Victoria.[27]

John McArthur knew that many Aboriginal people had 'formed an attachment' to his men. And he was touched by 'the sensitivity and tenderness of affection' they displayed towards one another in their daily lives. With every acknowledgement of shared emotional bonds between black and white, the awareness of shared humanity became harder to ignore. But emotion was also a marker of difference. Shocked by the excessive emotion displayed by Aboriginal people in their 'domestic broils' and their incessant shrieking and wailing at times of grief, some cutting their bodies and tearing their hair, McArthur resorted to Old Testament allusions of 'demoniacal possession': 'I never saw anything more fearful to look at; it is sufficient to make the heart of humanity bleed for them'. For McArthur and so many British settlers in colonial Australia, to be 'borne away' by passion was the telltale sign of infantile savagery, while to discipline one's emotions was a central tenet of civilised behaviour. Even Aboriginal people's fear of social isolation—'solitary confinement … [affects] them much in the same manner that it does children when shut up in dark closets'—pointed, they believed, to a lack of individual independence and self-discipline, two of the most celebrated qualities of nineteenth-century British character. The handful of Aboriginal men and women who learnt to live as honorary British by working as domestic servants were initially exalted as 'reclaimed' from a life of 'savagery' but were quickly disowned the moment they threw off their clothes and 'bolted' back to the bush.[28]

One young man, Neinmal, who waited on McArthur's table wearing a 'white jacket and waistcoat', his hair carefully brushed and parted, impressed the British so much that he sailed to Singapore, Java and Sydney in 1845 with the Scottish naturalist John MacGillivray, before returning with Sweatman on the *Bramble*, and learning to read and write on the way. With fluent English, impish wit and a fine singing voice, Neinmal revelled in his new life as a roving exhibit of the 'civilized savage' and became 'much attached' to MacGillivray as well as being extremely popular with McArthur and the marines. Understandably, 'older members of [Neinmal's] family' were envious of 'the attention he received' and resentful of his long absences from home. When a marine shot and killed an Aboriginal man accused of theft as he attempted to escape custody (the first violent death at the settlement), Aboriginal law demanded payback. Rather than choose a marine, which would have been far more dangerous, Aboriginal elders chose Neinmal because of his popularity. They knew that his loss would be much mourned by the British. When Neinmal returned to the bush one morning, he was speared and clubbed to death. As payback for his murder, his family then killed a member of his assailant's tribe. The shooting of one Aboriginal man had led to the murder of two more men.[29]

For every step that broke down the chasm of cultural difference, there was a countervailing push to remind both sides of the enormity of the divide. Although there were a handful of others like him—the most celebrated being Mildun (Jack Davis), who was only a young boy at the time of the settlement and later sailed to Hong Kong and England—Neinmal was an exception. The majority of Aboriginal people preferred to keep a respectful distance from the British. As Sibbald shrewdly noted, 'they have a language they speak to us in & another we do not understand'. McArthur too had learnt that 'they seem averse to our learning anything concerning them, and ... prefer the adoption of some of our language rather than we should acquire theirs'. While the British at Victoria tried to lure 'the natives' with what they saw as the tremendous advantages of civilisation, Aboriginal people remained determined to preserve their cultural integrity.[30]

––––––––––

By 1845, the prospect of Victoria Settlement surviving was slim. Despite the arrival of more marines from England, a series of determined but gloomy dispatches from McArthur combined with reports in the Sydney press condemning the settlement as a complete failure had virtually sealed its fate. In late 1844, McArthur reminded the Colonial Office that when Botany Bay had proved unsuitable, Phillip moved to Port Jackson. Victoria, he insisted, was 'too far up' Port Essington, 'cut off … from a stream of trade which is silently but certainly gliding past our front door'. The much-promised opening up of the interior to settlers had never occurred. Everything had proved a struggle—diet, physical and mental health, communication and the anticipated trade with Asia. The garrison could barely exist let alone thrive. Reluctant to forsake his intention to settle the north, New South Wales Governor George Gipps had already written to the Colonial Secretary in London suggesting that a settlement be established 'at or near Cape York', admitting in the same breath that the 'advantages have not been reaped' from Victoria Settlement. In the pages of McArthur's notebook a more poetic verdict had been reached: 'To the shape of a rat had this world been subjected, at the tip of its tail Victoria's erected'.[31]

In December 1845 and early May 1846, McArthur's mood was temporarily lifted by the arrival of two men, one of whom he would befriend for the next two years. The first man came not by sea but overland, emerging from the bush on horseback. On 17 December, the German explorer Ludwig Leichhardt and his party arrived in Victoria Settlement after a 14-month journey. They had travelled over five thousand kilometres from the Darling Downs in south-east Queensland in their quest to become the first overland explorers to reach Port Essington. Even today, Leichhardt's arrival at the settlement appears little short of miraculous. After losing John Gilbert in a violent clash with 'Aborigines' near the Gulf of Carpentaria, he had battled on, almost failing at the last hurdle when he became lost only three days out from Port Essington, led astray by buffalo tracks. Luckily, he stumbled upon the 'original blackfellows' footpath', heard their 'cooee' piercing the bush and followed the call. Coming upon an Aboriginal camp he was greeted by two men who spoke excellent English—'Backi, Backi', an old, lame man and 'Rambo Rambo', a 'short sturdy fellow with remarkably large testicles'. For the next two days, Leichhardt was provided with food and water—'the black-fellow showed us how we could easily take out the young shoot [of the cabbage palm] by splitting the leaves and we enjoyed a fine meal'—and led along ancient paths until his ultimate goal was finally within reach.[32]

Approaching the settlement from the south early on the morning of 17 December, he was led past waterholes and termite mounds, through an open forest of melaleuca, stringybark and ironwood.

After more than a year's journey the sight that greeted him moved him to tears. Passing through the garden with its 'fine row

Bushland close to the ruins of Victoria Settlement, 2014

of coconut palms', he was taken aback as 'white houses' and a 'row of snug thatched cottages' 'burst suddenly' upon him. It was Europe in miniscule, a momentary vision of all he had longed for after so many days and nights without the trappings of 'civilization'.

> They treated us with the greatest kindness and provided us with the necessary clothes and food. I was deeply moved in finding myself again in civilized society. I could scarcely speak, the words growing big with tears and emotion. And even now, thinking that I have been enabled by a kind providence to perform such a journey with no small means, my heart sobs with gratitude within me.[33]

Leichhardt had arrived at the height of the wet season, his skin irritated by scores of pus-inflamed boils—'appearing at the joint of the knee, at the loins, buttocks, anus [and] elbow'—his eyes clogged by conjunctivitis. After the initial relief subsided he saw the settlement as a 'lonely, solitary place' sustained largely by the sheer determination of that '*rara avis*', John McArthur. Leichhardt was anxious to return to Sydney where he had long been given up as dead. A lament for his party's 'bleaching bones in the deserts of central Australia' had already been 'published and set to music'. Four weeks later he found passage on the *Heroine* to Sydney, sailing down the east coast dreaming of his father—'silent and melancholy, his complexion sallow'—and his 'love of a girl' he knew could 'never be found embodied in real life'. When he arrived in Sydney he was greeted as a national hero, his triumphant overland trek to Port Essington fuelling yet another flurry of wildly ambitious schemes to develop the north, despite the fact that the settlement at Port Essington already appeared doomed. Until the entire continent could be claimed as 'civilised', colonial Australia could not imagine itself secure.[34]

In Sydney, Leichhardt gave great encouragement to an Italian priest who was about to board the *Heroine* for its return journey to Port Essington. He was an unlikely passenger. Although the British government had promised Catholic missions the same support as their Protestant counterparts in Australia, they had not expected that Port Essington would be high on Rome's list of priorities. At only thirty-three, Father Angelo Confalonieri was Australia's first Catholic missionary in northern Australia. Given the august title 'Vicar Apostolic of Port Essington' by his superiors in Rome, he eventually arrived at Victoria dressed in rags and clutching his crucifix after the *Heroine* was wrecked on a reef in Torres Strait during its return passage. His journey had been long and arduous. After leaving his home near Lake Garda and studying to be a missionary at Propaganda Fide, the Vatican institute for evangelisation in Rome, he travelled via Lyon, Paris and London in 1845 in an effort to recruit more priests to his mission and secure financial support. In September that year he sailed from London with more than twenty Irish, French and Italian missionaries bound for Perth, Sydney and Port Essington. Their mission was to realise Pope Gregory XVI's intention to evangelise the Australian continent. Like his counterparts in the Colonial Office in London, Gregory ruled a vast empire. From his Vatican office he carved the map of Australia into spheres of Catholic influence and had the related documents filed under 'Oceania'. Bishop Brady was to preside over the 'diocese' of Perth, Angelo Confalonieri, Port Essington and Northern Australia, while another priest was appointed 'Vicar of King George Sound' in south-west Australia. It was another form of magical possession, assumed rather than negotiated and blissfully ignorant of the practical difficulties of placing territories ten times the size of Italy in the hands of one man.[35]

In lieu of knowledge there was always faith. By all accounts Father Angelo—the naive soldier of Christ—fervently believed that he would convert the Aboriginal people of Port Essington to Christianity. Tossed into the sea when his ship struck the reef and dragged to safety by Nelson, the captain's 'great Newfoundland dog', he lost his two Irish assistants, James Fagan and Nicholas Hogan, and all of his worldly possessions. God, he believed, had saved him for one reason: so that he might carry out his mission to save the souls of the 'poor and naked savages' in the 'forests' of northern Australia before 'a Protestant mission' could 'establish itself' there. Writing to church authorities in Sydney only three days after he arrived, Angelo told the story of his shipwreck and miraculous survival, pleading for a pair of 'spectacles'—'my short sightedness is so great that I can hardly perceive objects until I touch them'—a 'breviary, some books of devotion', an 'altar-stone' and the 'necessary sacred vestments' that would allow him to say Mass. He was convinced that he faced 'a terrible probation of a whole year replete with fatigue, misery, and danger'. Desperate for funds and material support, he was also adept at dramatising his plight: 'alone, abandoned upon these inhospitable shores—without money, without aid, without clothes, without hopes, pale and emaciated, almost torn to pieces by the breakers—the poor Don Angelo lives as it were by miracle'. As a young priest (if his hagiographer can be believed) he had spent months walking alone in the Italian and Swiss Alps with little protective clothing and few provisions. In order to pass the test of physical and mental endurance to prepare for his life as a missionary, he attempted to emulate his Saviour's ordeal of forty days and nights in the desert. Trekking in the Alps, where village inns were usually within reach, would prove almost luxurious compared to the travails of life at Port Essington.[36]

Because Angelo had lost all his papers in the shipwreck, McArthur had to take him on trust. Heartened by the priest's enthusiasm, he provided labourers—both his own tradesmen and Aboriginal men— to build him a small house at 'Black Rock near the entrance of the harbour', 25 kilometres removed from the settlement. Angelo referred to it as his 'little shack'. This situation would allow Angelo to be undisturbed in his effort to 'live among the savages, and thus learn their language, and observe their customs and manners'. To walk along the low-lying, red-rock shoreline at the harbour's entrance today is to understand something of the isolation Angelo experienced. Writing to Propaganda Fide at the Vatican from the almost preposterous address 'North Australia, Port Essington', he complained regularly of *'immensa distanza, e difficile communicazione'*. Rome was an eternity away.[37]

McArthur kept Angelo supplied with 'food and clothing' from the 'Government stores', although by all accounts, self-sufficiency was not his forte. Years of having had his meals placed in front of him had left Angelo unprepared for life alone. Sweatman was amused: 'in all worldly matters he was … ignorant & helpless', especially in 'domestic matters … when he had his flour, he did not know how to mix or cook it! He was a terrible beggar too, and pestered us without ceasing, though always in the most polite language and with a thousand apologies'.[38]

To gain the trust of Aboriginal people, Angelo 'lived wholly in their manner', including eating 'roots' and 'half-cooked possums with entrails'. He was often seen with Aboriginal people wandering through the bush, sometimes far inland, 'notebook in hand', aided in his efforts by a young Aboriginal boy, 'Jim Crow', who served as his 'interpreter' and occasionally waited on his table. Once he had the confidence of Aboriginal people, he offered to take 'care of their children', teaching them to 'repeat prayers in Latin'. He saw immediately that he had more chance of indoctrinating them than he had of converting their parents. An outstanding linguist, Angelo 'mastered their language', boasting to his superiors that 'after having spent a year of almost continuous, hard, miserable life in the forests together with these poor savages, I can now speak their language perfectly'.

Entrance to Port Essington harbor, 2014, close to where Father Angelo Confalonieri lived, 1846–48

He reckoned rightly that 'almost all speak nearly the same language …
but with different dialects that are easy to understand'. Yet what he saw
of their culture was merely the half-glimpsed surface gloss refracted
through his own prejudices. Everything was more complicated
than it seemed.[39]

He produced a map of the 'Aboriginal Tribes of the Cobourg
Peninsula', although as linguist Bruce Birch has shown, despite the
map's value, the 'tribal' names Angelo recorded were actually Malay
names for locations rather than Aboriginal names for groups of people.
Where Angelo did succeed was in his beautifully written 'Specimen
of the Aboriginal Language or Short Conversation with the Natives
of North Australia Port Essington'. When I held this document in
my hands in the Vatican archives in late 2014, I was immediately
struck by the enormous care and pride Angelo had taken in its com-
pilation and presentation. This was truly a work of devotion. Angelo
had sent the manuscript, which he described as a 'little essay on the
language of this poor family of human beings', from Port Essington
to Propaganda Fide not only because he knew that it would be a permanent record of his work there, but because it embodied his mission
and calling.[40]

The title page was painstakingly
inscribed in black, blue and red
ink while the fragile manuscript,
bound carefully with string, was
barely more than 8 centimetres
wide and 16 centimetres long.
Inside, every entry was immaculately
written, with subheadings brilliantly
coloured in red. After listing phrases
which reveal something of Angelo's
everyday transactions—'give to me
your spear and your pearls, your
turtle shell, basket and I will give to
you tobacco, rice and other', 'make
fire', 'bring small wood', 'little boy
come here be not afraid', 'I must

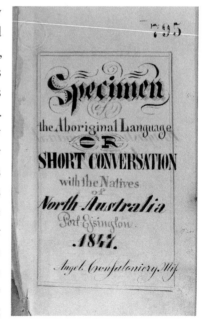

return to my house but tomorrow morning I will return and see you'—the manuscript ends with Angelo's raison d'être: 'Religious Questions and Answers'.

> Who made the Sun, the Moon, the earth?
> I do not know.
> My dear child, I will tell you. God made the sun …
> Did die your Soul?
> Never
> Where will go your Soul, when your body die?
> Before God
> What for before God?
> To receive reward if it was good; and to have punishment, if it was bad. The reward will have in heaven with God, forever, and the punishment in Hell with the Devil forever.[41]

Reading his exquisitely compiled manuscript and hearing of the 'love, attachment and affection' he was shown by Aboriginal people, Angelo's former teachers at Propaganda Fide could be forgiven for thinking that he had succeeded in converting 'the natives' to Christianity. But the truth was otherwise. Aboriginal people had actually succeeded in forcing Angelo to question the purpose and effectiveness of his mission. Sweatman described how they would trick 'the poor padre' when he asked them for translations of the liturgy. Instead of giving him the correct word in their language they would offer him obscenities. When Angelo came to say Mass he could not understand why they 'laughed at his sermons'. Others told of Aboriginal men and women repeating their prayers in the main square of the settlement 'with many gestures as rather a good joke than otherwise'. Parroting prayers was not evidence of conversion. More often than not it was a way of securing 'a bag of rice'. Indeed, Sweatman claimed that Angelo 'despaired' of ever succeeding. 'Had they had any idolatry of their own, [Angelo] said, he might have rooted it out and taught them Christianity instead, but having no idea of religion whatever, he feared it would be impossible to make them understand anything about it.' Although he had lived with them (or at least near them) and learnt some of their language, Angelo had still not grasped the importance of their Dreaming and creation stories—an oral gospel that bound the people of the past, present and future to the land and all that inhabited it.[42]

In 1847, by which time his initial enthusiasm had worn thin, Angelo told McArthur that he was not making sufficient progress. His only hope, he said, 'was to maintain and teach the children', ideally after they were taken away from their parents. In his correspondence with church authorities in Sydney, he came close to admitting defeat: 'their poverty and misery is so very deep, their condition is so degraded, their debasement is so terrible that it presents the hardest difficulties for the Mission'. The man who had learnt more of the closely related local Aboriginal languages (Garig and Iwaidja) than any other European at Port Essington and earnt the admiration of the majority of Aboriginal people he lived with, so much so that he was given a 'skin name' ('Nagojo') and thus adopted into their kinship system, nonetheless saw them as 'people altogether brutale' with 'no understanding but for their belly'. He gave others the impression that he wanted to leave the settlement and even doubted his mission. The surgeon Crawford, who had many long conversations with Angelo, claimed that he found him 'wholly without religious feeling', 'well acquainted with theology and a strong stickler for the doctrine of his church, but more like an advocate than a believer. Indeed he frequently gave occasion to doubt whether he himself gave credence to what he thought'. The longer Angelo lived with Aboriginal people at Port Essington the more his piety dissolved. It was he who was being converted.[43]

In early June 1848, Lieutenant Dunbar, McArthur's boatman, who normally delivered supplies to Angelo, 'went down in [the] deck boat ... not having heard that he was ill'. On landing at Black Rock he found him lying in his house 'complaining of want of sleep' and 'headache'. Concerned, Dunbar persuaded Angelo to come back with him to the settlement hospital. Within less than a week Angelo had died, yet another victim of malaria. Second-hand accounts claimed that his last moments were 'fearful'. He allegedly 'denied that there was a God'. Far more likely is that the thought of dying in such a godless place as Port Essington terrified him. On 11 June, McArthur and all the officers and soldiers at the garrison attended his funeral and burial 'with the respect due to a highly esteemed man'. McArthur, who over the previous two years had supplied him with provisions and occasionally taken his boat out to Angelo's and dined with him, was deeply saddened by his passing. Perhaps also because his death was yet another reminder of how the climate and isolation at Victoria had claimed the lives of so many of those who originally arrived full of hope. At the time of Angelo's death the cemetery contained nearly fifty graves. Soon the number of dead would outnumber the number of residents.[44]

At 'daylight' on 15 November 1848, the artist Oswald Brierly decided to 'take a stroll' around the settlement 'before it became so intolerably hot', eventually finding his way to Victoria cemetery. Brierly, who had spent the last six years managing Ben Boyd's pastoral and whaling interests at Twofold Bay, had arrived only a week earlier on Owen Stanley's *Rattlesnake*, together with John MacGillivray and the brilliant, moody, 23-year-old assistant surgeon and later renowned biologist Thomas Huxley. That morning, it took a while before Brierly realised that the fenced enclosure he had stumbled upon was the 'burying ground of the Establishment'. 'Forty four' graves 'altogether in one spot surrounded by trees' surprised him for a settlement 'containing so few people'. Angelo's grave was the most recent, his name and date of death still to be inscribed on the gravestone. As the *Rattlesnake* entered Port Essington harbour a few days earlier, the first thing to catch Brierly's attention was Angelo's house at Black Rock: 'Why there's a house', he exclaimed, 'with a curtain blowing out of the window'. After learning of his death, Brierly heard from McArthur and others how 'Don Angelo the Roman Catholic missionary' had 'devoted his time to acquiring [the Aborigines'] language and teaching [them] the Lord's Prayer ... but without producing the slightest change in any way'. 'Nor', he wrote, 'did they show the slightest regret when he died—I saw a vocabulary which he had left. He was a man about

39—a Tyrolese'. Angelo's 'fearful' last moments were burdened by the knowledge that his mission had failed.[45]

Looking around the cemetery, Brierly saw that white ants had consumed the marrow of the small wooden crosses that marked many of the graves. When he touched them they crumbled to dust. 'As the sun rose' over the graveyard, he watched as a goanna 'stopped with his head raised and his eye fixed upon [him]'. 'Green ants … ran over

96

Father Angelo Confalonieri's grave, Victoria Settlement cemetery, Port Essington, 2014

everything', dropping down from the trees and covering the ground on which he stood. At that moment, in the dawn's half-light, he thought of the 'church yard with its very records all decaying, devoured by blackness' and felt 'the most nervous [he had] felt anywhere'. He was glad to 'hurry away' from the place. Later that day, Stanley introduced him to McArthur—'a tall, thin old man who appeared to warm up at the sight of strangers'. When Brierly walked up the verandah steps and entered McArthur's private residence, he found a 'large gloomy apartment lined with cedar and many squares of ... [faded] calico', which 'hung down in shreds'. McArthur's papers and documents were spread out on every available surface. The 'theatrical melancholy' that enveloped him inside reflected the air of deterioration in the 'rickety old fort' outside. Brierly was struck by the way in which the white ants' activities lent the 'appearance of Antiquity in a settlement of so few years standing'. The atmosphere of 'utter decay' was unmistakable. The white ants had demolished an entire quarter of 'Victoria Square'. It was the same when he walked over to the hospital: table legs standing in tin cans, patients' beds constantly being moved to avoid the leaks in the roof or strung over with makeshift umbrellas, the ward presided over by a 'tethered eagle', a 'tame kangaroo' and an ornamental backdrop of 'native spears and barks', the patients' droll greeting—'a nice cool day'. Victoria had only existed for a decade and yet it appeared ancient: the long-lost remnant of a distant civilisation slowly being devoured by the tropical environment.[46]

For the nineteenth-century British imagination, which longed for deeply embedded settlement and at least the outward appearance of permanence in a colonial setting, there was something decidedly unnatural and unnerving about such images of decay. The ever-present sensation of impermanence undermined the garrison's security. The environment appeared to deny McArthur and the marines grand statements of imperial presence. It constantly reminded them that they were interlopers—not so much colonisers as disappointed speculators. Yet at the same time as it brought them to their knees it continued to entrance them. When Brierly saw McArthur's map of the harbour and his 'beautiful' sketches of the settlement, he could not help being moved: 'it was quite pleasing to see how in this uncongenial corner

of the world he had cherished his remembrance of an art'. To see how
the solitary McArthur had devoted so much of his time to capturing
'the passing effects of Sky and Shore … half caught in colour or …
recorded in pencil' inspired Brierly to record his own impressions of
Port Essington.

> 6 am Morning 11 Nov … Point Record and Land on the Eastern
> shore smoky and colourless—the settlement side on which the sun
> is shining is rather more clear—startling white and red Bank, water
> under it a Glassy calm, light currents of air passing and carrying
> grey colour across and Breaking the dark reflections of the Land.
> Jolly Boat and one of the Cutters with seaman and marines
> watering party going on Shore. Sun seen thro the Port Essington
> haze at this hour exactly resembles the attempts at Sunshine one
> sees in London—sun forming the centre of a smoky yellow spot of
> light being lost in the Surrounding haze.[47]

It was a photographic record that would later be developed in
Brierly's floating studio. Employed as the *Rattlesnake*'s artist for
Stanley's survey of the Great Barrier Reef, the Louisiade Archipelago
and part of the New Guinea coast, his journal remains one of the
most revealing depictions of life at Victoria Settlement in its final
years. Determined to record every scrap of knowledge regarding
local Aboriginal people, Brierly provided a snapshot of their society
in late 1848: describing corroborees attended by 'about 80 people'
from 'three different tribes'; noting the small number of elderly and
large number of children (some of them 'half cast'); watching as men
mixed colours in seashells and painted baskets with chewed-down
sticks for 'brushes'; observing Aboriginal people's consumption of
seasonal food such as long-necked turtles and the nut-like bulbs of the
waterlily, both of which became readily available as the swamps and
floodplains dried up; and detailing their contact with the Malays, who
arrived in about 'twenty' vessels at the end of the monsoon season
and stayed for a month or more. 'They collect tortoise shells for the
Malays—which they keep hidden in the Bush—will sooner sell it
to Malays than Whites. They also assist the Malays in getting the

Trepangs—and sometimes accompany them in the vessels—returning the next trip—three went away this season ... There have been no collisions [between Malays and Aborigines] since the establishment of the settlement—and it is thought that the presence of the whites has prevented any.' Although Brierly had devoted countless hours to documenting Indigenous cultures on the south coast of New South Wales, he arrived at Port Essington as if he were seeing Australia for the first time and he found much that was different, particularly 'the native mode of disposing of their dead—which is singular and different from anything I had seen amongst other Aboriginal tribes'.

> When one of their number dies the Body is carefully wrapped in Grass and Bark and laid upon a small stage or platform formed of Branches, one end resting against a tree the other being supported by two forked Branches which raise it about five feet from the ground—on this the Body is placed and left exposed to the action of the weather until the Bones whiten.[48]

The body was left alone for months until the ants and birds of prey had completed their job—an offering to nature after the spirit ('Imbarbar') had departed. 'The bones were then collected' by family or friends and carried about 'from place to place' until they were

99

Oswald Brierly,
*Native Bier, Port
Essington,* 1853

eventually lost. Women could often be seen carrying the bones of children around the settlement in baskets. Sibbald, for example, noticed how unwanted bones were sometimes buried in the sand and covered by a small raised heap of stones. He also referred to 'infanticide', which he said was practised when there were twins or 'diseased' children: 'the child is killed by crushing the head with a stone, the mother not being able to carry or suckle more than one'. All of these practices mystified the British. Did they revere their dead? Did they believe in life after death? In their efforts to discern whether Aboriginal people possessed spiritual beliefs they came to the conclusion that they indeed believed in evil spirits and the 'transmigration of souls', their dead returning as 'Malays'. The sight of spirit beings was sometimes seen as a portent of death, as Sibbald saw firsthand: 'an old man very well known in the colony went out fishing one day, when he came back in great alarm & said he saw two ghosts, one white & the other black, he stood stupid with terror & on looking up again they had disappeared, he had previously been unwell & he said he would soon die. He died in two days'.[49]

For all of the sincere attempts made by the British to understand Aboriginal people at Port Essington, it was impossible to deny the gulf that separated the two cultures. The longer the British remained, coexisting on relatively peaceful terms, their failure to found their new Singapore and prove their superiority appeared all the more galling. The longer they clung to their tiny patch of cleared forest without moving inland and conquering all before them, the more they appeared to lose the very fabric of their 'civilised' culture. Lurking not far beneath the many descriptions of Port Essington as unsuitable for 'European constitutions' was a more profound existential crisis. McArthur hinted as much when he complained to the Colonial Office in 1844 that Victoria Settlement could not even 'be viewed as a European population', but rather as 'a mimic Babel of the extreme East', a place where race, language and culture were disparate and confused. With only a handful of marines and labourers in the garrison, both the Malays and Aboriginal people outnumbered the British. They arrived as the representatives of the most powerful and advanced civilisation on earth—toasting their possession of the entire north

coast of the continent, quickly erecting their prefabricated buildings and mounting their guns on the headland—and yet they had
degenerated into just another racial group, unable to gain even the
slightest foothold. The land was 'barren' and unsuitable; the waters
'sombre, dismal and monotonous'; the heat and humidity not con-
ducive to work. Once the settlement was established there was little
to do 'beyond keeping the houses, stores, gardens &c. in order, and
looking after the stock'. Busyness was replaced by siestas; roast beef by
'Malay curry'; shoes by bare feet. They were reduced to roaming the
bush like the 'natives' to search for food. And with a 'great desert on
one side, and islands peopled principally by savages on the other', their
isolation and vulnerability was magnified a thousand times over.[50]

Many of the patients lying in their hospital beds at Victoria suffered not only from malaria but depression, or what d'Urville called
'nostalgia'. To live in the garrison was to grapple with the loss of
culture and country. Brierly noticed how the climate induced in
him a 'pent-up close feeling' that he 'could not escape'. Not even the
dogs at the settlement seemed to manage 'the exertion of barking'.
McArthur, too, felt as if he was living 'from the world shut out'. Port
Essington, he wrote sardonically on the first page of his journal, was

Hospital ruins, Victoria
Settlement, Port
Essington, 2014

'World's End'. His notebook is full of maudlin poems in which he longs to 'tread on English ground'. Painfully exiled from his 'dear Kent', McArthur's deepest anxiety was that he might 'never' see his homeland 'again', that he would die in soil that did 'not bear culture well', a place where no 'house or plough' would ever disturb his grave. Even Thomas Huxley's infamous denunciation of the settlement as 'the most useless, miserable, ill-managed hole in Her Majesty's dominions' was an exasperated cry of recognition: in such a place as Victoria, the supposedly natural superiority of the British was exposed as fiction. Despite the fact that they longed to escape, they were haunted by the realisation that their failure to found a new Singapore was 'a blot on the national character'.[51]

At daylight on 16 November 1848, Brierly, MacGillivray, Huxley and Stanley prepared to leave Port Essington on the *Rattlesnake*. Shortly after the *Rattlesnake* got underway, a wooden canoe manned by twelve Aboriginal men approached them from the west. Brierly could see four men 'paddling', 'the rest sitting down in the canoe—their heads and shoulders only just showing above the Gunwhale'. The men were so closely packed together, Brierly feared that if it met even the smallest wave 'she must have gone down'. The canoe pressed on, the paddlers 'trying with all their strength to get to the ship'. But just as they succeeded in coming 'very near', the next 'Board' took the *Rattlesnake* away from them and the canoe turned back to shore. What explained their desperation to reach the ship? Was it last-minute trade, the giving of gifts, the wish to accompany them or simply the desire to come aboard and say goodbye? McArthur was more successful, sailing out on his decked boat and deciding to sleep on board the ship that evening, returning before the *Rattlesnake* sailed out of the harbour the following day. He would miss their company. The conversation on board that evening over dinner undoubtedly turned at some point to the future of Port Essington. Like McArthur, MacGillivray, Brierly, Huxley and Stanley were all convinced that the settlement should be abandoned immediately. But until the orders arrived from the

British government, McArthur, who had already suffered a bout of malaria, was bound to remain there with his ailing band of marines. The time spent waiting for a decision that everyone believed to be inevitable was interminable. It would take another year before the moment finally arrived. On the evening of 12 November 1849, when Captain Henry Keppel, commander of HMS *Meander*, arrived in Port Essington and 'immediately communicated' to McArthur that he had 'come to remove' the settlement, the garrison rejoiced. It was as if war had ended. Although they had expected the decision, they were surprised by its immediacy. Keppel's instructions were to 'take all stores and personnel to Sydney'. While the marines' wives and their children celebrated at hearing the news, Keppel watched as Aboriginal women, some of whom possibly had relationships with McArthur's men, 'showed their grief by cutting their heads and faces with sharp flints'.[52]

They had little time to lose if they were to beat the monsoon season. Over the next three weeks, the settlement was quickly evacuated. Everything Keppel saw during this short time—'the heat and moisture of the climate, the land-locked harbour, the swamps and mud-banks, the mangrove marshes; and, in the case of Europeans, want of fresh … and vegetable diet, and of mental occupation and excitement'—confirmed his view that Victoria could never succeed. He was the last of the British to arrive and be immediately transfixed by Aboriginal culture. He walked inland with Aboriginal guides, watched corroborees of over two hundred and fifty people—three days of singing, dancing and feasting—and left praising their intelligence, 'talent for mimicry' and humour, although he was 'disgusted' by many of their cultural practices. One experience in particular remained with him: the burning of Country.

The conflagration spreads with fearful rapidity and violence, consuming everything in its way, creeping up the dry bark of the trees, running along the branches to the withered leaves, and involving everything dead or alive in one common ruin, until the whole country, as far as the eye can reach, is in a grand and brilliant illumination, which, to be fully appreciated, should be seen. It is accompanied by a low murmuring sound, interrupted now and then by the loud report of the fall or bursting of some large tree, well calculated to increase the melancholy of poor wretches worn out with sickness, and without hope of relief.[53]

Unlike Aboriginal people, for whom fire represented the promise of renewal of Country, Keppel imagined 'the final destruction of our world'. He saw a land unfit for European settlement, consumed by an Armageddon-like inferno, devoid of both history and future. While he was busy loading the *Meander* with the settlement's stores, Keppel lost his surgeon and one seaman to 'fever'. They were buried in the cemetery, McArthur not even able to abandon the settlement before presiding over two more funerals. Just as Aboriginal people had helped to off-load Bremer's ships a decade earlier, they now assisted McArthur and Keppel to evacuate, making the long trek from the settlement to the jetty and back again. For their help they were given some tobacco and several banteng cattle, 'kangaroo dogs' and horses that could not be taken on board. Keppel asked one Aboriginal man whether he would 'take possession of the Governor's house' after they had departed. 'I suppose I must', he replied.[54]

On the morning of 30 November, when the garrison 'marched down' from the settlement to the pier led by the *Meander*'s band, the majority of Aboriginal people were busy searching 'for what they could find among the ruins of the buildings'. After the initial waves of grief, they appeared uninterested in their friends' imminent departure. Arriving at the pier, the 21-gun salute that had heralded British possession of the country in 1824 now signalled their retreat. That evening, before sunset, Keppel and McArthur carried out their orders: 'We destroyed … what still remained of the settlement'. All leftover stores and provisions were smashed. The decked boat was blown up. This would apparently ensure that 'other parties' such as the Dutch or French would not 'try their hands at a settlement on the same spot'. The very people who had struggled for more than a decade to build the settlement now reduced it to ruins. What Aboriginal people made of this almost gleeful act of destruction is difficult to know.[55]

On 1 December 1849, McArthur left Victoria Settlement never to return, the chalk-white cliffs that beckoned him in 1838 receding into the distance as the *Meander* sailed out of the harbour. He had devoted ten years of his life to a misadventure. The British government's attempt to take advantage of the many 'busy pushing capitalists, who [were] searching every quarter of the globe' for trading opportunities had failed miserably. Over forty lives had been lost. Aboriginal people had been right all along. The white birds that had brought the British to Port Essington had come again to take them away, just as they had done at Raffles Bay.[56]

There had been other failed colonial settlements in Australia such as Risdon Cove in Tasmania (1803–04) and Kingscote on Kangaroo Island in South Australia (1836–39), but none had lasted as long as Victoria Settlement. After more than a decade's struggle, what had been gained? In the eyes of the British government, the decision to abandon Victoria was not a relinquishment of sovereignty. On the contrary, the garrison's decade-long existence demonstrated British sovereignty over Australia's north and the entire continent. Any attempt by a rival power to usurp that sovereignty would be seen as an 'infringement of the rights of the British Crown'. Strategically, it had been a success. Rival imperial powers had been warded off.

Remains of the 'magazine', Victoria Settlement, Port Essington, 2014

The 'ring-fence' around Australia had been closed. Victoria could be left to the Aboriginal people to whom it once belonged. Only two years after the settlement was abandoned, Thomas Beckford Simpson, commissioned by the New South Wales government, arrived at Port Essington searching for Ludwig Leichhardt, who had mysteriously vanished on his third overland expedition. 'Jim Crow', who 'spoke English well', greeted him warmly and even slept on board his ship. Simpson was disappointed by the devastation that greeted him. 'All the houses in the barrack Square were destroyed … the new hospital had been burnt in fact all the buildings with the exception of the Commandant's house (which was gutted) and the officers' Cook house had all been destroyed … the various roads and pathways through the settlement were scarcely discernible'. Only the cemetery was undisturbed.[57]

The legacy left behind by McArthur and Keppel—particularly introduced wildlife—became the seed of future environmental destruction throughout northern Australia: banteng cattle (now the largest population in the world), water buffaloes, pigs and wild dogs. In their wake came cattle farmers and pearlers in the late nineteenth and early twentieth centuries. Aboriginal people like 'Jack Davis' and 'Flash Poll', who were children during the days of the settlement, survived into the early twentieth century, surprising European visitors to Victoria with their Queen's English, ability to recite prayers and psalms and their fond memories of McArthur and the marines. Eventually, however, Aboriginal people on the Cobourg Peninsula fell prey to the same lethal combination of violence, disease and forced removal encountered by so many others throughout Australia. After the ravages of a smallpox epidemic in the late nineteenth century and their removal to Croker Island in the 1950s and 1960s, not one Aboriginal person remained on the peninsula in the 1970s. Not until the passage of the Northern Territory government's *Cobourg Aboriginal Land and Sanctuary Act* in 1981 did a small number of Aboriginal communities return to live on the peninsula. Today, only forty to fifty Aboriginal people reside there, sharing the management of the Garig Gunak Barlu National Park. Aside from the National Parks Office, situated 20 kilometres from the ruins of Victoria Settlement, no Europeans live there. More than one hundred and fifty years after the British deserted Victoria Settlement, Europeans remain occasional visitors to Indigenous Country. In 2015, some of the artefacts that were collected by the British at Port Essington and eventually deposited with the British Museum in London—including 'the oldest known didgeridoo in existence' and one of the oldest bark paintings in Australia—were exhibited at the National Museum in Canberra. Muran clan representatives Carol and Don Christophersen saw the objects not only as an opportunity to connect with their cultural heritage but also as a 'sad' reminder that 'the collection of artefacts and the collection of human remains during the English occupation' went hand in hand. Today, the Natural History Museum in London still holds the remains of 'two West Arnhem Land people—a man and a girl'.[58]

As the *Meander* sailed away from Port Essington in December 1849, Keppel described how his crew held 'corobories [*sic*] and dances so often, that frequently afterwards the kangaroo dance was as well performed on the main deck of the *Meander*, many thousand miles from the place where it originated, as we had seen it on the spot'. While Aboriginal people were left with English and the storied ruins of the settlement, the British left Port Essington dancing like the 'natives' they had originally disparaged. Both cultures had been transformed by their encounter with one another. Yet no-one on the *Meander*, McArthur included, realised that Victoria Settlement was close to the place where many Aboriginal people in Arnhem Land and beyond believed that the creation ancestor Warramurrungunji first 'emerged from the Arafura Sea at Cobourg Peninsula'. In 2004, Croker Island Aboriginal elder Tim Mamitba told the story to Nick Evans and Murray Garde.[59]

We're not certain where Warramurrungunji came from, but she came ashore on the northern part of Croker Island, having crossed the ocean. Once she was here, she gave birth to many children.

And she healed herself by sitting on a combination of sand and hot ashes in that place where there are now many sand dunes ... She first came ashore at Malay Bay ... In each place she left some of her children. She kept on like that, leaving children in many places. She used to carry them on her shoulder in a dilly bag. She would assign each group a country, telling them, 'You're going to speak this language'. She also went to Eastern Arnhem Land, and she travelled inland, placing all the groups of children in different places and giving them different languages. We don't [know] where she lay to rest. Maybe much further inland, where the kangaroos and wallabies live. The escarpment country. We don't really know where she's buried, where she is now, but we know she started from here on Croker Island ...[60]

In one variation of the story recorded by Paul Foelsche, an inspector of police, in 1881, it was said that Warramurrungunji reached Port Essington and found it 'good country'. There 'she made a large fire'. 'When this burnt down, the sea rose to its present level, while inland fresh water filled in all the springs and waterholes. [She] then left there the first group of humans, gave them their language and name, and continued inland.' These were the stories that Aboriginal people chose not to communicate to McArthur, the creation stories that could not be overwritten by Father Angelo's prayers or eradicated by a decade's contact with British civilisation. Aboriginal people from Port Essington and beyond had found a way to coexist with the newcomers and retain their culture. At the same time they recorded the detail and drama of this encounter in their stories, songs, dances and art. Across Arnhem Land, world-heritage rock art sites document every stage of the region's contact history: Makassan prau (the earliest painted before 1664), European ships, decorated hand motifs that probably have their origins 'in the gloves worn by Europeans at the Victoria Settlement', four-wheeled horse-drawn buggies, rowboats, English letters and numbers, pipes, coffee mugs and tobacco tins, Ludwig Leichhardt astride his armour-plated horse, images of Europeans on horseback brandishing Martini-Henry rifles, and also of missionaries, steamships, cattle, buffalo hunters, Chinese gold seekers, bicycles and early Qantas planes, all sitting side by side with the more familiar X-ray images of traditional art thousands of years old.[61]

The memory of this history is imprinted indelibly on every aspect of Indigenous culture in Arnhem Land. The rock art is their 'history book'. They can never forget. Yet even today, non-Aboriginal Australia has forgotten much of its own colonial history and remains largely ignorant of Indigenous history. Few better examples can be found than the story of Victoria Settlement at Port Essington, one that was unwittingly played out in the place where the creation ancestor first came ashore many thousands of years ago to lay the foundations of Indigenous culture in the far north of Australia.[62]

CHAPTER THREE

'Hip Bone Sticking Out': Murujuga and the Legacy of the Pilbara Frontier

T̲HE 'CENTRALISED CONTROL room' is dominated by two giant 15-metre screens which allow complete 'visibility of performance' from any vantage point; each huddle of computers represents a distant site or function centre. Employees gaze up at monitors stacked two or three high, shifting their attention constantly between as many as eight different screens. Everyone is somewhere else.

From this extraordinary technology hub in Perth, Rio Tinto 'integrates production' across the company's mines in the Pilbara, all of

Rio Tinto Operations Centre, Perth, 2015

which are more than fifteen hundred kilometres away. Four hundred operators synchronise 'a system of 15 mines, four port terminals, and a 1700 kilometre rail network'. Trains and trucks are controlled and repaired remotely, while every step of the supply chain—mines to rail to port to ships—is closely monitored. Closed-circuit television in 200 locations across the Pilbara provides Rio with what it proudly calls 'whole system visibility'.

The Rio Tinto 'Operations Centre' brings to mind television images of NASA's Kennedy Space Center at Cape Canaveral, in which engineers and scientists appear anxiously before their computers, tracking every moment of a rocket's flight into space. I later discovered that Rio had consulted NASA when designing the centre. No other space in Australia reveals as much about the way in which technology has changed our relationship with place. We not only observe places and people from a comfortable distance, as Joseph Banks spied

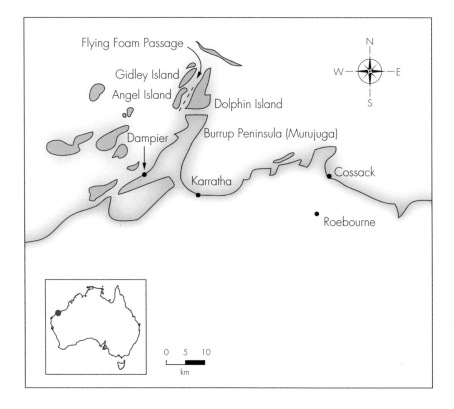

Aboriginal people with his hand-held telescope in 1770, we haul them in from thousands of kilometres away, entering, controlling and altering their distant environments without being physically present. The natural cycles of 'real time' no longer apply. Rio's Operations Centre never sleeps, operating twenty-four hours a day, 365 days a year, saving many of its employees from working in an indescribably hot, semi-arid region that many believe is best experienced by remote control.[1]

Vast areas of Australia exist in the national imagination in conveniently one-dimensional terms. Few better examples can be found than the Pilbara, a region of over 500 000 square kilometres in Australia's north-west that George Seddon aptly described as 'not precisely defined: the land between the Murchison-Gascoyne to the south and the Great Sandy Desert and the Kimberley to the north'. In geological terms, the Pilbara is one of the oldest regions in Australia, containing rocks over 3600 million years old and one of the world's 'best preserved fragments of ancient continental crust'. For geologists, the area is internationally renowned as a 'field laboratory' for 'studying the early history of the Earth'. But for the majority of Australians, the Pilbara is a metaphor for mountains of iron ore, a fly-in fly-out El Dorado—the site of the mining boom that began in the 1960s and erupted most spectacularly in the early twenty-first century, driving the nation's economy and enabling the Australian government to save the country from the Global Financial Crisis.[2]

In Perth, the corporate logos of the Pilbara's mining and energy companies tower over the CBD skyline—BHP Billiton, Rio Tinto, Woodside. There is no doubting the major source of the city's wealth. But like most Australians, few of Perth's residents have firsthand experience of the Pilbara. The mining revenue flows in as if from a faraway galaxy, the physical reality of Pilbara the place always kept at a safe distance. Even when mining magnate Lang Hancock first saw the region's iron ore in the early 1950s, he did so by flying over the landscape. Surveyed from above, excavated from afar and scanned for every last ounce of its mineral wealth, the landscape of the Pilbara is frequently reduced to its economic potential alone. As Fortescue Metals Chief Executive Andrew Forrest lamented in 2012, 'there is literally several billion tonnes of iron ore in the Pilbara *stranded* by lack of infrastructure'.[3]

Few Australians know the Pilbara or its sub-regions intimately; the area entered national consciousness as a vast, history-less quarry when industrial development began in the 1960s. And like many other regions of the country, its past is known only by a handful of historians, archaeologists, geologists, local enthusiasts and, of course, Aboriginal people, whose oral, story-bound culture is inherently historical. To date, the connection between the rivers of lucre extracted from the Pilbara's mines and the history of the region since Europeans arrived in the 1860s has not been understood. Nor has Australia managed to fully comprehend the source of the Pilbara's most exceptional and enduring wealth—its Indigenous cultural heritage. In a region where many towns were established barely fifty years ago, the pre-industrial past can often appear insignificant compared to the scale and pace of recent development. History of all kinds—geology, archaeology, Indigenous and non-Indigenous—is easily obscured by industry's gargantuan shadow.

On the rock-covered slopes of the Pilbara's Burrup Peninsula—the largest island in the Dampier Archipelago and home to one of the oldest, most concentrated and culturally significant galleries of rock art on earth—there is one place that graphically captures the confrontation between rampant industrial development and the struggle to retain Indigenous heritage. Archaeologist Ken Mulvaney, one of the leading authorities on the Burrup's rock art, brought me here on a fiercely hot afternoon in November 2015. Over the last decade or more, he has devoted much of his time to surveying the extensive areas of the peninsula's art that still remain largely unidentified, repeatedly calling on the Australian government to nominate the area for World Heritage listing. He knows the significance and contradictions of this place better than anyone.

Straight off the plane after an 8-hour journey from Sydney, the sensory impact of the Burrup overwhelmed me: oppressive heat that immediately sapped my strength, irrepressible squadrons of tiny flies bent on crawling into my eyes and mouth, and all around me, abutting the Indian Ocean, the landscape's breathtaking palette of colour—piles of burnt, iron-red rocks that appeared to have been thrown down at random from above; a sea of spinifex that dissected the bare, rock-strewn hills and from a distance, softened the country to the eye, changing from straw-yellow to gold in the late afternoon light; and in the valleys and gorges, small, gracefully gnarled, white-barked gums that emerged like beacons from the bone-dry ground; all spread under the vault of an achingly blue sky.

As we drove out along the peninsula it was impossible to escape industry's footprint. The Burrup is Australia's Ruhr and Lascaux in one: towering industrial plants on one side of the road, ancient World Heritage–significant rock art on the other. Even the road we travelled on existed because of the establishment of the North West Shelf Gas Project in the 1980s. Stopping the car opposite Woodside's liquefied natural gas (LNG) plant, we crossed the road and walked no more than five minutes until 30-metre-high rock walls surrounded us, the narrow floor that ran between them no more than a few metres wide. Ken stopped and pointed up above our heads. 'There it is', he exclaimed. Although I had seen photographs of the 'Climbing Men' petroglyphs—art created by removing part of the rock's surface by pecking or pounding—to stand before them was both an act of recognition and to experience something else entirely. They were smaller and more intricate than I had imagined, a series of images 20 to 40 centimetres long, imprinted on a flat, outward-facing rock no more than 1 metre wide. Not far above head height, they looked down on me like a painting hung high on a gallery wall.

Some images appeared to show men climbing a tree (although this is only one interpretation), while others showed human figures and a 'face-like motif' with enormous eyes, possibly in ceremonial dress. The lizard on the left of the panel is probably the most recently engraved. Geologist Mike Donaldson, who spent years photographing and documenting the Burrup's rock art, has explained how 'different levels of repatination' indicate that the 'Climbing Men' images were 'produced at very different times, perhaps thousands of years apart'. Remarkably, the large eyes also bear strong similarity to the so-called 'archaic faces'—rare petroglyphs found far away in the Cleland Hills in Central Australia. I soon realised that all the images were in

'Climbing Men', Murujuga, 2015

conversation with one another: art produced in response to earlier traditions, sometimes embellished with new images placed side-by-side, sometimes overlaid completely. The result was an extraordinary open-air museum, a library of cultural knowledge and expression that linked Aboriginal people across millennia. In the weeks that followed my departure from the Pilbara, it was this site above all others that left the most lasting impression, not only for the quality of its art but for the mammoth industrial complex that stands only a few hundred metres away.[4]

The starkness of the juxtaposition was unforgettable. Standing at arm's length from the 'Climbing Men', I could see Woodside's plant in the near distance (now known officially as the Karratha Gas Plant). It was alarming to think that such ancient and priceless cultural heritage stood within a hair's breadth of obliteration. To hear the roar of the plant's spitting gas flames was to feel the force of industrialisation itself, one that threatened to steamroll everything in its path. In Europe or the United States the equivalent of the Burrup's rock art would be a proudly managed World Heritage tourist site. Yet in the Pilbara, Indigenous heritage struggled for recognition amid the push for

Karratha Gas Plant,
Burrup Peninsula,
Murujuga, 2015

industrial development. How had Australia allowed this to happen? The answer lies not only in the way successive governments have continually encouraged the expansion of industry since the 1960s, but in the long history of the Burrup Peninsula, the period that includes what writer Nicolas Rothwell has labelled 'one of the least-examined questions in the story of Australian settlement': 'the dramatic depopulation of the [Indigenous] northwest'. Long before the names 'Pilbara' and 'Burrup' were inscribed on European maps of north-western Australia, the Burrup Peninsula's traditional owners, the Yaburara, knew their Country as Murujuga ('hip bone sticking out'). They first encountered European settlers on the shores of their archipelago in the mid-nineteenth century, almost eighty years after Arthur Phillip arrived in Sydney Cove with the First Fleet in 1788. The history of this ever-expanding frontier, little known and largely severed from the history of industrial development in the late twentieth century, is nothing less than the ground on which Australia's resources boom was built.[5]

The opening pages of Australia's European history are all too familiar: a series of Dutch, British and French navigators—the sun-struck creation ancestors of white Australia—brush up against the continent's coastline, mapping and naming places as they go. Once ashore, they are quick to judge, summing up the entire country in a throwaway phrase (usually pejorative), observing the bizarre flora and fauna and the trails of smoke from the 'natives'' fires, searching desperately for fresh water and invariably condemning the few Aboriginal people they meet as savages. Seeded with the pessimistic pronouncements of an ad hoc collection of maritime explorers and buccaneers, Australia was imagined as a land outside God's creation and entirely lost to European civilisation; a discordant place without culture and history that many Europeans had seen, but about which, in the words of the seventeenth-century French author Denis Vairasse, they had only 'been able to give the most superficial observations'.[6]

Two months before Phillip Parker King charted and named Port Essington in April 1818, he explored Dampier Archipelago, which had already been named by Louis de Freycinet in 1803 in honour of William Dampier's brief visit in 1699. On board with King was Bungaree, the famed Aboriginal mediator and explorer from Broken Bay, New South Wales, who had circumnavigated the continent with Matthew Flinders fifteen years earlier. Unlike his predecessors, King sailed the archipelago for several days, christening islands as he went. In some respects he was no less convinced than Dampier that the country was the 'most barren place on earth', yet his observations were far from superficial; he noted how it was crisscrossed by 'the tracks of the natives' and 'the mouths of the creeks were planted with their weirs'. While he made no mention of engravings, he thought that he could detect some purpose in the rocks that were 'piled in all directions' across the landscape.[7]

On 26 February 1818, sailing close to where the town of Dampier stands today, King saw three Aboriginal men paddling on logs in the direction of 'Lewis Island'.[8] As he sailed towards them they immediately became 'alarmed and cried out in loud tones'. Every time his men managed to manoeuvre the *Mermaid*'s cutter close by, the men jumped into the water, dived under the ship and 'swam astern'. After eluding King several times, one of the men was finally seized by the hair and dragged from the water, resisting so strongly that it required 'two men to hold him'. Only when he saw Bungaree did the man calm down and 'allow himself to be lifted on board'. Probably in his early twenties, he was not the only one protesting his capture. After anchoring the cutter near the 'central island' nearby, King noticed about forty men, women and children on the shoreline. 'The whole party', he wrote later, 'appeared to be overcome by grief', the women crying out 'and rolling on the ground and covering their bodies with sand'.

On board, King placed a bead necklace around the man's neck and a 'red cap' on his head, upon which everyone applauded his regal appearance. They were rewarded with a brief smile. By adorning his prisoner with colourful gifts, King was demonstrating his good intentions. As he explained, the man was 'greatly caressed, in order to induce him to give a favourable account of us to his companions'. In retrospect, this was not what happened. Held captive, the man was reduced to a plaything, half an hour's amusement for King's men: force him from the water, dress him up and feed him biscuits (he spat them out) and offer him sugared water in a saucer (he lapped it up). When King took him to the side of the ship where he could see his people on the beach, he shouted out to them for help. Finally, King allowed him to paddle ashore, lashing an axe to his log and tying a bag around his neck that contained 'a little of everything he appeared to fancy'. Then he watched the ripple effect of his actions as the man was reunited with his friends and family.

As soon as the man stepped ashore he was met by a group of his fellow countrymen, their 'spears poised and pointed towards him'. 'Huddled together in the greatest alarm', they ordered him to 'stand at a distance' and throw away his red cap, bag and axe, which he duly did. Women and children peeped over the nearby bushes and rocks, riveted by the interrogation that followed. All this time, the man stood 'as motionless as a soldier at drill' until the questioning ceased. Then, tentatively, the men advanced towards him, spears still at the ready, until they had him completely surrounded. One by one, they examined his body carefully to be certain that he was still one of their own. Finally reassured, they allowed the women and children to approach before everyone seated themselves 'in a ring', the man sitting 'in the middle', where 'he told his story, which occupied about half an hour'. The elaborate process of his re-entry to society was almost complete. His story told, everyone stood at once and shouted loudly at King's party, before removing themselves 'to the opposite side of the island' and leaving the unwanted gifts behind them on the sand.

Over the next few days, King continued to meet Aboriginal people, determined to 'collect a vocabulary of their language' (a forlorn hope as he later admitted) and to establish good relations. For the Yaburara these meetings involved every possible response: fear, anger, confusion, laughter, affection, curiosity and awe. They were perplexed by Bungaree's 'strange language' and astonished to see his 'scarred' body, shouting with delight when he removed his shirt. 'When he pointed to the sea' to show them where he came from, 'they set up a shout of admiration and surprise'. King soon realised that they were more interested in Bungaree than him. In fact, the Yaburara were trying to incorporate both the British and Bungaree into their worldview. How they explained their appearance in the waters of their archipelago is difficult to know: departed ancestors briefly returned, evil spirit beings to be feared, powerful foreign visitors who potentially threatened their livelihood, or all of the above.

On one occasion, as King approached a group of men, he noticed that they were 'trembling with fear'. But after he took 'the chief by the hand' and placed a 'red cap' on his head—its striking colour and theatrical manner of bestowal confirming his authority—both parties relaxed and 'were soon gabbling each in [their] own language', somehow managing to enjoy their 'mutually unintelligible' conversation. As King's party returned to their boat, they walked 'hand in hand' with five Yaburara men like lifelong friends preparing for a reluctant parting. They then shook one another's hands, a 'mode of leaving', King thought they 'appeared perfectly to understand', perhaps from prior experience with other European visitors. It was easier for both parties to display the rituals of friendship when the newcomers were not intending to stay. Later the same day, when King tried to land on a nearby island to replenish his water supplies, he was prevented from going ashore by thirty Yaburara men who threatened him with 'spears and stones'. Although he saw that their intent was not to kill them—'we were in their power and had they been inclined, they might have speared the whole of our party'—he was equally convinced that it was pointless to risk destroying 'the friendly intercourse' he had established with the previous 'tribe'. On this occasion, 'their object', he noted pointedly, 'seemed to be merely to get rid of us, and in this they completely and very fairly succeeded'.

Unlike Dampier at Lagrange Bay in 1699, who shot one Aboriginal man during a fruitless search for water, King had avoided violence, but his intention to establish friendly relations had only been partly successful. With the exception of one friendly meeting, the Yaburara wanted him gone. Before he sailed to Nickol Bay, he named the islands where he had walked hand in hand with Aboriginal men 'The Intercourse Islands', now the site of one of Rio Tinto's iron ore shipping ports at Dampier. While the stories of his encounters there would live on in Aboriginal culture, they would never become founding myths of the Pilbara's settler history. Despite his intentions, King left with an understanding of Aboriginal society that confirmed the ascendance of European culture—their huts 'nothing more than a bush struck in the ground' and their means of water transport the 'extreme case of the poverty of savage boat-building all around the world'. He saw the Yaburara as even more primitive than Aboriginal people elsewhere in Australia, a view that would ultimately prefigure the beliefs of those who settled the Pilbara more than forty years later. The day he dragged the young Yaburara man from the water and restrained him on board the *Mermaid* would prove indicative of much of the future race relations on the north-western frontier. Aboriginal people were to be used as the settlers saw fit.[9]

Until the surveyor and explorer Francis Thomas Gregory arrived in the Dampier Archipelago in 1861, the Yaburara's contact with Europeans was limited. American whalers certainly built temporary structures in the mid-nineteenth century on some islands, but they left little evidence of their activities and their presence appears not to have seriously disrupted Yaburara culture. As so often in Australian history, the story of Aboriginal people's contact with Europeans is comprised of meticulously documented encounters (sometimes of little more than a few days duration, as with King's visit in 1818) punctuated by decades or even centuries of silence. In these tellings, Aboriginal people can remain curiously static in their cameo role, entering history only when Europeans visit their Country. To grasp the subtle changes in culture and shifts in perception wrought by their contact with Europeans for over two centuries before the settlers finally arrived in the 1860s is almost impossible. We are left with snatches of knowledge—noting the gradual introduction of English words and the use of tools such as metal axes or knives, or a liking for tobacco and other gifts—Indigenous oral history aside, their existence is nearly always mediated through European eyes.

The Yaburara had no way of knowing that Gregory's appearance on the south-eastern tip of Murujuga in 1861 heralded the arrival of permanent settlement. That realisation would dawn slowly. What had been for the last two centuries merely fleeting moments of contact with Europeans was about to become a brutal frontier, one that has figured little in Australia's understanding of the north-west. How the land was 'opened up' has been relegated to a minor footnote in the triumphant narrative of development.

Gregory, who had already surveyed the Murchison and Gascoyne rivers to the south, was appointed by the British and West Australian governments to explore the north-west and assess its potential for development, particularly pastoral activities and growing cotton, then in short supply due to the American Civil War. For nearly three months in 1861, his ship, the *Dolphin*, remained anchored off Hearson's Cove (named after his second mate, who was accidentally injured as the ship off-loaded) while he explored the surrounding country. From his first days ashore, Gregory had difficulty keeping the Yaburara away from his camp. Convinced that they would steal his horses and provisions given the chance, he tried to make them understand that he had 'taken possession for the present and did not want their company'. They took no notice of him and continued to approach, 'ordering [him] back to the ship'. Only when Gregory fired on them did they finally withdraw. Later, further inland, he drew a line in the sand, 'twenty

Hearson's Cove, Murujuga, 2015, where Francis Thomas Gregory arrived in May 1861

paces' from his camp, but Aboriginal men responded by setting fire to the grass around the camp. Again, it was gunfire that forced them to keep their distance. Although Gregory made it clear that he 'did not wish seriously to hurt them', his method of asserting his right to camp on their land would be repeated hundreds of times over in the years to come. Guns and bullets were the ultimate expression of the settlers' authority, the brute, lethal instrument of frontier administration.[10]

When Gregory returned to Perth, his sanguine description of the north-west gave more than enough encouragement to the British government to declare the area 'open' for colonisation. He pointed to the great 'commercial value' of the 'the beds of the pearl oysters', identified two to three million acres of Crown land as suitable for grazing, talked up the potential to grow cotton on the 'arable lands on the De Grey and Sherlock' rivers, and reassured potential settlers that the small numbers of 'Aborigines' would not prove 'particularly troublesome … if properly treated'.[11] He gave the impression that profits were there for the taking. Within the space of a few years the settlers arrived, encouraged by generous government land grants—up to 4000 hectares rent-free for three years—and funding from private investors and wealthy squatters from the eastern colonies eager to capitalise on Gregory's predictions. Because the government had banned the use of convict labour north of 'the 26th parallel', the settlers would immediately turn to Aboriginal people for their labour force.[12] 'The North District' that the government was about to 'unlock' stretched all the way from the Murchison River north to the Timor Sea, including the Kimberley and the vast arid regions to the colony's border with South Australia, a territory so great that it gave rise to dreams of another empire. When the first shipload of settlers left from Perth in April 1863, the editorial in one of the city's newspapers wondered whether the colony was witnessing the 'colonization of an entirely new country' that would one day break away from the colony and form an independent state. Perth, a lonely island of British settlement, was about to give birth to another island of British 'civilization', one that was so far away in its citizens' imagination that it might just as well have been another country.[13]

In the early 1860s, there were between forty and fifty thousand Aboriginal people living in north-western Australia in approximately fifty clearly defined territories. On Murujuga and the islands of the archipelago, there were at least one hundred and fifty to two hundred Yaburara, possibly more, their numbers probably fluctuating throughout the year according to the season. Although they had no idea, in the eyes of British law their land was no longer theirs. When Major Edmund Lockyer, determined to pre-empt any possibility of French settlement in the west, hoisted the Union Jack at Albany on 21 January 1827 and claimed British sovereignty over the western third of the Australian continent, Aboriginal land became 'Crown land' and Aboriginal people became subjects of the Crown. What the law had claimed without negotiation—the 'wandering natives' were not deemed to own the land—would take many years of bloody conquest to secure.[14]

When the settlers arrived in 1863, Yaburara society was still intact. As custodians and practitioners of the countless rock engravings that covered Murujuga and the nearby islands, they lived in four to five distinct groups, and appeared to be on good terms with their neighbours—Ngarluma (to the east) and Mardudunera (to the west), both of whom visited them regularly. Their language, 'meaning northeners', was closely related to that spoken by the Ngarluma. Beyond archaeological and firsthand evidence of their diet—'they netted, [trapped] and speared fish and turtles and, from their [log] watercraft, caught dolphins, dugongs, turtles and sharks'—we know little of their culture. Like many tribes on the north-west coast of Australia, they had long had contact with the Makassans, who had sailed the region in search of trepang since at least the mid-eighteenth century.[15] As the first British settlers arrived on the shores of Murujuga, the Yaburara sometimes showed them the rock engravings, pointing out images on Dolphin Island of fish, 'turtles, lizards, and different kinds of birds, including emus'. Gazing at these 'drawings', a handful of the newcomers recognised evidence of their 'ingenuity and artistic skill'. But most who remarked on the engravings in the late nineteenth century saw only 'rude figures on stones' and 'many men and women in a variety of vulgar attitudes'.[16] Shocked by images of men with elongated penises and women in provocative sexual poses, they could only see what offended them. Little did they realise that for the Yaburara, who sometimes restored the images, merely to touch them was to 'release the spiritual essence in order to maintain the balance of the natural order'.[17]

Within three years of the first settlers' arrival, the north-west was transformed. Over one million hectares of land leased, a port established 40 kilometres east of Murujuga (eventually named Cossack in 1871), and an administrative centre founded 15 kilometres south-west of Cossack at Roebourne, which became the first town in north-western Australia. By the late 1860s there were well over thirty thousand sheep in the region, the first hard-hoofed animals to tramp the fragile Pilbara soils to dust. In May 1863, when Charles Nairn established the first settlement for the entrepreneur Walter Padbury, he landed his sheep at Cossack and immediately met several Ngarluma men on the beach—'great strapping fellows … very noisy but friendly and incessantly begging for tobacco'. Three days later he asked them

Pilbara Country, inland from Karratha, 2015

to lead him to water, which they promptly did. But Nairn found it too brackish. The next morning several of his sheep were dead after the water in the well 'turned quite salt'. He watched them in the throes of death 'frothing at the mouth and nose', their carcasses swelling to 'a great size'.[18]

Travelling north to the De Grey River in search of better country, Nairn soon realised that the 'fine grassy country' he saw from a distance was in fact 'spinifex plains as far as the eye can reach'. As he journeyed north-east, he learnt from his Aboriginal guides to burn the spinifex ahead of him, the new green shoots sprouting so quickly that his stock had feed most of the way. Unaccustomed to the scale of the land, he kept looking for visual relief, exasperated by 'nothing but the same kind of country'. The 'dry sandy soil' of the river channels he imagined 'would absorb all the Rain of Australia & [still] be barren'. Not until he reached the De Grey did he become more enthusiastic: 'this will be fine country for Maize Tobacco or in fact anything requiring good land & a warm climate'. Two years later, and not long after Nairn marked a 'great event'—'the first ground turned by a plough on the De Grey'—a severe drought brought the pastoralists to their knees. The country was far hotter than they had expected. Many settlers departed, convinced that the whole enterprise had been a terrible mistake. Meanwhile, the Ngarluma's supply of roots, seeds and game was even more depleted due to the erosion caused by the sudden introduction of sheep. Long before conflict occurred, Aboriginal people struggled as Europeans occupied their most fertile land and disrupted their hunting grounds and traditional patterns of movement.[19]

In 1866, as the nascent pastoral industry languished in the face of the drought, the squatters turned to the other half of Gregory's prospectus: pearls. Emma and John Withnell, wealthy squatters who held one of the largest runs at Roebourne, noticed Aboriginal people on their station wearing pearl shell necklaces. Intrigued, John joined them 'beachcombing' and soon had them out on his boat diving for pearls, which he immediately shipped to Fremantle and London. Other squatters told similar stories of observing 'Aborigines' near Nickol Bay wearing 'pearl shell pendants' before rushing to set up 'a company' to harvest pearls. It was not only Aboriginal land that Europeans assumed as their 'property' but the coastal waters and ocean beds too.[20]

Aboriginal people had collected pearl shells for thousands of years. 'Carefully curated' objects of adornment and ritual significance, they were 'wrapped in soft bark or cloth and kept with an individual's personal possessions'. Many were moved through national trade networks into the interior, far north, south and east of the continent, including Arnhem Land. The Aboriginal community at Port Essington would have known pearls from Murujuga and the Pilbara and Kimberley coasts, as would the Makassans. But European pearling entailed a completely different economy: international trade networks, exploitation of Aboriginal labour, enormous profits for a select few and intensive harvesting until resources had been totally exhausted. It was a model of development that would be repeated many times over in the Pilbara. By 1868 there were 'swarms' of pearling boats on the north-west coast and islands around Murujuga 'contracting' more than three hundred Aboriginal people. It was at this point that the Yaburara experienced the tidal wave of European invasion.[21]

With Cossack serving as the major port for a flourishing pearling fleet, pearlers were active in several sites near Murujuga, including Dolphin and Gidley islands. From 1866, they relied on a mix of 'voluntary and forced [Aboriginal] labour', competing with one another to secure the best divers, many of them women, and children as young as ten.[22] Working along the north-west coast, they removed Aboriginal people hundreds of 'miles from their home and friends' to dive for pearls.[23] As coastal people, the Yaburara were among the most accessible sources of labour, and they were regularly 'contracted' to dive for pearls. Essentially, this meant being cajoled or forced to sign indentures that placed them under the terms and conditions of the 1823 *Master and Servant Act*. Once they had placed their mark on the contract they became the property of the pearlers for months at a time, or as long as the diving season lasted. They were also subject to imprisonment with hard labour—either on faraway Rottnest Island or in temporary lockups in Roebourne—if they were caught absconding from their employment.[24]

At the same time as the Yaburara's families and social networks were torn asunder by the removal of their men and women to dive for pearls, a smallpox epidemic, which began in 1866—probably brought by Malays who were also working as divers—severely depleted their population. It is difficult to tell how many died, but reports of many deaths along the coast and inland suggest that the impact was critical throughout the entire region. For the Yaburara, these were cataclysmic events. In order to survive, they took whatever they could from the stations nearby. At night, they left the islands and peninsula and raided the closest station at present-day Karratha, taking 'bread ... bullock meat' and other provisions back to their campsites.[25] As competition for resources increased and the large number of unattached white men began to 'take' Yaburara women, the seeds of violent conflict were sown. Seemingly oblivious to their own theft of Yaburara land, the enforcers of frontier justice hunted down Aboriginal 'thieves', captured them, chained them by the neck, walked them to Roebourne, convicted them of petty theft and sentenced them to lengthy gaol terms. Few of their captives had any idea why they had been imprisoned. In February 1868, one such expedition led to a series of events that would end in the almost total destruction of a culture that had survived for thousands of generations.

———————

It began with a seemingly minor incident: a Yaburara man stealing 'flour and other stores' from a 'small boat' pearling in Nickol Bay. On 30 January, Constable William Griffis, already bent on apprehending another Aboriginal man guilty of 'petty thefts', set out from Roebourne together with his Aboriginal guide 'Peter' and the 'sailor' George Breem to search for the culprits. 'As usual, [they] were well armed, Griffis having a revolver, Peter a carbine, and both carried a good supply of ammunition.' The story of what happened next and why will always be contested. The official account claims that after six days searching, Griffis finally found the man responsible for stealing the flour—'Coolyerberri'—'put a chain around his neck' and tied him to a tree. That night, 6 February, Griffis, Breem and Peter camped with a pearler, Jermyn, on the shores of Nickol Bay, not far from Murujuga. Incensed by their friend's capture and detention, a group of Yaburara men debated how to respond. According to the later testimony of the 14-year-old 'Jacky, a native of the North West Coast', who witnessed the discussion, considerable division emerged among them as to what they should do. Most argued that Griffis and his men should be speared to death as soon as they were asleep, while a minority such as Jacky insisted that this course of action would only incur the wrath of the settlers. The more determined among them argued that they were not afraid of the inevitable white reprisals: when they came searching for them 'they would spear them' too. By this time the decision was made.[26]

When 'the moon had not risen high', Jacky left them and went with the women and children and 'the native men who were not savage' to camp 'over the hill', barely four hundred metres away. Then, as he learnt shortly afterwards from one of the assailants, two hours before dawn, the others crept along the track towards Jermyn's tent and set Coolyerberri free. As Griffis woke he was speared 'in the chest', his skull crushed by several men wielding tomahawks. Peter was 'speared in the belly just as he was rising up', and Breem, who tried to escape, was chased down and speared. Jermyn had apparently left only hours earlier for Cossack. No further trace of him would ever be found. After taking all the ammunition and 'ransacking' the tent, the murderers fled 'to the westward'. Early the next morning, two 'native boys' alerted the pearler Henry Davis to what had taken place. Davis went immediately with them to the scene, covered the bodies, and after questioning a reluctant Jacky, who was 'afraid' to tell the truth, he learnt the identity of the three murderers and communicated the news to Horace Sholl, whose father, RJ Sholl, had been Government Resident at Roebourne since late 1865. Just before noon the following day, 8 February 1868, Sholl senior heard firsthand from Davis what he had seen. Sholl, who had already been pushed out of the Camden Harbour settlement further north by Aboriginal resistance three years earlier, was not about to allow the same thing to happen a second time. His response was swift: 'as there seemed no doubt but that the intelligence was true, I ordered three coffins to be made. Our arms were also got out, and cleaned and loaded'.

Yaburara Heritage Trail, in the hills above Karratha, 2015

Sholl wasted no time in requesting a 'few of the inhabitants of the town' to meet with him and 'discuss matters'. Reconnaissance parties were sent out promptly. The wealthy squatter Withnell and two other men left Roebourne that afternoon, 'intending to ascertain the fate of Jermyn and warn the other men'. Sholl started at sunrise the next day, travelling with his son Horace and a '"Swan River" native, Jimmy'. The two parties met near Jermyn's tent four hours later. They unsaddled their horses about three hundred metres from the murder scene and walked in carrying the coffins. The first body they saw was Breem's, 'about 50 yards to the westward of the tent'. 'He was lying on his face with his arms stretched in front of him ... [his] hands being clenched'. The spear that killed him was 'broken off under his left arm' having 'penetrated his heart'. His remains were so badly 'decomposed' that his clothing had 'been burst by the swollen body' and 'too much distended' to enable Sholl to 'put them in the coffin'. He had no choice but to bury Breem's remains on the spot. Griffis's decomposed, 'naked' body was 'lying at the western entrance of the tent'. He had been so badly 'mutilated' that there was 'no vestige of a face below the eyes'. Sholl wrapped his body in a 'boat sail' and placed it in the coffin. He then dealt with Peter's 'much battered' body, which lay nearby, his 'face (crawling with worms) a mass of corruption'. Peter was covered with 'bags' and placed in a coffin. The 'stench' from the bodies was so 'dreadful' it made them 'all sick'. All of this Sholl reported in clinical detail, reading the landscape strategically, like a military officer in the heat of battle:

> [their campsite] was a very badly chosen spot. From the slope, or even the summit of the hill, spears might be thrown with effect into the creek, while the mangrove belt, though thin, would afford cover for an attacking party. Even an armed party, prepared for an attack, would have to fight at a disadvantage in such a position.

Surveying the scene, he was appalled by the 'reckless destruction'. He noticed that 'the [victims'] clock had been thrown on the fire, but had slipped down the heap of ashes and was not burnt'. 'It had stopped at 20m. to 4', which Sholl thought the approximate time 'when the murder was committed'. Picking up Griffis's sextant and handcuff keys from the ground, he prepared to return to Roebourne with the two bodies. Jermyn's horses had come back to camp the day before, their bridles cut, which convinced Sholl that he had probably met a similar fate to the others. Intending to bury the bodies the next day, his plans were thwarted by heavy rain, which filled the two freshly dug graves at Roebourne cemetery. Unexpectedly, he was forced to deal with the 'awfully sudden death' of the man who had originally made the coffins for him, carpenter James White. White drank himself to death, dying at 5 p.m. on 10 February, 'during the heaviest of the rain'. 'He was placed in the coffin he had made himself for Breem' and the following morning, Sholl 'read the service over his remains and those of the other poor men'. He had known all the men who had been killed, but none more so than Griffis, who he had worked with closely. Burying him was particularly hard. Sholl thought 'his loss' would be 'much felt' in the district. As he told his superiors, Griffis 'was bold and fearless in the discharge of his duty, and was much dreaded by native offenders. He died while executing the law upon those who would, if not apprehended and punished, most probably have been more severely dealt with by those whom they had robbed, and possibly in that case the innocent would have suffered with the guilty'. In Sholl's eyes, the 'feared' Griffis had saved the 'natives' he arrested from deadly reprisals by the settlers, an allegedly benign consequence of zealous law enforcement that would soon be shown to be false. His ministerial duties done, Sholl now turned to administering justice.

Aware that the 'native murderers' had fled to the islands near Murujuga, Sholl issued warrants for their arrest and appointed two search parties: one on land, headed by the Victorian squatter Alexander McRae, and another on sea, led by John Withnell. Lacking sufficient police officers for the job, he swore in twelve 'special constables', including McRae and Withnell, agreeing to pay them two shillings per day for the duration of the expedition. Several 'Swan River' natives also joined them. It did not begin until 14 February, once the 'horses were caught and shod, arms repaired, and provisions packed'. With the memory of the carnage at the campsite still vivid in his mind, Sholl asked McRae to read the funeral service for Breem. At 10 p.m. that evening, the members of the two expeditions departed Roebourne determined to apprehend 'the principal murderers' and avenge the death of their comrades.

After two days' travelling, McRae's land party met with Withnell's cutter at Hearson's Cove on the south-east edge of Murujuga. Neither party had sighted any of the men they were seeking. After agreeing to meet again at King Bay on the opposite side of the peninsula the following day, McRae's Aboriginal guide noticed 'a number of native tracks leading to the west' and they headed off in quick pursuit. At nightfall, they spotted fires on the beach near the southern side of King Bay. McRae decided to make camp and surprise the 'natives' early the following morning, assuming without any evidence that this group was 'likely to contain many of the men [he] wanted'. They started 'before daylight' on the seventeenth and soon came upon their prey. 'They were camped on a clear sandy beach.' But before they could surround their quarry, the men bolted into the mangroves and hills. Giving chase, McRae managed to 'cut some of them off' but 'they would not stop to be arrested'. At this point, McRae claimed that he had 'no alternative but to fire upon them'. 'One of the murderers' was shot dead, and 'several others wounded'. It was no good, he insisted, allowing them to 'escape without a lesson' because this would only lead to 'further outrages against the settlers'. McRae did not state exactly how many of the 'wounded' died. But every shot he and his men fired into the backs of those trying to escape was designed to instil fear into the hearts of Aboriginal people. Capturing those responsible for Griffis's death was only part of the equation. Their motives were far more basic: revenge, intimidation and silencing 'the natives'.[27]

In the blazing sun, McRae continued hunting the escapees for the next few hours, scrambling 'over the high rocky hills' in a 'fruitless' search. Every time he caught sight of someone, they 'just as quickly disappeared into the rocks'. He soon gave up and returned to his camp, claiming to have found 'a Crimean shirt and hat belonging to Griffis [and] Peter's red cap' in the Yaburara's possession. Later the next day he learnt that some of the 'natives' had gone north towards Flying Foam Passage, the narrow stretch of water between Dolphin and Angel islands. Withnell had returned from there to King Bay and

Beach on the east coast of Angel Island, Flying Foam Passage, 2015

told him that he had captured two men the previous evening, one of whom, 'Mulligang', was allegedly one of the murderers. But having 'no chains or handcuffs' (a curious omission for 'special constables' apparently appointed to apprehend the murderers) he was unable to stop them from slipping overboard. On the morning of the eighteenth, the two men swam ashore to an island only 'a short distance off' and hid in the mangroves. Withnell 'gave orders to fire upon them' because, as he argued later, if he had attempted to 'retake them, they would probably have escaped'.

The next morning Withnell conveyed McRae's party to Dolphin Island where they 'found the natives had crossed to some of the islands in Flying Foam harbour'. Catching sight of several men 'crossing the bay in canoes', they gave 'chase' in a small boat, shooting one man dead. The others managed to land on a nearby island. McRae could see them 'standing on the shore' and as they 'made for the mangroves' he ordered his men to fire. His official report stated simply that 'several were shot or wounded'. Like Withnell, he claimed that it was impossible to capture them and that he therefore had little choice but to shoot them. Who he was shooting did not appear to matter. The object was to shoot as many of the Yaburara as possible.

On the twentieth, Withnell's party went ashore on one of the islands 'to the north of Flying Foam harbour', most probably Angel Island or Gidley Island, where they 'came upon a native camp'. The country was 'rugged' and as the Yaburara were 'armed', Withnell and his men 'had a sharp skirmish with them' and only narrowly escaped being speared. He reported that 'none of them were taken' but failed to mention how many were shot. For the next two days both parties continued searching without managing to take any prisoners. By 22 February, both McRae and Withnell had returned to Roebourne and Cossack. McRae thanked the members of the expedition for the 'performance of their duties' on such an 'unpleasant trip' and then gave Sholl a firsthand account of their expedition. On paper, Sholl interpreted their efforts as something of a triumph, telling the Colonial Secretary five days later that as a result, the 'loss of life amongst the isolated whites has been prevented, the well disposed natives confirmed in their amity towards us, the wavering made steadfast, the guilty terrified, and the old feeling of security revived amongst the whole white population'. Despite the fact that not one of the guilty had been brought back to Roebourne, Sholl still saw the expedition as a resounding success, a conclusion that suggests his intention was always to demonstrate the settlers' power over Aboriginal people by punishing them indiscriminately and spreading terror. Only then would 'the old feeling of security' among the settlers return. It also seems extraordinary that Sholl could claim such extensive impact for the expedition from the mere handful of encounters he mentions in his official report. Far more likely is that his reports omitted much of the 'unpleasant' detail and that many more Yaburara were killed than he had claimed. His public statements differed markedly from his private accounts. As he confided to his sister, he had led a 'strong party to go out and give them fitz ... [and] a great many were lost'. In any case, Sholl had not yet finished the 'lesson' he was teaching.[28]

Over the next three months, the search for the murderers and thieves continued. On 18 March, Sholl despatched another party, which resulted in the shooting of at least three more men. In May, two others who were allegedly involved in Griffis's murder were arrested and sent to Rottnest Island gaol for twelve years. Again, it is possible that many more Yaburara were shot during these confrontations. By June 1868, Sholl was 'glad' to inform his superiors that 'the natives [had] been quiet' since he last wrote.[29] Estimates of how many Aboriginal people were killed between February and June 1868 would be forever disputed. Official accounts placed the number at less than ten. But only one year later, when the settler William Taylor wrote to the Colonial Secretary critical of the treatment of Aboriginal people in the north-west, he referred to the manner in which Sholl's expedition 'murdered the blacks ... committing the most cowardly and diabolical acts both on innocent women and children'. Taylor also alleged that Griffis was murdered because he had abducted Aboriginal women, an allegation that would become the cornerstone of the surviving Aboriginal oral history relating to the massacre that was recorded in the late twentieth century. Ngarluma elders spoke of Griffis 'raping' Yaburara women:

> Lots of Yaburara people [at Murujuga] long time ago. This policeman took a young girl into the bush, with a rifle. The old fella (the girl's husband) he got a spear in his hand, he put the spear right through the policeman's chest. The other police all got their guns, went out there, got all the Yaburara up, got them all together, shot them down. Must be 30, 40 people killed.[30]

While definitive evidence of the numbers killed will never be found, the circumstantial evidence of frontier language and settler attitudes towards Aboriginal people at the time is far more conclusive. Only three years before he led the expedition to avenge Griffis's death, Alexander McRae was in Roebuck Bay, just south of Broome, having already been forced out of Camden Harbour by the Worora. 'The niggers are a savage, determined race of people,' he told his sister in August 1865, 'the worst that have been met with on this side of the continent. A good many have been shot, but it does not seem to have had the desired effect'. Three months later he complained to her again: 'the natives are still very troublesome although a great many of them have been shot'.[31] McRae was no stranger to a culture in which Aboriginal people were shot at first sight. Nor was his approach to frontier conflict shaped exclusively by his experience in the north-west. When the results of his expedition were reported in his home district in Victoria, the local paper noted proudly that the son of a local squatter and his men had 'shot several of the murderers' before adding in the next sentence: 'The new country is, however, progressing favourably, copious rainfalls have fallen, and the increase of lambs has been 100 per cent'.[32] Despite the fact that the lives of Aboriginal people were protected equally under the law, many settlers viewed them as subhuman, a mentality that was certainly not exclusive to the 'lower orders' of society. Sholl's well-read son Trevarton, who assisted his father in administrative matters at Roebourne from 1865 and spent his 'fearfully hot' days waited on by his 'nigger servant' while reading Samuel Johnson, Jane Austen and Byron, remarked casually after his return from a 7-week expedition south to Exmouth Gulf: 'Saw any amount of niggers, obliged to pepper one lot, others friendly'. Once British settlers had a stake in the land, they would not tolerate interference. The clear instructions given to Charles Nairn by the investor Walter Padbury left no doubt as to how he should deal with 'troublesome' natives: 'you must shoot at them'. The settlers, he told Nairn, 'must fight and subdue the natives' in order to provide greater 'security to property'.[33] A similar approach was adopted at sea.

Although legislation was passed in the 1870s to regulate the employment of Aboriginal people in the pearling industry, it was constantly dismissed on the distant ground of the frontier. As pearling began in earnest in the late 1860s, disobedient Aboriginal divers were sometimes shot in the water as they tried to swim away. In August 1868, in the wake of the shootings at Murujuga and Flying Foam Passage, John Watson was one of the main witnesses in the trial of fellow pearler Robert Rowland, charged with murdering three Aboriginal divers near Port Hedland. Rowland, who had already spent time in prison for attempted murder, had also been a member of

Withnell's punitive expedition. Watson described how he saw 'three natives' accused of trying to strangle a white man taken on board a pearling vessel, the *Little Eastern*. 'Six or seven white men' surrounded them on deck. As Watson's boat came close by he heard someone shout: 'We will shoot them'. The 'master' of the *Little Eastern* insisted that he would have 'no bloodshed' on his vessel, to which another of the pearlers replied: 'I'll take them on board my own boat and shoot them'. Watson tried unsuccessfully to persuade the men 'not to shoot the natives'. One of the prisoners, a 'young man', his face 'marked all over with smallpox', was then forced into the water after which several of the pearlers took their shotguns and fired at him repeatedly, 'perhaps twenty shots'. 'We have settled him', one of them declared. The same was done to the next man. Watson saw his body rising to the surface, 'blood and bubbles coming out of his mouth'. He left before the third 'native' was dealt with.[34]

In the late 1860s, 'shooting natives' was standard practice on the north-west frontier. Yet there was also a fierce debate within settler society regarding the morality and justice of such brutality. As Watson tried to persuade the pearlers not to shoot their captives, so Charles Nairn tried in vain to stop the shooting of Aboriginal people near Gregory River in 1863.[35] It was little different on the other side of the frontier. Aboriginal people debated whether they should kill white settlers, especially in cases such as the murder of Griffis, because they knew that to do so would result in massive retaliation. Watson's depiction of the pearlers also highlights the isolation of frontier life and the tendency of settlers to see their communities as threatened and vulnerable, forced by the vast distances that separated them from 'civilised society' and for their own 'protection' to take the law into their own hands. Many pastoralists and pearlers in the north-west, including experienced administrators such as Sholl, believed that it was their right and duty to do whatever it took to secure their foothold on the land. Burying the mutilated bodies of law officers such as Griffis only fuelled their anger and further steeled their resolve to assert their authority.

Until recently it was thought that allegations of a massacre at Murujuga in early 1868 did not surface until the late nineteenth

137

century. But during the same court case held in Perth in August 1868, in which Watson gave evidence, the defendant's counsel, Parker, attempted to excuse his client's actions by referring to the events at Murujuga and Flying Foam Passage months earlier. At that time, 'there was a kind of *war* between the whites and the natives', Parker proclaimed, 'referring to the *massacres* which had taken place near Roebourne'. This evidence is crucial because it reveals that only six months after Sholl's expedition, the terms 'war' and 'massacre' were used in court to describe what happened at Murujuga. It also confirms that there were multiple 'massacres', not just the one that occurred at King Bay on 18 February. Twelve months later, even Sholl implied that the cost to the Yaburara had proved devastating. When two of the alleged murderers came to Roebourne of their own accord in February 1869, Sholl granted them an amnesty because, he said, 'the natives have received a severe lesson and much blood has been spilt'.[36]

In the decades before responsible government was granted to Western Australia in 1890 and the state belatedly joined the Australian Federation in 1901, the story of the 'Flying Foam Massacre' lay at the heart of a fiercely divisive debate over the treatment of the state's Indigenous population in the north-west. From the 1870s to 1890s, as pearlers gradually combed the inland areas to capture more and more divers—a practice known then as 'blackbirding' or 'nigger hunting'—allegations of forced labour, chain gangs, incarceration, severe beatings, stockwhip floggings, shootings and an 'unquestionable system of slavery' abounded. Letters to the Colonial Secretary in London (where slavery had been abolished in 1833), written in the hope that the British government would be more likely to protect Aboriginal people than their representatives in Perth, testified to the most horrific cruelties. In one instance, in 1878, Lionel Gould claimed to have witnessed the flogging of Aboriginal women for failing to harvest sufficient pearl shells. When one of the women working on De Grey station attempted to 'steal' pearls, the station owner boasted to Gould: 'I made a grab and caught her by the hair and flogged her till she pissed and shit herself'. Letters and articles published in the Perth press by those willing to speak honestly about the shameful treatment of Aboriginal people in the north-west were loudly denounced by the city's establishment and those who had once lived in the region.[37]

In 1886, the divisions between the humanitarians who were convinced the colony had lost all sense of morality and those who defended the settlers' 'stern justice' came to a head when the Anglican missionary Thomas Gribble published *Dark Deeds in a Sunny Land*, in which he detailed countless examples of settler brutality. Gribble would eventually be run out of town, penniless after losing a libel case and disowned by many in the church hierarchy in Perth, the government and conservative press. But his courage and that of many others resulted in the British government refusing to cede responsibility for Aboriginal affairs to the new colonial government in 1890. In a controversy that exposed the deep fear in Western Australian society that the colony had been established illegitimately, the Flying Foam Massacre stood as a flashpoint of settler anxiety.

Gribble had quoted the evidence of the former Roebourne resident David Carly, who stated categorically that it was 'very well known around Nickol Bay and Flying Foam Passage that in one day there were quite sixty natives, men, women and children shot dead'. He claimed to have been shown the 'skulls of 15 who were shot dead', including three children.[38] The controversy that erupted in the wake of these allegations simmered for almost a decade, with claims surfacing in late 1892 that up to 150 Yaburara 'were massacred in cold blood'.[39] Twenty-five years after Sholl authorised the punitive expedition from Roebourne, debate still raged as to how many Aboriginal people had been killed. Many in Perth were so appalled by the stories that trickled down from the north-west they would gladly have cut the region free. But in the pages of the Perth papers, former pastoralists of the north, incensed by the suggestion that they had presided over gross injustice, vehemently denied allegations of a 'massacre' and blamed atrocities on the 'worst class of pearlers'.[40] The victims, apparently, were the settlers, not the Yaburara.

As Charles Harper, newspaper editor, politician, one-time pearler, pastoralist and business partner of Alexander McRae, wrote to *The West Australian* in November 1892: 'remember the Foam Passage

139

massacre. Yes, I remember the time well. On riding into Roebourne in the early part of 1868 I found the few people there in a most excited and nervous state, armed men patrolling the town at night, and women too terrified to sleep'. Harper admitted that 'some [blacks] were shot' but 'how many was never exactly known, but it was doubtful', he thought, 'that more than 10 were killed'. He then claimed that after the shooting, 'a little child was found accidentally wounded in the thigh, the wound was bound up, and it was taken off to the boat and tended with care, though it ultimately succumbed'. Each time an irate pastoralist sought to defend Sholl's party they revealed (or invented) previously unknown detail in an attempt to justify what occurred. In the same letter, Harper also detailed other examples of frontier conflict in the north-west, admitting that one 'severe engagement', carried out not under the instructions of government but 'the first law of nature—self preservation' could indeed be classed as a 'massacre'.[41] But with regard to Flying Foam, he remained extremely defensive and protective of Alexander McRae's reputation. Others, like the wealthy pastoralist of the north-west AR Richardson, a member of parliament who would soon become Western Australia's Commissioner of Crown Lands, were more brazen:

> The blacks, elated with victory, and like bloody hounds madly excited with a first taste of the white man's blood, sent in a message to the little settlement [of Roebourne] that they now intended to serve all the rest of the white fellows in the same way, and drive them right out of the country … The settlers that were in … [Sholl's] party were as justified in obeying orders as British soldiers when they shot at either Kaffirs, Zulus, Abyssinians or any other inferior race, and for which they are frequently decorated with medals … and their names sounded forth as heroes and brave soldiers, the pride of the nation … as to these silly allusions to the 'settlers' having taken away their country from the natives, I always thought the country was taken possession of in the name of the Queen, and that the Crown leased it to the settlers, taking payment of rent from them for the use of it. Please censure the 'flag' for taking the country and not the subjects who merely occupy it.[42]

The settlers in the north-west did much more than 'merely occupy' the land. They forced Aboriginal people to submit to their occupation. Richardson denied that there had been a massacre, only the application of 'stern justice' to 'savages' who he insisted were 'incapable of understanding any lessons but those of Might is Right'. The result of the expedition, he argued, was overwhelmingly positive. There was 'never any further trouble with natives. They became … good servants on the most friendly terms with settlers, and soon gave up bush life and poverty to enjoy plenty of good food and other luxuries'. For Richardson, all those who had lost their lives in the cause of bringing 'civilisation' to the north-west were apparently war heroes, like the leader of Sholl's boat party, John Withnell.[43] When he died in 1898, the author of his obituary lauded him as one of the colony's founding fathers. Yet the dispute over the legality and morality of what occurred at Murujuga in 1868 had continued to dominate Perth public culture to such an extent that he was forced to defend Withnell's role, threading fabrication with outright denial.

The time came, as it comes to all new settlements in Australia, when the blacks meditated a slaughter of the whites, and they began by killing a policeman and several other white men on the shore of Nickol Bay. When the news reached Roebourne considerable consternation arose, as the whites were few and the blacks many. However, Mr. Withnell went out with his team and one or two others and brought the bodies in for burial. A meeting was held to consider what steps should be taken to assert and maintain law and order. The general opinion was that the murderers should be at once arrested, if possible, but who was to do it? For there was only one policeman left. Those present at the meeting could all find excellent reasons why they could not form members of a party to aid in the work. Finally … [Withnell] broke his accustomed silence and said, 'Any man who could see his fellow-man brutally murdered, as those had been, and not take steps to bring the murderer to justice had no British blood in him'. After that excuses were forgotten, a party was formed and the murderers were captured.[44]

By the early twentieth century, the Flying Foam Massacre was increasingly remembered as an example of a handful of exposed settlers who had no alternative but to resort to violence in order to assert their possession of the land. In 1900, when the former pastoralist John Slade Durlacher finished his memoir of life in the Pilbara, in which he sympathetically (if patronisingly) documented Aboriginal culture, he typically glossed over the evidence, depicting the 'bold' natives as the aggressors who 'threatened the small band of settlers at Roebourne', before defending the settlers' right to 'give the offending natives a lesson that they would not forget for some time'. For Durlacher, violence and intimidation were essential components of the white man's 'civilising influence'. What began as an example of merciless settler violence that deeply unsettled many Western Australians in the late nineteenth century slowly lodged in settler memory as an allegory of white vulnerability.[45]

When John Withnell's wife Emma (the 'mother of the north-west') died in 1928, her obituary included her reflections on her friendship with Aboriginal women: 'they seemed to delight to take down my hair, of which I had plenty, and hold it out in the sunlight while the others danced around me. They not only gave me their friendship and protection, but those remaining wept in grief when I left the district'. Yet when it came to the struggle between the settlers and Aboriginal people for land and resources, the author portrayed the settlers as victims, pointing out that 'a number of the new settlers' around Roebourne in the early days 'were killed by the blacks'. No mention was made of the blacks killed by the whites.[46] The wealthy pastoralists of the north-west who had profited most from the 'silencing' of the 'natives' went on to become esteemed figures in Perth society, condoning and even applauding what had taken place at Murujuga in 1868. Not until 1933, when John Watson, the same man who stood in a Perth courtroom sixty-five years earlier to bear witness to the callous and inhumane actions of pearlers in the north-west, published his memoir *Pearling in 1868: A Tragic Adventure*, were the foundation myths of British settlement in the north-west again disturbed by the Flying Foam Massacre. Watson, who had heard eyewitness accounts of what happened and was enlisted by Sholl only months later to arrest some of the culprits on Legendre Island, recalled the events at King Bay on the morning of 18 February, when McRae's men attacked the Yaburara's camp.

> At daylight next morning the land party came upon a number of natives in camp, several of whom may or may not have been concerned with one or other of the murders They were shot down while others took to the water only to be finished off by the boat party. I leave it to the imagination of my readers to picture the public indignation that would he aroused to-day by such slaughter, perpetrated as it was with the colourable approval of the responsible Government official of the district. The men really guilty of the murders of Bream and the constable were not in the camp where these reprisals were made.[47]

Watson's recollections were indictments of colonial administration, his accusation of 'slaughter' yet another reminder that McRae's and Withnell's expeditions were less concerned with apprehending sus-pects than killing as many Yaburara as possible. At the time Watson's allegations were published, Indigenous people in Western Australia were not citizens, and even when citizenship was finally granted in 1944, state legislation stipulated that 'full rights of citizenship by Aboriginal natives' would only be given when they had 'dissolved tribal and native association except with lineal descendants or native relations of the first degree' for two years prior to their application.[48] Indigenous citizenship in Western Australia was first predicated on the eradication of traditional culture. By the 1930s, Aboriginal people in the Pilbara were being moved by the government to ration camps and coastal reserves such as the one at Roebourne, 50 kilometres from Murujuga, in which different tribal groups were forced to live together under the control of the Native Welfare Department and the police. The circles that the first settlers had marked out around their homesteads to signal to the 'natives' that they should keep out were now placed around Aboriginal people to fence them in. Watson's memories of the Flying Foam Massacre surfaced in a settler culture that was still preoccupied with managing the Aboriginal 'problem'.

Ever since the first settlers had arrived in the north-west, government, churches and administrators had sought to determine the course of Aboriginal people's lives—dispossessing them, enslaving them, 'protecting' them, civilising them, converting them, imprisoning them, assimilating them, removing their children and deciding where they should live, work and play. There was no escape from the meddling hands of white Australia. Although Aboriginal labour had enabled the establishment of the profitable pearling and pastoral industries and formed the backbone of the Pilbara gold rushes in the 1890s, their pivotal role as founders and pioneers was rarely if ever acknowledged. For all they endured, the most remarkable feature of Aboriginal societies was their ability to adapt and survive in the face of enormous dislocation, men and women walking hundreds of kilometres back to their Country when the pearling season was over, and their elders keeping their families and culture alive as they worked and lived on pastoral stations or the ration camps and reserves created for them by the government. Yet there was no denying the dramatic impact of the invasion.

Within thirty years of first settlement, the Indigenous population of Australia's north-west had been severely depleted by a combination of disease, violence, sudden loss of land and disruption of traditional culture. It was nothing short of a revolution. At its forefront was the experience of the Yaburara, custodians of a Country imprinted with some of the most astonishing examples of ancient Indigenous culture in Australia, and who became the first Aboriginal people to succumb to British settlement in the north-west. In the seven years between 1863 and 1870, a culture that had existed for thousands of years was decimated. For years afterwards, the evidence of mass shootings continued to mount. In 1946, Edward H Angelo recalled a 'holiday cruise' he took through Flying Foam Passage in 1892: '[We] landed on a small, unnamed islet about two miles south of Angel Island. Here we discovered numbers of skeletons. On inquiring later we were told that many years previously a white man had been murdered by natives … the band had been chased in boats, found on this island and wiped out. Judging by the skeletons the punitive expedition had done its job thoroughly'.[49]

In 1983, the scholar who did most to document the Flying Foam Massacre, Tom Gara, concluded that he was unable to find any examples of Aboriginal people living a traditional lifestyle in the archipelago after 1870. In the 1890s, the few Yaburara who remained had 'sought refuge in an out camp of Karratha Station'. In the twentieth century, anthropologists and archaeologists referred to them as 'extinct', lamenting the fact that the people who knew most about the petroglyphs of Murujuga could no longer be found, their cultural knowledge having vanished with them. Today, there are only a handful of Aboriginal people who claim ancestral links to the Yaburara.[50]

In October 1869, as he sailed through Flying Foam Passage, Richmond Thatcher remarked on the strangely 'beautiful echo', 'the plainest he ever heard', his words coming back to him 'with a rapidity and force quite startling', broken only by the shouts of pearlers 'anchored in the passage' and 'natives camped ashore'. By the late nineteenth century the echo of the pearlers and the 'natives' had fallen silent. The Yaburara were 'no more'. All that remained were the mysterious 'tattooed' figures that John Withnell had observed on the rocks of 'every hill'. In the memory of white Australia, Murujuga became a place like so many others, one briefly lit by a frenzy of commercial activity before being discarded—a place of no utility.[51]

Conveyors at Parker Point near Dampier shifting iron ore from stockpile to ship, 2015

In 1968, Charles Court, Minister for Industrial Development and the North West, and later Premier of Western Australia (1974–82), addressed a symposium in Perth on the prospects for the Pilbara in the 1970s. Court's portfolio said it all: he was charged with responsibility for overseeing what would become the most rapid and extensive industrial development in Australian history. Since the establishment of iron ore mining at Mount Tom Price and the first shipments of ore from Dampier in 1966, the Pilbara had changed, said Court, 'from a mendicant area to a great producer of national wealth'. It was time to think 'big enough and bold enough', he declared, time to show those in the 'eastern states' and the 'timid types' who doubted the gospel of development that the north–west was not 'just a piece of nothing'. The 'starry-eyed dream' of blooming deserts was close at hand. With injections of overseas capital, the government would harness the rivers to provide water for new cities and towns and vast agricultural projects. The development 'multiplier' would begin to take effect and very soon, Court told the Institute of Engineers, '2 + 2' would equal '9'.[52]

It was an old dream. Western Australian politicians and 'development leagues' had long been concerned that 'Asiatics' would swamp the north–west. Rapid development was the only solution. For all those intent on 'keeping Australia white', decentralising 'the white population' was seen as paramount in a state where over 95 per cent of Western Australians lived in Perth, a city which had a population of only 900 000 in the early 1970s.[53] As far back as 1888, geologists had known that the 'iron country' of the Pilbara had sufficient reserves 'to supply the whole world' but the cost of extracting it was too high.[54] Even when new markets emerged and the technology existed to overcome these difficulties, the Commonwealth government, fearful of inadvertently providing the raw materials for Japanese expansion (and much to the dissatisfaction of the Western Australian government), placed an embargo on the export of iron ore in 1938.[55] Not until the embargo was lifted in 1960 did Court's vision of transforming the 'vulnerable' and 'virtually unpopulated' north into the engine room of the state's economy become a reality.[56]

The Pilbara, which owed its name to a creek in the north-west goldfields, underwent the most dramatic transformation seen in any part of Australia since the Victorian gold rushes in the 1850s. From 1960, in a succession of booms over more than four decades, the fever for Mammon that had driven the pearlers and goldminers in the late nineteenth century would strike with even greater intensity. By 1971, when vast reserves of natural gas were discovered on the North West Shelf, 100 kilometres north-west of Dampier, government ministers spoke of their obligation to 'seize the initiative' and 'collectively live up to the great promise' handed to them 'by nature'. Relying on age-old tropes of emptiness and God-given lands, they saw no reason to negotiate with Aboriginal people. Having unleashed the potential for profit on previously unimagined levels, the forgotten, 'almost empty' region of the Pilbara was once again open for business.[57]

In the space of only five years, new towns were established—Dampier and Tom Price (1965), Karratha (1968), Newman (1969) and Wickham (1970)—and massive infrastructure projects completed: power, water, housing, airports, roads and railways. By any measure, the sheer speed and scale of the development was staggering. Murujuga, previously separated by tidal mud flats, was connected to the mainland by road and rail causeways. And in 1979, Woodside Petroleum, the company planning the development of the North West Shelf Gas, bestowed its own name on the area—'the Burrup', after Mount Burrup, the highest peak on the island, originally named after Henry Burrup, a bank clerk who was murdered during a robbery in Roebourne in 1885.[58] The irony of linking a place where more than fifty Aboriginal people had been murdered with the name of one murdered white man seemed to escape almost everyone. The tsunami of industrial development had little time for such historical curiosities.

Only four decades after the first iron ore shipments from Dampier, Murujuga was home to a raft of industrial sites: Woodside Petroleum's LNG processing plant at Withnell Bay, Woodside's port at King Bay, Yara Pilbara's ammonia plant (the world's largest), two of Rio Tinto's three iron ore port facilities at Parker Point and East Intercourse Island near Dampier, and Dampier Salt's crystalliser ponds and port facilities at Murujuga and Mistaken Island, all of which continued to hunger for expansion. In the process, an even greater irony emerged: as industry stamped its mark indelibly on the landscape of Murujuga, it inadvertently led to greater knowledge of the Pilbara's flora and fauna and recognition of 'one of the most important sites of Aboriginal art in Australia'.[59] What the Yaburara had known for millennia was finally 'discovered' by Europeans more than a century after the first settlers arrived on their land.

One of the first moments of discovery occurred in 1962, when proposals emerged to place an iron ore shipping port on Depuch Island. Zoologist David Ride led a team from the Western Australian Museum in a preliminary survey of the island's rock art and flora and fauna. Astonished at what he saw, and unfamiliar with Murujuga, Ride mistakenly thought that the island was home to 'probably a greater concentration of Aboriginal engravings than any other place in Australia'. He immediately saw the rich heritage value of the art, despite the fact, as he admitted, that they knew virtually nothing about its cultural meaning and production. But it was Ride's ability to convey the awe he felt before the island's rock art that shattered conventional perceptions:

> I, for one, will never forget the wonder of going up Watering Valley for the first time, pausing to rest on a stone slab by a small pool and then, suddenly, coming to realise that the rocks on all sides of me and above me were covered with carvings—birds, fish, turtles, boomerangs, little stick-men, and dancing men … and there, above all, high in the wall of the gorge were the two carved men described by Wickham [during the visit of the *Beagle*] more than one hundred years before.[60]

When the crew of the *Beagle* landed on the same island in 1840 they carved their ship's name on a rock, leaving their own mark on the 'lonely picture gallery' that looked down on them from the walls above.[61] Ride, the first of many professionals who would come to the north-west on the coat-tails of industry in the years that followed, had seen what others before him had failed to see. A century after they were first seen by Europeans, he provided one of the first positive descriptions of the Aboriginal engravings, acutely aware as he was that they represented a depth of cultural expression far beyond the brief presence of European Australia. His findings appeared to have an immediate effect on the Western Australian government. Depuch Island was abandoned as a site for industrial development and the government turned instead to the Dampier area, where even less was known about the rock engravings. Edgar Lewis, the minister who wrote the introduction to Ride's 1964 report, stressed the need for governments and industry to 'behave responsibly' and avoid the 'needless destruction … of our unique native rock art and Aboriginal culture'.[62] But his admirable ideals, rare for a government MP in the 1960s, would not be heeded. Large-scale industrial development was unleashed on Murujuga, the place that would later be described by Ken Mulvaney as one of 'outstanding and unique ecological and cultural value; with combinations of arid and tropical flora and fauna, and a sequence of rock art production possibly spanning tens of millennia'. The Western Australian government could not have chosen a more inappropriate site to exploit the 'natural wealth' of the north-west.[63]

149

Rio Tinto iron ore train, outside Karratha, 2015

Throughout the 1960s and 1970s, archaeologists such as Sylvia Hallam began the task of surveying, mapping and photographing what they would eventually realise was only a small percentage of Murujuga's petroglyphs. The effect the petroglyphs had on many who saw them was life changing. Engineers Robert Bedarnik and Enzo Virili, ostensibly employed to establish mines, roads and townships, devoted much of their spare time to examining the engravings. The ancient, mysterious presence of the images, imprinted on a jumbled, burning red canvas that at first glance was almost alien to European eyes, appeared to eclipse the transitory nature of the industries they had come to establish. Bedarnik eventually gave up his job and devoted the rest of his life to the study of Australian and global rock art, campaigning to save Murujuga's art from the effects of industrial development. Few who took the time to climb the rocky slopes and observe the images closely came away unmoved. To stand surrounded by art that stretched far into antiquity, inscribed with a cultural significance that would forever remain obscure, was to be reminded of how little Europeans understood of Australia's deep past. Impressed by the enthusiasm of engineers such as Virili and Bedarnik, local newspapers in the early 1970s reported on 'one of the little-known benefits' of the 'mineral boom', 'the discovery of Aboriginal rock paintings and engravings'.[64] Discovery, however, would not necessarily lead to protection. Although industrial development resulted in the first surveys of Murujuga's Indigenous heritage, neither these nor the state's 1972 *Aboriginal Heritage Act* could stop the destruction and removal of almost 5000 images, which began in 1980 when staff from the Western Australian Museum moved rock art from the building site of Woodside's gas plant to a compound at Hearson's Cove. The rocks would remain there for more than three decades, caged ruins of a cultural heritage Australians had yet to fully respect.[65]

For Aboriginal people, the mining boom offered little succour. After award wages for Aboriginal pastoral workers were introduced in the 1960s, many had little choice but to leave the large stations for Roebourne Reserve, where more than three hundred people

Petroglyphs, Murujuga, 2015

resided in Third World conditions, prey to high rates of disease and infant mortality. Segregated from the rest of the community, they struggled to adapt to life on the reserve, where many of them were entirely severed from their homelands. With the sudden influx of miners into Roebourne in the early 1960s, they faced yet another onslaught. Thirty years later, long-time resident of Roebourne and Banjiyma elder Alice Smith described how Aboriginal communities 'just fell apart':

> The 1960s mining boom was a lot like the pearling boom a century earlier, because both booms brought an influx of single white men and grog, violated our women and filled the jail with our people. The difference was that while pearling made us slaves, mining left us out of the work force … police, pub and welfare, that's all we got left …[66]

In 1975, the reserve was closed. More than two hundred and fifty people from over fifty families were moved without consultation into 'the village', a new collection of government-funded houses near the old Roebourne Cemetery. 'Homemakers, all ladies' came from the 'family service' to assist with the finer points of domesticity. After finally becoming accustomed to life on the reserve, the suburban model of housing broke down surviving social structures. Many teenagers turned to crime and alcohol and drug abuse. Incarceration rates increased dramatically. In September 1983, a fight broke out between police and Aboriginal people outside the Victoria Hotel in Roebourne. One of the many arrested, 17-year-old John Pat, died in his cell after allegedly being punched by a policeman, his head hitting the ground during the melee in front of the hotel. A Karratha jury later acquitted the police charged with Pat's murder. The Aboriginal community in Roebourne erupted in anger. On television news, the town's main street, with its sadly familiar scenes of Aboriginal dysfunction and public drunkenness, became the symbol of a similar malaise in communities across the nation. As rapid industrial development continued only 50 kilometres away, the events at Roebourne became the catalyst for the establishment of the Royal Commission into Aboriginal Deaths in Custody (1987–91). Few Australians were aware of the brutal frontier history that had brought Roebourne to such a parlous state. While the epicentre of the nation's 'economic powerhouse' at Murujuga powered ahead, Aboriginal communities imploded. The new towns built during the boom had sucked resources from Roebourne, once the region's largest town. The Roebourne gaol and an ever-increasing police presence appeared to be the only growth sectors in the town's economy. Subjected to wave after wave of displacement and oppression for more than a century, many Aboriginal families had been brought to the point of total collapse, the face of their Country changed forever.[67]

In 1984, the construction of the Harding River Dam flooded 'Yawajuna' (Lockyer's Gorge), 'a beautiful valley of pools and paperbarks', and dried up the Ngurin River downstream near Roebourne, a favourite camping place of the Aboriginal community. As elder woman Lilla Snowball exclaimed in the 1993 documentary film *Exile and the Kingdom*, the dam had 'insulted' her Country: 'Everything's busted up'. Mining renamed and reshaped Aboriginal Country.[68] Wakathuni Hill, virtually cut in half by mining, became Tom Price. Across the Pilbara, places that had carried Aboriginal names for thousands of years—beaches, hills, headlands, valleys, gorges, rivers and plains—became nameless features on maps. Europeans named the places that mattered to them economically, but had no interest in naming every feature of such a vast landscape. Many beaches and headlands on Murujuga and surrounding islands remain unnamed today, 'No Name Point' being one of the exceptions. Inland, at Tom Price, the area's largest hill, Jarndunmunha, became 'Mount Nameless'. In 1979, mining executive Roderick Carnegie brought Australian artist Fred Williams to the Pilbara. Williams, seduced by the country's 'red-violet' hues, produced one of his greatest series of landscape paintings. 'Anyone who could *not* paint this particular country', he mused, 'is probably in the wrong profession'. *Mount Nameless, Afternoon* was one of his most memorable paintings in the 'Pilbara' series.

Williams had managed to capture the landscape's heady sweep of colour and also point to its deeper Indigenous significance, one that would take decades to resurface.[69] The new mining community at

Tom Price embraced their 'nameless' hill, founding the 'Nameless Festival' in 1971, a week-long carnival that included a 'beer festival', '2-day shoots', art exhibitions, firework displays and the crowning of the 'Nameless Queen'. By the 1980s and 1990s, 'wood chopping', camel races, the 'Wild West Ball', and rolling pin and iron ore throwing competitions had been added to the program. Exasperated, Yinhawangka elder Lola Young offered her view of the mountain's renaming: 'non-Aboriginal people named the biggest hill around here at Tom Price, Mount Nameless. They didn't ask the Aboriginal people here if that place had a name already. And it had. Its name for thousands of years has been Jarndunmunha: there's nothing nameless about that'.[70] Not until 2011, on the occasion of the festival's fortieth

Fred Williams, *Mount Nameless (afternoon)* 1981
Oil on canvas, 122.3 x 152.8 cm
National Gallery of Victoria, Melbourne
Presented through the NGV Foundation by Rio Tinto, Honorary Life Benefactor, 2001 (2001.596) © Estate of Fred Williams

anniversary, did the hill's traditional name return when the festival was officially renamed the 'Nameless Jarndunmunha Festival'.[71] The shared name was one sign of the dramatic change in race relations that had taken place since the High Court's Mabo (1992) and Wik (1996) decisions and the decade-long movement for reconciliation that began in 1991. The recognition of native title empowered Aboriginal communities legally and politically. Mining companies were now obliged to negotiate with the country's traditional owners. In the early 1990s, Aboriginal elders could rightly point out that for all the profits mining companies reaped from their lands, 'blackfellas got nothing'.[72] Now they would be able to strike million-dollar compensation deals and become mining entrepreneurs. Companies such as Rio Tinto and Woodside funded research into Indigenous heritage and soon agreed to cultural heritage and conservation protocols. These new relationships were potentially liberating and empowering but they also led to internal divisions and power struggles within and between Aboriginal communities. Who would benefit from these new legal and political instruments? Which groups had the right to claim traditional ownership and negotiate deals with mining companies? Who had the right to speak for whom?[73]

After more than two hundred pieces of rock art were removed under Aboriginal supervision in 2007, during the construction of Woodside's five-billion-dollar Pluto Gas Plant, Indigenous elder Wilfred Hicks criticised Aboriginal groups in the Pilbara for failing to stand up for Murujuga. Hicks, who described Murujuga's rock art as an 'Aboriginal Bible', pointed to the fact that some Aboriginal people had received up to five hundred dollars a day from Woodside as heritage consultants to oversee the rock art's removal. 'Once the rock has been moved the spirit of that rock has been broken', he lamented. 'It makes me feel sick.' Because only a handful of Aboriginal people with Yaburara ancestry remained, Murujuga and its extraordinary rock art were even more susceptible to competing claims of ownership and those in government and industry eager to pursue development at all cost. Native title would prove to be of little use.[74]

In 2004, the Federal Court ruled that native title rights over the Dampier Archipelago had been extinguished. It was virtually impossible for any Aboriginal group to successfully mount a legal claim of continued association with Murujuga and the islands nearby. In any event, only one year before the Federal Court decision, the Yaburara's traditional neighbours, the Ngarluma Yindjibarndi, struck an agreement with the Western Australian government in which they relinquished any native title claim they might have held over the Dampier Archipelago. They allowed industrial development to go ahead in exchange for control of the remaining land, funding for a visitors' centre, '5.8 million dollars in up-front payments' and state funding for housing and transport infrastructure in Roebourne. This remarkable deal, which effectively saw Aboriginal people forgo their native title rights, has divided local Aboriginal people ever since, with one Ngarluma custodian, Robyne Churnside, arguing that many of her 'old People' who signed the agreement 'were illiterate and did not understand the terms of the deal'. Yet regardless of the consequences for native title, the 2003 agreement led to the creation of Murujuga National Park (2013) and its administrative body, the Murujuga Aboriginal Corporation, which today manages 42 per cent of the peninsula and comprises Murujuga's custodians, now known collectively as 'Ngarda-ngarli'. Throughout this process, industry's ever-increasing presence was always underwritten by strong government support.[75]

In 2007, when the Commonwealth and Western Australian governments struck a deal with Woodside and Murujuga's custodians, they secured National Heritage listing for 368.3 square kilometres of the peninsula at the same time as they allowed Woodside's new gas processing plants to proceed and earmarked 48 square kilometres for further industrial development.[76] Those politicians who had warned that national heritage listing would be a 'catastrophe' that would jeopardise 'the very core of the Australian economy' were proven wrong.[77] Politically, the deal appeared the only way to proceed. Acknowledge all 'stakeholders' by recognising the heritage value of Murujuga's rock art and reassure industry that this recognition would not compromise its plans for further expansion. The truth, however, was that governments of all persuasions had consistently failed to place the protection of 'the densest accumulation of engraved rock art in the world' above the demands of industry.[78] Despite National Heritage listing, insufficient funds for adequate management and protection continue to leave Murujuga's rock art vulnerable to vandalism, possible damage from industrial pollution and perhaps the greatest threat of all—indifference and ignorance.

Over the last decade, more than twenty sites have been defaced with chisels and power drills or covered in graffiti, often with spray-paint. The vandals carve names or images into the rock or disfigure the original images in any way they can. Aboriginal rangers have been forced to devote considerable time to fighting the vandalism and restoring the damaged art (often in vain).[79] The desecration of ancient sites has also occurred at King Bay, where a memorial has been erected to the victims of the Flying Foam Massacre. Across the bay from the memorial site, Woodside's Supply Base glistens in the distance. The inscription on the plaque reads: 'Hereabouts in February 1868, a party of settlers from Roebourne shot and killed as many as 60 [Yaburara] people in response to the killing of a European policeman in Nickol Bay. This incident has become known as the "Flying Foam Massacre"'. Directly above the memorial site, a striking collection of standing stones appears to commemorate the event.

Standing stones,
Flying Foam Massacre
memorial site,
King Bay, 2015

At various intervals over the last ten to fifteen years, many of these standing stones (which resemble other ancient geological features constructed by humans throughout the archipelago) have been pushed over, smashed or otherwise damaged. Robert Bedarnik, who first visited the site in 1968, claimed in 2004 that of the original 138 standing stones only forty remained undamaged. Since that time more have been pushed over, some with their tops lopped off.[80] It is as if the vandals, knowing that Aboriginal people believe that the survivors of the massacre erected the stones in memory of those killed, are even more determined to knock them down. Whether the stones were placed in position thousands of years ago or more recently, they stand over the place where Aboriginal people were murdered. The knowledge of what happened there transforms the meaning of the site. The stones appear to carry the aura of a memorial. In the words of elder Wilfred Hicks, 'it is important that people remember this massacre, and learn the history of this Country. It is also important that we protect the sacred rock art here, which connects us to our ancestors'.[81]

In 2013, local Aboriginal groups and others from across Australia came together to inaugurate the first National Day of Commemoration of the Flying Foam Massacre. Aboriginal leaders from the Pilbara stood on the steps of Parliament House in Perth to draw public attention to the day. The fate of the memorial site at King Bay and the story of the Flying Foam Massacre are now undeniably connected to the protection of the Yaburara's extraordinary cultural legacy. So too is industry's presence on Murujuga. The home of Australia's largest industrial development, the North West Shelf Gas Project, stands on the very ground where one of Australia's worst frontier massacres took place. On the shores of Murujuga, the protection of ancient cultural heritage, the memory of the violent history of colonialism and the mighty hands of industry are messily entwined. They are all part of Murujuga's future.[82]

———

In November 2015, I saw rock art almost every day that I spent on Murujuga. It was impossible to avoid. Walking into one of the most accessible sites, Deep Gorge, the cathedral-like atmosphere grew heavier as the walls of the gorge closed in above me. It was difficult to find a rock that was not engraved. Images rained down from every direction: stick figures, female figures, masked faces, dugongs, kangaroos, mysterious circles, fish, turtles, emus, lizards, birds, spirit beings and many images that could not be easily deciphered. The further I walked, the more the larger engravings on the vertical rocks on either side of the gorge seemed to cohere, accentuating the gallery effect. Some were faint and weathered, while others virtually leapt out, intensely lit by the early morning sun, the temperature already 35 degrees at 9 a.m. It seemed impossible to grasp the deeper meaning of the ancient cultural heritage that surrounded me.

A few days later, on my last morning in Dampier, I took a boat to Angel Island, close to one of the places where many Yaburara were killed in 1868. Approaching the island from the sea, it was already possible to make out a collection of striking, tablet-like stones standing atop one of the rock piles near the shore. Walking past more remarkable standing stones on the beach, through the spinifex and low-lying

Tablet stones, Angel Island, Flying Foam Passage, 2015

scrub and climbing up the hill, I was standing before the tablets in less than half an hour. Packed tightly together, they stood almost perfectly upright surrounded by even more engravings on rocks nearby. The largest and most striking image was just over 1 metre in length and probably engraved long before the sea levels rose at the end of the last Ice Age six to seven thousand years ago. Older than Stonehenge or the Pyramids, it stood facing the sea, a majestic reminder of Australia's ancient heritage before which all we have done in this country can easily appear ephemeral by comparison.

As I returned to the boat and looked back at the stone tablets from the sea, I found it difficult to believe that the Western Australian and Commonwealth governments had failed to nominate Murujuga and the Dampier Archipelago for World Heritage listing. Putting aside the presence of so much heavy industry and the threat that it undoubtedly poses to Indigenous heritage, this is a place of international significance, a place that tells the story of our shared human heritage. If international tourists flock to see Ubirr and Uluru, given the provision of proper funding and infrastructure, why would they not come to Angel Island and Murujuga to view such extraordinary art? There is no other place like this in the world. The range and historical depth of the art on display—more than one million images—is astounding. Thylacines became extinct in north-west Australia between three and a half thousand and four thousand years ago. Throughout Murujuga, Ken Mulvaney has found many thylacine engravings, further evidence of the area's outstanding heritage status despite the fact that so much of the peninsula's art still remains unmapped. The history of Aboriginal occupation is well 'beyond 20 000 years' and Mulvaney believes the art will eventually 'challenge the Kimberley's status in antiquity and artistic endeavour'.[83] The facts speak for themselves.

Murujuga National Park comprises only 42 per cent of the peninsula. Angel Island and the entire Dampier Archipelago are excluded. Despite the fact that anywhere between five thousand and ten thousand examples of the peninsula's rock art have already been lost due to industrial development since 1965, countless images continue to remain unprotected in the land earmarked for future industrial development. For decades, politicians have pleaded that they were

Thylacine petroglyph, Angel Island, Flying Foam Passage, 2015

161

'unaware' of Murujuga's significance. Even when they belatedly acknowledged that the peninsula was 'the greatest cultural heritage site in Australia' and perhaps 'the world', as the current Premier of the state Colin Barnett claimed in 2006, they have continually failed to honour their words when granted the opportunity to govern. Their ears are tuned to the siren song of development, one that has already littered Australia with the wastelands and deserted towns left by past mining.[84]

The struggle to value Murujuga's Indigenous heritage is the struggle to truly 'see' Indigenous cultural heritage as worthy of the same protection as non-Indigenous heritage. The thylacine engraving on Angel Island, which has stood for many thousands of years, is entirely unprotected. Yet the remains of European settlement such as Cossack, barely one century old, have been carefully preserved. Others, like Roebourne gaol, a place of immeasurable suffering for so many Aboriginal people in the Pilbara, has been saved as a heritage tourist destination. Our failure to 'see' is rooted in the long history of prejudice that we have yet to fully overcome. The legacy of the frontier endures in Australia's national imagination, with its lingering visions of a vast, 'empty' country that must be made useful at all cost.

Out on the waters of the Dampier Archipelago, the view back to the coast is unforgettable. Mountains of salt and iron ore stand piled on the shoreline. Ships queue to load their cargo. Gas flames burn on the horizon. The clattering din of industry drifts across the waves. The town of Dampier appears encased in the development that gave birth to it. Yet long after the reserves of gas and iron ore have been exhausted and the industrial plants and ports have turned to dust, the rock art will hopefully remain, its abiding presence transcending all that we have rushed to establish on Murujuga in so little time.

CHAPTER FOUR

On Grassy Hill: Gangaar (Cooktown), North Queensland

THE HILL RISES abruptly from the water's edge. From its wind-swept crest the eye scans 360 degrees: north towards Hope Vale Aboriginal land and along the wilderness coast of the Cape York Peninsula; south over Cooktown, its handful of grid-pattern streets and 'historic' buildings dwarfed by Mount Cook; east to the Great Barrier Reef and the Coral Sea; and west across the snake-trail of the Endeavour River and the Great Dividing Range beyond. Here, on

163

The Endeavour River, Cooktown, from Grassy Hill, 2016

Grassy Hill, where the south-easterlies blow so hard they would take you away, the vastness and majesty of the continent seems tangible. The tip of Cape York Peninsula is still 800 kilometres to the north, the sprawling cities of Australia's south-east two to three thousand kilometres away. Whichever way I turned, the undeniable presence of the country—ancient, abiding and storied—towered over the meekness of the tiny settlement below. I had come, like so many others, with the knowledge of what happened here in 1770, drawn by the sheer weight of the story. It was impossible to stand on Grassy Hill and not imagine James Cook's ailing ship out on the water, desperately seeking 'refuge' in the harbour below.

Long before the Guugu Yimithirr saw the *Endeavour* on the horizon in June 1770 they had heard news of its progress along the coast. Far to the south, on the beaches of K'gari (Fraser Island), the Badjala and Dulingbara had followed the path of 'a mysterious white-winged object passing along the surface of the ocean like a gigantic pelican'. Some on the island saw it 'coming up and going back with the wind at its rear, like a sand crab'.[1] While the Guugu Yimithirr were prepared for the vessel's appearance—reports of the sighting of a 'strange large canoe' had travelled north from Cape Tribulation—they were certainly not prepared for its entrance into their waters nor did they expect the visitors to stay. They were accustomed to seeing the smaller, transitory craft of the Torres Strait Islanders and the Makassans 'looking for fish, dugong, beche de mer, trochus or shells'. What they saw on this day was otherworldly. Early on the morning of 17 June they watched as James Cook's *Endeavour* entered the river mouth, its white sails billowing like clouds floating on the water's surface. Led by two small boats that Cook had sent ahead to warn him of the danger-ous shoals that 'lay in [his] way', he anchored the leaking ship about a mile offshore before finally beaching it on the southern riverbank. For the next three weeks, as Cook's men patched up the *Endeavour* and until tentative contact was finally made, the Guugu Yimithirr closely observed the visitors' every move. In years to come, they would refer to Cook and his crew as 'Wangaar': ancestors who had finally returned from the east, ghostly white. It was a deeply spiritual explanation that would prove ominously prophetic.[2]

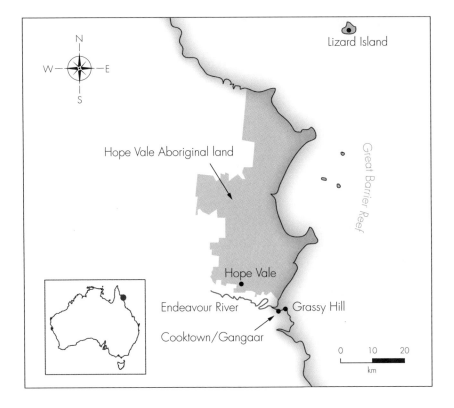

Little more than one hundred years later, the foot of Grassy Hill would be inundated with thousands of white men 'hurrying to and fro, [their] tents rising in all directions'. A police station, courthouse and customs office would quickly follow.[3] Close to where the *Endeavour* was repaired in 1770, at the 'foot' of Grassy Hill's 'western slope', 'sailors and labourers' landed 'horses and cargo' in their rush to reach the Palmer River goldfields.[4] From the summit, the arrival of a procession of steamers was signalled daily from the flagstaff. Whitewashed timber buildings clawed their way up the slopes. 'Old whalers' set up their boiling-down works below, extracting oil from the livers of sharks and dugongs.[5] In the 1870s, a complex culture that had evolved over 30 000 years and managed a rich and delicately balanced environment was ripped apart by hordes of miners and pastoralists in pursuit of Mammon. For the Guugu Yimithirr who survived, and for many Aboriginal people across Australia, 'Captain Cook' became the first of the British invaders and all of them—a series of cataclysmic happenings both past and present—more a body of story than a man.

James Cook climbed Grassy Hill alone on 30 June 1770. Sending some of his younger men to 'take a plan of the harbour', he walked at low tide 'upon the hill over the south point to take a view of the sea'. Looking through his telescope, he scoured the harbour, trying to gauge the extent of the shoals that blocked his safe passage out to sea. He was uneasy with what he saw. There 'were a number of sand banks or shoals laying all along the coast'.[6] The thought surely crossed his mind that he would never see England again. In the future, many would climb Grassy Hill in his memory, combing over every word of the 'immortal' navigator's journal, highlighting the 'perilous' situation of his ship after it struck the reef, praising his resourcefulness and ingenuity and that of his men, and seeking to erect 'a shrine to the man' who 'found Australia for England'.[7] They remembered fondly that it was at Gangaar that Cook's crew first saw the kangaroo (an approximation of 'gangurru' in the Guugu Yimithirr language) and where the *Endeavour*'s artist, Sydney Parkinson, created the first written record of an Aboriginal language (about 150 Guugu Yimithirr words), and they dutifully printed his name on their maps. Gangarr became Cooktown. Waalumbaal Birri became the Endeavour River. Gaya became Mount Cook. Milngaar became Mount Saunders.[8] Overwriting Indigenous Country with the names that Cook had sprinkled along the coastline of the peninsula, they managed, as one newspaper columnist quipped in 1954, to 'convey nothing appropriate', because names such as Cape York and Prince of Wales Isles were taken from the titles of 'the disreputable' family of King George III, 'giving a raffish Regency air to the place'.[9]

In June 1819, when Phillip Parker King landed the *Mermaid* in 'the very same spot that Cook landed his stores upon forty-nine years' earlier, he was mindful that he was the first British navigator since 1770 to visit the site of the 'enterprising commander's' ordeal. In early July, he found pieces of coal near his tent. Consulting Joseph Banks's journal he realised that Cook's crew had taken the ship's 'coals' ashore. King was jubilant. He had found a 'relic' from the *Endeavour*. He was the first in a long line of souvenir hunters who would give anything to hold even the tiniest vestige of Cook's presence in their hands.[10] In 1886, the 'Working Men's Association' of Cooktown offered a 300-pound reward for the cannons that Cook had thrown overboard to lighten the *Endeavour's* load.[11] The 'historic' tree to which Cook had allegedly moored the *Endeavour* was destroyed by fire in 1917. Undeterred, locals preserved the 'old relic' by propping up the 'piece of blackened and ancient log'.[12] By the 1930s, the town itself was imagined as 'sacred' to Cook's memory, 'a place of pilgrimage' for all those who valued the 'history of the new nation'.[13] There were claims (apparently supported 'by Aborigines') that a 'cairn of stones' erected by Cook stood at the summit of Mount Saunders, his name—'carved with a chisel'—still visible on one of the stones. The search for the ship's 'ancient British naval guns' and anchors continued.[14] In 1969, an American scientific expedition found the *Endeavour's* cannons, telling *The New York Times* that Cook was the 'Christopher Columbus of Australia'.[15]

Two years later, divers found the Holy Grail—the only anchor that Cook failed to retrieve from the seabed before his departure in August 1770, which now rests in the James Cook Museum in Cooktown. Carried away by the discovery of the relics and the increasing enthusiasm for local history, Sir Raphael Cilento, former president of Queensland's National Trust and one of the founders of the museum, described Cook's storage tents, blacksmith's forge, pigpens and sheep drying nets spread at the foot of Grassy Hill as a 'transient British settlement' which had 'the appearance of a tiny sea-side village'.[16] If the Guugu Yimithirr saw Cook as the embodiment of all that happened to them in the process of British colonisation, their usurpers came to worship him as the saintly father of white Australia, the first white man to plant the seed of 'civilisation' in far north Queensland. By the late twentieth century, Cook's name was everywhere: inscribed on the highway north from Cairns, memorialised in Cooktown's parks and museums, emblazoned on motels and tourist memorabilia, and eulogised on the lookout at Grassy Hill. The place that had been his for only seven weeks became his eternally in his absence. Far more than Botany Bay, Cooktown remains very much Cook's town. The great man has never left.

Courthouse and other
buildings at the foot
of Grassy Hill, circa
1890

168

The story of Cook's narrow escape from shipwreck on the Great
Barrier Reef and the seven weeks he spent at the mouth of the
Endeavour River in 1770 gradually came to obscure much of the
history of Cooktown and the far north. For most of the twentieth
century, it not only helped to conceal the land's true discoverers and
custodians—the Guugu Yimithirr—it hammered home their dispossession with every telling. Cooktown's 'historic' status in Australian
history, reaffirmed annually from 1959 through the re-enactment of
Cook's landing, initially offered only one role for Aboriginal people:
polite withdrawal. As Guugu Yimithirr elder Eric Deeral often pointed
out, the Discovery Festival that accompanied the re-enactment from
the 1970s only tended to reinforce the myth that Cook discovered
Australia. And it cast a pall over what another Guugu Yimithirr
elder, Noel Pearson, has described as 'one of the bloodiest episodes
in the colonial occupation of this continent'.[17] The history of this
brutal frontier—its remembering and forgetting and the society that
emerged in its wake—lies at the heart of a remarkable transformation.
Nearly two hundred and fifty years after the *Endeavour* was repaired
on Gangaar's shores, the story of 'Captain Cook'—long seen by many

Guugu Yimithirr as synonymous with their dispossession—became an instrument of reconciliation and the basis for a new understanding of Cooktown's and Australia's founding moment.

———————

In the 1870s, at a time when many parts of south-east Australia had already been settled for well over fifty years, far north Queensland was still imagined as a 'silent wilderness'.[18] The settlement of Gangaar that followed the discovery of gold was nothing less than an overnight invasion. There was little time for the Guugu Yimithirr to adapt and little possibility of negotiation. The newcomers—'men of all nationalities': British (including a large Irish contingent), French, German and Chinese (who came from other colonies and southern China)—had only one object in mind: to 'ventilate the rich … resources of the district'.[19] After James Mulligan returned with almost 3 kilograms of gold from panning along the Palmer River in September 1873, waves of miners followed in his wake. Other fields nearby were quickly exploited. Within months, thousands of ramshackle dwellings were 'struck up' close to where the town stands today—'miserable huts, zinc sheds, any blessed thing that would shelter from the sun's fierce heat was used as habitation'. The British talked of Cooktown as the 'next capital of northern Australia'. For the Chinese, whose commercial acumen and market gardens quickly made them essential to the viability of the town, it was the 'new Canton of the south'.[20]

In 1874, three to four thousand people were camped at the foot of Grassy Hill alone. Estimates of the influx in the first few years varied enormously; some said 15 000, with 12 000 of those being Chinese; others thought as many as 30 000, with 18 000 Chinese. The constant stream of new arrivals outstripped the harbour's capacity. In the rush to land animals and cargo, horses were slung up suspended by the stomach; after being launched over the ship's side they were 'plunged into the water' just inside the mouth of the Endeavour River. Many drowned as they swam or were towed ashore. No sooner had men arrived and made their first forays inland to the Palmer goldfields than many returned complaining that Cooktown's reputation was unfounded. Rumours of 'thousands of ounces' turned out to be 'hundreds'. Conditions were harsh. On the long trek to the fields, food and water were often scarce. The sharp-edged grass stripped 'the skin and flesh' from horses' legs. Rain was either non-existent or came down in 'incessant' tropical downpours. Tracks were barely passable. By May 1874, 'the first comers' had already taken up the best mining sites. Ships full of 'disappointed men' began to return south.[21] But those with more patience and resilience persisted. Still more came than left. Ashore, the whole scene was 'noisily busy with workmen'. Pubs sprang up faster than general stores—the 'Captain Cook', 'the Sovereign', 'the Red Lion', 'the Royal' and 'The Digger's Arms'; more than fifty were erected within the first two years, along with a thriving Chinatown, joss house and market gardens. Nearly everyone's aim was to get rich and leave. The highly mobile population was constantly replenished by new arrivals. Even today, much of north Queensland retains a large itinerant population. Yet for all the 'hazy and mysterious' dreams of a northern capital, few were committed to building a new society.[22]

To read the Cooktown and Brisbane newspaper reports of frontier violence on north Queensland's goldfields in the 1870s and 1880s is to confront one of the most brazen examples of a 'relentless war of extermination' in Australia's colonial history.[23] The violence is forever etched in the language used to describe what occurred. As miners headed out into the fields determined to extract their share of riches, competing with one another as much as with the untamed environment, the attitude of many was to shoot the Guugu Yimithirr on sight. As the *Cooktown Herald* trumpeted as early as 1874: 'when savages are pitted against civilisation they must go the wall. It is the fate of their race'.[24] Observers remarked on the miners' 'warlike appearance' as they walked to the goldfields in gangs: 'arms and ammunition form as much a part of the digger's outfit as his pick and shovel or his blanket'.[25] 'Protected' by the ruthless Native Police Force that had arrived with them on the first ships, many miners saw the experience as an opportunity to hone their military skills: 'rifle and revolver practice during camping time has become quite an institution'.[26] While they noticed the natives' 'wonderfully constructed dams in the river for catching fish', they also occupied their campsites, eating the food that had been left behind as Aboriginal people retreated to higher ground.[27] Wary of attack, the miners regularly burnt the grass around their camps for protection, which they guarded day and night. The names they gave to the places where the terrain left them vulnerable to ambush ('Hell's Gate') or alternatively marked their glorious victories ('Battle Camp') indicated the ferocity of the 'race war' that would last for nearly two decades.[28]

From the very first incursion inland, there is overwhelming evidence that the war was the result of unprovoked violence on the part of trigger-happy miners eager to assert their authority. Initially ignorant of the lethal power of firearms, there were reports of Aboriginal men 'grasping the very muzzles of the rifles' as they attempted to 'wrest them from the hands of the whites, standing to be shot down rather than yield an inch'.[29] When the Guugu Yimithirr and their southern neighbours, the Guugu Yalandji, adjusted their strategies and responded by spearing cattle and horses or attacking groups of miners on their trek to the fields, reprisal killings were swift and merciless in their execution. Newspaper accounts of such expeditions from Cooktown require little elaboration: 'they murdered two out of one party and had to pay dearly for it'; 'whenever the black troopers came across … [Aborigines] they made short work of them'. When the 'diggers' surrounded groups of 'natives', wrote one letter-writer, 'then commences the work of slaughter; they are fired upon, and those who are only wounded, are knocked on the head by either tomahawk or Snider [rifle] after which bloody scene the bodies are burned'.[30]

Specific reports detailed mass killings within one year of the miners' arrival. In October 1874, after 'the blacks' had speared large numbers of horses near 'Pine Creek', 'diggers' were 'apprehensive' of further 'raids' and decided to act:

22 diggers, well armed, mustered one evening and proceeded up the creek in quest of the blackfellows' camp. After travelling nearly all night, their fires were at last sighted, and the avengers, dividing into two parties, and posting themselves conveniently for the work of dispersion, waited patiently for the dawn. When at last day broke, something like 200 blacks were seen squatting

171

about the fire. The white men soon made their presence known, and in a moment the yelling of the blacks, thus taken by surprise, was horrible. ***** They did not show fight but ran right in the direction where the second party, who had not yet shown themselves, were posted *****[31]

Each asterisk spoke volumes about the law as practised on the ground of north Queensland's frontier. *The Cooktown Courier* summed up the general policy towards Aboriginal people in 1878: 'Putting in plain English this is what we Queenslanders do ... we set the Native Police on [the Aboriginal inhabitants] to make them "quiet". This is effected by massacring them indiscriminately'.[32] The editor's bald statement was partly an attempt to deny community responsibility. For as the same paper's editorial acknowledged only one year earlier, the Native Police, comprised largely of Aboriginal men from southern Queensland, were not solely responsible for the killing on the Palmer: since the district was settled, it stated bluntly, 'armed police have been waging continual war with the blacks and private individuals have been doing a good deal of shooting among them'.[33] The Chinese, usually unarmed or carrying rudimentary weapons, were rarely, if ever, among them. While they were certainly involved in conflict—reports of Chinese being speared and killed were not uncommon—there is no evidence that they were involved in reprisal parties.[34] Despite a government inquiry into the first allegations of 'slaughter' at Battle Camp in late 1873, the war against the Guugu Yimithirr continued unabated. It was fought on the goldfields by miners and police and also on the streets of Cooktown, where it was fought in words. Belligerent, shrill and often sensational editorials in the town's newspapers regularly whipped up community anxiety about the 'murderously hostile' natives. It was in the editors' interest to present themselves as the megaphone of the miners' phobias about 'the blacks' and to champion their pleas for government and police 'protection'. Sensational language mobilised fear and fuelled violence. And it reflected the deepest insecurities of the British: a handful of 'savages' could not hold their enterprise to ransom. After all, they were supposedly the superior race. The leaders of Cooktown opinion could see 'no middle course'.

In their eyes the choice was either 'the abandonment of the country or the complete repression of these pests'.[35]

The Guugu Yimithirr and the Guugu Yalandji fought tenaciously for their land. They were widely believed to be far more formidable fighters than Aboriginal people in the south. Reports from the front line emphasised their bravery, strategic cunning and skilful use of the country to launch raids and avoid their enemy, such as sending smoke signals 'from a special wood' or placing 'small twigs ... in various positions' to warn of an impending attack.[36] Despite the fact that the odds were stacked against them—they were outnumbered and faced large numbers of men armed with repeating rifles—they continued to fight valiantly. In 1876, after three years of the more belligerent whites 'sending a rifle bullet after every blackfellow they saw', their numbers (anywhere from 1500 to 2000 when the miners arrived) were reported as 'greatly thinned'.[37] Yet 'in the unoccupied country', they were thought to 'hold their own', and were still largely in control of all the country 'right down to the north bank of the river estuary on which Cooktown [was] built'.[38] The following year locals admitted 'the blacks [had] been driven not quite six miles from the very town of Cooktown' and remained 'not a bit cowed'.[39] By the 1880s, however, when the alluvial goldfields were already exhausted, the Guugu Yimithirr and their neighbours also faced pastoralists who had quickly claimed large swathes of land. In 1884, according to Hervey Fitzgerald, the Cooktown police magistrate, the graziers' policy towards Aboriginal people was little different to that of the miners: 'extermination'.[40] News of these horrors travelled quickly to other colonies. In 1882, South Australian MP William J Sowden was travelling with a parliamentary party to the Northern Territory. He described what he was told about the north Queensland frontier with a candour that remains shocking today.

> Even now it is considered a joke all along the coast beyond Cooktown in many quarters to shoot down blackfellows by way of retaliation, and some men pride themselves on the 'row of stiff-uns' they have made in their time, and others talk pleasantly of 'black-crow shooting' ... Oh! We Christianise the natives, we Europeans;

we initiate them by baptism into the mysteries of religion, but the baptism too often is a baptism of blood.[41]

Forced out of their traditional territories, often into the lands of other clans, which only created further animosity, their resources and livelihood taken from them or severely compromised (the bêche-de-mer trade saw men, women and children abducted and traded along the Cape York Peninsula coast), their women forcibly taken or traded for sex by miners and pastoralists of all nationalities in an overwhelm-ingly male-dominated society, Aboriginal people's capacity to resist was severely weakened. By the mid-1880s, nearly all their watercourses had been occupied. It was around this time that reports emerged of 'a great quantity of blacks going [into Cooktown] begging during the day' and spending their nights on 'the reserves on the north shore' of the bay.[42] Years of war had left them deeply scarred, as CH Tongue, a new arrival from Manchester in 1884, observed: 'If they see anyone with a gun they keep far away from them and if you point one at them they will run as fast as their legs will carry them. They go from door to door calling out ... [for] bread. They will eat anything that is thrown to them'.[43] Depictions of Aboriginal people as fringe dwellers became more common. In 1885, curfews were put in place banning them from the town after dark (they would remain in place until the 1960s). In the same year, one Cooktown paper suggested they be 'rounded' up and kept by police in the 'North Shore Reserve' or on the mission at Cape Bedford. Only then, the editor argued, would 'the town ... be cleared of an intolerable nuisance and the demands of the fishing labour market met'.[44] Concerned about the ongoing 'problem', Cooktown residents held an urgent meeting in 1889 to discuss measures to keep 'the blacks out of town'. They were deemed by many residents to be 'a disgrace to the town and the people in it'. Before the meeting adjourned, others argued that they had 'more right' in Cooktown 'than the Chinese and many others who objected to them'. 'We had taken their land', one man told the meeting, 'and the hunting grounds which supplied them with food, and now it was sought to prevent them from picking up our scraps'.[45] But for every person who stood courageously in public to question the morality of

Charlotte Street,
Cooktown, circa 1890

their society's callous indifference towards Aboriginal people, or who
wrote eloquently in the Brisbane papers, describing the 'treatment'
of 'Aborigines' as a 'stupendous blunder' and a 'damning blot on the
history of Australian colonization', there were countless more who
took the law into their own hands or remained silent onlookers.[46]
The Lutheran mission established in 1886 at Cape Bedford, north of
Cooktown, arrived just in time to throw a mantle of protection over
the Guugu Yimithirr and many other Aboriginal people throughout north Queensland who had survived the frontier wars. Noel
Pearson's grandfathers experienced both sides of the war's aftermath.
'Arrimi', a 'Kuku Warra' man whose people had been 'almost entirely
annihilated' in the 1870s, died 'a fringe dweller on the outskirts of
Cooktown'. Ngulunhtul, 'also known as Charlie', 'was taken away as a
ten-year-old' to the mission at Cape Bedford. Placed with Aboriginal
people from all over the Cape York Peninsula and as far away as central
Queensland, he became 'a Guugu Yimithirr-speaking Aborigine'.[47]

————

To contemplate the overwhelming evidence of the brutality of the
frontier that accompanied the Palmer River gold rush challenges our
ability to understand what occurred. The newspaper language strips

Aboriginal people of their humanity, reducing them to obstacles or 'pests', inferior beings who are merely *acted upon*. The reports of the killing, particularly 'the mundanity and casual parsimony' of the language, as Pearson has reflected, remain profoundly disturbing.[48] Yet while the language clearly reflects the racial ideology of those who wrote the words, it disguises as much as it reveals, and it often seems difficult to reach the many encounters in which violence was not involved. Noel Loos, one of the first historians to grapple seriously with the brutality of the north Queensland frontier, estimated that almost twice as many people were reported killed by Aborigines in the Cooktown–Palmer district than any other mining field in the far north. While the toll of Aboriginal dead, he concluded, was far greater, he also argued that disease, alcohol, opium, displacement and the continued denial of Aboriginal people's humanity under the guise of 'protection' (from 1897 in Queensland) were even more significant contributing factors than violence in explaining population decline.[49] The thundering racism of the era, in which Aboriginal people were condemned to a future-less existence on the margins of settler society, continued the destruction of their society at the same time as it undoubtedly tended to hide the many examples of accommodation and cooperation that ensured their survival, such as working as stockmen and domestic servants. After the initial period of violent confrontation subsided, the two-sided confrontation presented by the Cooktown papers—an illusion in any case given the large number of Aboriginal policemen involved in the killing—became a far messier terrain. What began as the meeting of separate cultures gradually evolved into a murky entanglement in which the power relationship nonetheless remained starkly unequal, the unjust and inhumane policies of colonial and later state governments seeking to control every aspect of Aboriginal people's lives. No matter how much our present-day sensibilities might wish to 'move on' from histories of violence and oppression, it remains a perpetual obligation to remember the way in which the land was conquered. By the late 1890s, the Guugu Yimithirr had been pushed off their traditional lands and suffered significant population loss, while further north, the language of war would continue for many years. In 1905, the Brisbane

Telegraph carried a warning that 'white residents' from Cape York to the Jardine River would be 'compelled' to act against the 'natives' who were 'showing signs of depredations and discontent'. In the midst of this long conflict and in its aftermath, Aboriginal people would never forget how they had been dispossessed.[50]

In the Guugu Yimithirr's remarks to Europeans that remain on the documentary record, and in their art and oral history, they stressed that their land and people had been violently taken from them. Paintings of Europeans on horseback and Native Police brandishing rifles can be found in at least seven remote rock art sites in the escarpment country above the Endeavour, Laura and Palmer rivers, where the Guugu Yimithirr and their neighbours had often sought refuge. Some images show Native Police depicted in the 'horizontal … position', reflecting the belief that if they were painted in this way they would soon lie down dead.[51] Detailed illustration of the killing can also be found in unexpected sources. 'Oscar', an Aboriginal boy who had been stolen or traded from Cooktown in 1887 and sent to work on a pastoral station, left behind a disturbing 40-page sketchbook in which he drew Native Police shooting 'Aborigines', including 'hanging them from trees' or 'executing them' while they were tied up.[52] Long after the most intense period of killing had subsided, Aboriginal men told missionaries their people had been 'killed by tribal enemies, or they were shot by policemen or whites'.[53] They also recalled particular events such as the massacre in 1879 at Dumin bigu (Indian Head), just north of Cooktown, in which twenty-four Aboriginal people were 'trapped in a ravine and shot' by Native Police. Another four people were 'presumed drowned'.[54] As a young man, Noel Pearson learnt from his elders at Hope Vale about the massacres that had destroyed so many of their people, including memories of Aboriginal stockmen further north at Cape Mellville in the 1950s 'finding the bones of their people littering the landscape'.[55]

Given that much of the killing on north Queensland's frontier took place between 1873 and 1900, these events were in living memory for many people until the mid-twentieth century. The stories were passed on to their children and grandchildren. The memory of frontier violence was part of the story of how they had come to live on the mission or work on pastoral stations. Today, these same memories are enshrined publicly in Cooktown's 'Milbi Wall' (1998), which tells the story of Guugu Yimithirr history from their perspective. Narratives of massacres have also survived in the memory of both Aboriginal and non-Aboriginal society because they more readily served as singular, dramatic and sometimes apocalyptic explanations of dispossession and cultural loss. Yet the descriptions of war and conflict that have survived in the historical record do more than just reflect the banality of the killing: they also reveal how the miners and pastoralists perceived themselves as *victims*. Despite their superior arms and numbers, they saw themselves as vulnerable and isolated, the helpless prey of 'black demons'.[56] 'Massacres' were committed not by them but against them—'dreadful massacre & outrages by Palmer Blacks'—and against their horses and cattle—'it was resolved to put a stop to this wholesale massacre'.[57] 'Apprehensive' of the 'natives' raids', they imagined 'the blacks' would 'either slaughter' them or 'burn' them 'out of their territory'.[58] Battling against drought, 'flooded rivers', treading the 'pathless forest' through 'the habitat of the wild savage' with 'Anglo-Saxon energy and perseverance', these envoys of 'civilisation' had their 'little homes upset' and their lives placed 'in jeopardy'.[59] Because Aboriginal raids hindered their mining activities, they complained of 'incalculable loss', their position 'perilous in the extreme'.[60] When Cooktown residents in the late nineteenth century were confronted by criticism from humanitarians in Brisbane or further south, they cast themselves as the sufferers.

> If some of those spurious philanthropists down south who are continually speaking of the 'poor blacks' were obliged to make the journey to the Palmer, if they were even living here in Cooktown and knew as well as we do what is passing around us, we have little doubt that their maudlin sentimentality would undergo a rapid change. We have had to chronicle many outrages by the 'poor blacks' in this district where the 'poor whites' have been the sufferers … It is very easy for people who are perfectly safe from such dangers to preach toleration, and humanity, and forebearance, and Christian charity, but were they posed to lose their property

or their lives by the spears of the 'sable bretheren', the Christian charity and all that would soon evaporate in the smoke of a rifle.[61]

Believing they were 'not sufficiently protected by the Queensland government … from the murderous onslaught of the fierce enemies who have made the road to Palmer a warpath on which every man risks his life', they called for more police, more arms, and 'good roads'.[62] Isolated and fearful of invasion—it seemed entirely fitting that the Queensland government's abortive bid to annex Papua New Guinea in 1883 was telegraphed to the world from Cooktown—they also saw themselves as victims of government indifference.[63] Cooktown was 'so remote from the seat of government that its interests [were] in danger of being overlooked', a sentiment shared by many towns in north Queensland and one that fuelled the push for the region to separate from Brisbane and become a self-governing colony.[64] Attitudes towards government were riddled with hypocrisy and double standards. Complaining that government did not protect them, miners and pastoralists blamed the government for forcing them to disperse the 'blacks' in their own self-defence. Yet when they were asked to account for their actions or provide assistance to the Aboriginal people they had dispossessed, they argued that it was 'the government who had benefited by taking the natives' land who should provide for them and not the townsmen'.[65] At no time during or after the frontier war did the miners or pastoralists accept collective responsibility for what had happened to Aboriginal people in the last decades of the nineteenth century. Distancing themselves from government, they refused to see themselves as the chief beneficiaries of the war they had waged.

On the streets of Cooktown, lurid tales of the murder of miners and their families by 'blood-thirsty savages' reinforced the perception of victimhood among the town's citizens.[66] Women's bodies were reportedly found 'stark naked … evidently ravished by the murderous wretches'. Fanciful stories emerged of parents and their children being 'run down like paddymelons by a merciless mob of infuriated cannibals'.[67] Their bodies were then placed on top of a 'great fire kindled on the hilltop to heat [a] huge oven', before 'the horrid

179

banquet' began. Punitive parties of 'outraged' miners and native police quickly avenged the deaths of such 'poor men'.[68] Every allegation, no matter how unsubstantiated, required an even more excessive response. Transfixed by fear and their own sense of vulnerability, one story in particular galvanised Cooktown's community and literally enshrined an undercurrent of victimhood for decades to come. In October 1881, Mary Watson, the young wife of Robert Watson who was away gathering bêche-de-mer, was reported missing from their cottage on Lizard Island, almost one hundred kilometres north-east of Cooktown. Wild rumours of her fate circulated in Cooktown and all over Australia. Well before her body was found, police had extracted a host of contradictory 'confessions' from various groups of Aborigines and exacted terrible revenge against scores of innocent people.[69] No-one will ever know how many Aboriginal people were killed. Without a scintilla of evidence, newspapers ran headlines such as 'Lizard Island Massacre'.[70] As the story unfolded, Mary and her two Chinese workers, Ah Leong and Ah Sam, were visited by a group of Aborigines for whom Lizard Island was the 'home of manuya, the sand goanna' (the island was not permanently inhabited), where they had long collected medicinal plants. Dismayed to find their sacred ground occupied and their law broken, they speared and killed Ah Leong and wounded Ah Sam before leaving the island.[71] Fearful that she would be their next victim, Mary decided to leave the island with Ah Sam and her 4-month-old child, Ferrier, floating out to sea in 'the pot that the bech-de-mer [was] boiled in'. She drifted for eight days and 65 kilometres in the tank before finally coming to rest on No. 5 Howick Island.[72]

In January 1882, a passing fishing vessel discovered the bodies of Ah Sam, Mary and her child. Mary was reportedly found with 'her head resting on the tank with baby Ferrier at her breast and a loaded revolver at her side'.[73] She had died from thirst while Ah Sam had died from his wounds inflicted at Lizard Island. As the press told the story, she had been forced from her home by the 'Northern blacks' and drifted helplessly at sea, bravely clutching her babe and revolver to the last, her diary at her side.[74] Her final plaintive entries—'self very weak really thought I should have died last night … have not seen any boat

Mary Watson's voyage depicted on Cooktown's history pavement, 2016

of any description (no water nearly dead with thirst)'—were repeated so often they became the cry of the whole community.[75] As soon as her body was found, Watson was exalted as a 'noble soul', the woman with a 'kind and loving heart' who became an Australian 'heroine' virtually overnight.[76] Lizard Island became synonymous with her disappearance and death. Few recalled that it was from the 'summit of Lizard Island' in 1770 that James Cook spotted 'openings in the reefs', through which he eventually passed out to sea.[77] When the bodies arrived in Cooktown for burial, 'every public organization' joined with the town's residents in honouring the 'courageous mother'. A memorial was erected in 1885 by 'public subscription', its white sheen of innocence still visible on the town's main street today.[78] For most of Cooktown's history, the Watson memorial stood not far from the Cook memorial, erected in 1887, as the only monuments in town.

Over time, Mary Watson's story became an allegory of the bravery, integrity and irreproachable nature of the entire settler community. In Cooktown, 'every child' had heard the story: Watson and Ah Sam were apparently 'greater figures' than 'Burke and Wills or any of the other tragic personalities' in Australia's history.[79] Well into the 1950s, the story was published in newspapers throughout Australia, often in melodramatic tones that repeatedly emphasised the 'treachery' of the local 'Aborigines', which it was claimed far exceeded 'that of the Aborigines in any other part of Australia'. Like the martyr Watson, the settlers were the noble victims of unjust Aboriginal attacks. They were not the perpetrators of war.[80]

For Cooktown and north Queensland, the legacy of a frontier in which extinction was seen as 'the blacks'' natural destiny was profound and long-lasting. Lutheran missionaries at Cape Bedford recognised the tragic effects of 'a number of terrible bloodbaths … in which almost all fathers of children who are now ten years or older were killed'. Observing the remaining 'Cooktown blacks' in 1898, WE Roth, Northern Protector of Aborigines, remarked on their 'demoralised' appearance and found it difficult to obtain information from them about 'the habits and customs of the old days'.[81] Suspicion, fear and animosity lingered on both sides well into the twentieth century. As the *Brisbane Courier* admitted as early as 1880, 'all these years of unrelenting hostility and indiscriminate murder … have not left very friendly feelings behind them'.[82] Interviewed a century later, Sister Denise Burns of Cooktown's St Mary's Convent, the great-great-granddaughter of John Savage, the town's mayor in the late 1880s, recalled her father's deep-seated fear of 'the blacks' in the early twentieth century.

> I know that my father certainly … talked about the blacks as he used to call them and they were obviously frightened of them the way my father used to talk … [he] had some stories where he could vaguely remember of things the blacks did that had made him a bit hostile … towards [them] … it wasn't a happy relationship … given just the attitude of my father and the fear in him about the blacks.[83]

The legacy of fear and hostility was passed down from one generation to the next. For Cooktown, north Queensland and Australia, it would take far longer to overcome the residue of mistrust than it took to create it. As the Guugu Yimithirr and Aboriginal people throughout Queensland entered the period of government 'protection' from 1897 and were moved onto missions and reserves, the settler economy that had displaced them was already in decline. By the 1890s, it was widely acknowledged that the alluvial goldfields were completely 'worked out'. In the space of thirty years, Cooktown's 'heyday of prosperity' was already gone. As one columnist observed in 1897, the future outlook was bleak: 'beyond the mineral fields Cooktown has few other resources ... [and] the pastoral industry, even at its best, cannot be counted as much'.[84] Although a handful of Chinese businessmen remained until the early twentieth century, most Chinese moved on to other mining fields once the gold and tin had dried up, many encouraged to return home by unfair taxes and the passage of legislation (1877) restricting Chinese immigration. In the 1920s, the thousands that had thronged in Cooktown's streets fifty years earlier had been reduced to a mere 600 people, and by the early 1950s the town's population had dwindled to several hundred.[85] The Aboriginal population of Hope Vale and Bloomfield missions, whose ancestors the first wave of miners and pastoralists had tried to 'disperse', now outnumbered the white population. The overwhelming image in the town was one of poverty and desertion; logs and rocks holding down corrugated iron roofing, pubs and businesses closed and goats wandering the empty dirt streets. Like so many other former mining towns across Australia, Cooktown had gone from boomtown to vanishing point in seventy years. In 1941, a visiting journalist described Cooktown as 'moribund', the 'Ghost Town of the North'.

A white road drooping amid palm-trees, broad-leaved bananas and weeping figs to a ramshackle wharf now seldom visited by large steamers; a dilapidated township with fine public buildings fast falling into decay ... a signal-station hill commanding one of the loveliest river views in Australia, a wide estuary of sapphire gleaming under a sky of king-fisher blue ... To-day, whole blocks of buildings in the centre of the town have fallen down ... It is hard to picture Cooktown in the days when it was the second port in Queensland ... the blacks have vanished from the environs of Cooktown, early Cooktown history recording more than one attack upon townspeople who ventured too far into the scrub. The blacks have disappeared, but so have the Chinese and most of the whites ...[86]

Beset by the ravages of fire (1919) and cyclones (1907 and 1949), its population further depleted by economic depression and war, Cooktown's tale of hardship and struggle continued. Yet it was now cast through an increasingly popular memory of the early mining and pastoral days as 'wild and romantic' in which the contribution of Aboriginal labour and the frontier wars were almost entirely absent. Remembering the town's 'historic association'—James Cook, the 'glories of the Palmer gold diggings' and Cooktown's natural beauty (the 'Queen of the North')—became another form of forgetting.[87] There were two histories separated by a deep chasm: Cooktown's, largely imagined as a 'non-Aboriginal space' and told as if Aboriginal people had barely existed, and Aboriginal oral history, which resounded with stories of the white man's destructive impact—'all these people gone'.[88] As the Europeans and Chinese slowly deserted Cooktown, the Guugu Yimithirr remained in their Country, thanks to the extraordinary figure of Georg Heinrich Schwarz, the Lutheran missionary who arrived in 1887 and presided over 'Hope Valley' mission near Cape Bedford from 1890 until 1942.

By the turn of the century, Aboriginal people who were not employed were potentially subject to forced removal onto reserves or missions. Men regularly left their communities to work as divers in the bêche-de-mer trade. Traditional patterns of movement, culture and kinship had long been disrupted. 'Whole clan areas were bereft of owners, and whole languages were left with few if any speakers.'[89] On this ever-shifting and still violent frontier, Schwarz's mission became even more important as a place of cultural refuge. Cooktown itself relied heavily on Aboriginal labour. In the 1920s there were up to forty women and children working as 'houseboys, housemaids and

nurses', most of them unpaid.[90] Despite the efforts to keep 'Aborigines'
out of town, they continued to 'come in', drawn by all the vices
that Schwarz was keen to protect them from, particularly prostitu-
tion, opium and alcohol. Determined to isolate Aboriginal women
and children from the corrupt influences of town life, Schwarz kept
children away from their parents in order to keep them at school.
He separated boys from girls, and by the time the girls had reached
marriageable age their presence drew many Aboriginal men from
across the peninsula to the mission. By the early twentieth century,
Schwarz, who was largely dependent on government funding for
his project's livelihood, was also receiving children who had been
removed from their families across Cape York Peninsula by the
government's protection agencies. Against the odds, he established a
tight-knit community that nonetheless remained open to constant
waves of outside influence. Hope Valley became home to Aboriginal
people from all over north Queensland, its mighty anchor a stern,
compassionate and strictly enforced Lutheran moral code. As a
self-described 'third-generation legatee of mission protection', Noel
Pearson explained how Schwarz believed that the Guugu Yimithirr
language 'best conveyed the gospels' to the 'hearts' of his people. For
the majority of the mission's residents, Guugu Yimithirr was not their
first language, but it gradually became the mission's lingua franca.
For Pearson, although 'the missionaries' kindness and humanity were
mixed with the racialism of the time', Schwarz was a 'hero' because he
preserved Guugu Yimithirr language and culture and that of countless
Aboriginal people across the peninsula. As another mission resident,
Guugu Yimithirr elder Eric Deeral, reflected towards the end of his
life: 'I would not be here if it had not been for the mission. Nor
would my language'.[91]

   In some respects, Schwarz and his Aboriginal community shared
a common bond. They were both outsiders. During World War II,
when fear of Japanese attack reached fever pitch in north Queensland,
Schwarz was interned in a camp for German 'aliens' while the mission's population was evacuated from Hope Valley to Palm Island and
Woorabinda, 170 kilometres south-west of Rockhampton. Aboriginal
people living on fringe camps around Cooktown were left alone,

The evacuation of Aboriginal residents from Hope Valley, 1942; image from Cooktown's Milbi (Story) Wall, 2016

suggesting that Schwarz and his community were targeted because of his German ancestry. But there were other reasons. As many Hope Vale residents later believed, their 'long association' (well into the twentieth century) working with Japanese fishing boats also marked them as suspect in the eyes of the government. While Cooktown's residents at least had prior warning of the evacuation—women and children were moved to Cairns as the town became an advance operational base—neither Schwarz nor anyone in the mission community was consulted about the move. On 17 May 1942, shortly after the Battle of the Coral Sea, trucks arrived and took everyone away. Eric Deeral, who was a boy of ten at the time, remembered the day for the rest of his life. 'We were shocked to see trucks with soldiers with tommy guns … we didn't know where we would be taken to.' Schwarz was barred from returning, while the mission was not re-established until 1950 when it was re-christened Hope Vale.[92]

Born in Hope Vale in 1955, Eric Deeral's niece, Alberta Hornsby, 'lived mainly with [her] grandparents', 'Uncles and Aunties', and for a short while on Starcke Station, north of Cooktown. 'My father applied for an exemption from the *Aboriginal Protection Act* in the 1960s', she recalled, 'and we left the mission and went to live in Malanda [on the Atherton Tableland]. My father worked on a dairy farm. Living on the outside was very hard for my parents, I think. I remember longing for the security of my grandparents'. When I spoke with Alberta in Cooktown, she recalled vividly how her father 'hated the fact that Aboriginal workers'—their wages were sent back to the mission—'were only given basic rations' during 'the station days'. 'Dad protested that they should all receive tomato sauce from the station owner.' But he 'got a hiding from his older brother' for making a stand. 'Don't you forget the station owner is the boss', his brother admonished him, yet another reminder of how loyalties were rarely if ever neatly divided between white and black communities. Sent away at the age of ten to attend high school in Albury—'a government and church initiative for assimilation' that her parents believed was 'the right thing to do'—Alberta was billeted to a Lutheran family. There, in the late 1960s, she found herself invited to the mayor's office to take part in 'National Aborigines Day'. 'Together with another girl, I must have been the only school-age Aborigine they could find in Albury', she said, smiling. Alberta fell pregnant at the age of sixteen and returned to live at Hope Vale, working in the mission's administration as a single mother. Within a year she had 'run away' to Cooktown. Her adult life was spent shifting from Cooktown to Cairns and Brisbane in 1972, where she worked in the Golden Circle canned fruit factory and spent time with her uncle, Eric Deeral, who, in 1974, as a member of the National Party, became the first Aboriginal person to be elected to Queensland Parliament. Lunching with Eric Deeral at Parliament House, Alberta was drawn closer to the world of political and historical discussion. As for the early frontier times, both Eric and her father preferred to look forward: 'they never dwelt on bad stuff', she said. After moving back to Albury for a while—'I had a good relationship with my foster family, it was my second home'— Alberta finally returned to Hope Vale in the early 1990s where she was reunited with her uncle Eric, with whom she already shared a passionate curiosity about Guugu Yimithirr history and culture.

Looking back on her youth in 2016, Alberta explained her attitude towards her Guugu Yimithirr heritage and life under government regimes that sought to dictate so much of her existence: 'I grew up being a victim', she said forcefully, 'and whilst I was a victim, I don't want to live with it now. If we go on being victims we'll always have that attitude—you owe me'. Alberta's cousin, Noel Pearson, has expressed his admiration for his people's 'determination to survive in the teeth of hardship and loss' and at the same time encouraged Aboriginal people across Australia to leave behind the destructive impacts of 'victimhood', so often linked to a culture of welfare dependence. One of the most striking aspects of the long history of Cooktown's frontier is that both Aboriginal and non-Aboriginal people emerged from the experience, albeit in very different ways, relying on narratives of adversity. From the 1870s until the last quarter of the twentieth century, stories of suffering, loss and survival underwrote both settler and Aboriginal cultures. Both believed they had rebuilt their communities several times over in the face of insurmountable odds. Both saw themselves as hard done by and as dogged survivors. Yet their histories and communities were still largely seen as separate entities.[93]

Looking north-west,
Cooktown harbour,
2016

Footprints 'upon the sand'; 'fires still burning'; clam shells and 'roots of wild yam' visible in the smouldering coals. 'Houses' and campsites deserted. No matter how far they pursued them, Cook's men could only find traces of their presence. On 16 June 1770, as the *Endeavour* tried to get ashore, Joseph Banks spied four 'Indians' through his 'glasses' and watched as they ran away along the beach. When the ship was finally moored 'within 20 feet of the shore' two days later, he was again disappointed to find only 'old frames of ... houses and places where they had dressed shellfish'. To walk five or six kilometres inland was unnerving. The 'steps of men' were everywhere yet 'neither man nor beast' could be seen. Even when the 'natives' could be glimpsed momentarily, 'they ran away as fast as they could'. For the next three weeks, while the *Endeavour* was repaired at Gangaar, the Guugu Yimithirr adopted one strategy towards the newcomers: avoid and observe. As Banks admitted, they had 'discovered us before we saw them'.

In the absence of face-to-face contact and finding themselves unexpectedly stumbling through unknown country in the wet tropics, nightmarish visions arose. One of Cook's men returned from 'the woods' claiming to have seen 'a creature as black as the devil ... [with] two horns on its head'. It was a flying fox. Everything about the country was 'strange': wolf-like creatures, 'slender', 'mouse'-coloured animals 'the full size of a greyhound' that 'jumped like a hare', and flowering plants with blazing colours that appeared other-worldly. Nature itself seemed to take on a monumental form: pyramid 'anthills' that Banks thought resembled 'stones' he had seen in 'English Druidical monuments' and that his fellow naturalist Daniel Solander likened to 'Rune Stones' in Sweden. Marooned until they could find a safe way out, they lived as hunter-gatherers: shooting 'dinner', collecting 'wild yams' from the 'swampy areas', hauling enough fish for a kilogram per man and searching for 'Indian kale' to supplement whatever meat they could find with 'a few greens'. When the foraging was over there was the never-ending task of collecting botanical specimens and other objects of interest. Over two centuries later, some of the cuttings that were eventually deposited with the Natural History Museum in London can still be found pressed in the pages of Banks's copy of *Paradise Lost*.[94]

By early July, the ship was almost ready. As Banks realised, having tried for so long to get in to the river mouth, they now had to turn their minds to 'how we should get out of this place'. Climbing Grassy Hill, he was confronted with the 'melancholy' prospect that they would again be wrecked attempting to leave. 'Innumerable shoals' as far as he could see, no 'straight passage out', and a 'trade wind' that blew directly in their 'teeth'. Like Cook, he wondered if they would ever 'escape'. Resigned to waiting until the conditions were ideal, Banks returned to his collecting. Meanwhile, he discussed the natives' shyness with Cook. He thought them timid and cowardly for not coming forward. So much of their behaviour mystified him. Cook, too, was unable to understand why they failed to harvest the 'shell fish and other small fish' which were easily caught at low tide 'in holes in the rocks'. Perhaps their canoes would not take them 'so far out to sea'. How was it possible after three weeks here that curiosity alone did not cause them to show themselves?

On 10 July, the stand-off was finally broken. Close to where the *Endeavour* was still moored, four Guugu Yimithirr men landed their canoe and stood on the beach with their spears. With reassuring signs, Tupia, Cook's mercurial Tahitian cultural broker, tactfully managed to persuade them to lay down their arms and sit with him on the ground. Cook soon joined them, struck immediately by their 'soft and tuneable voices' and striking talent for mimicry. Within a matter of minutes they could pronounce English words perfectly. Although they declined to stay with them for 'dinner', they would now return daily, exchanging fish, receiving 'cloth nails and paper' (with which they remained distinctly unimpressed) and even introducing one man—a 'preposterous' bone 'as thick as a man's finger' placed through his nose—by name: 'Yaparico'.[95] Over the coming days, while Cook's men busied themselves harvesting green sea turtles weighing up to 'three hundred pound', a kind of trust seemed to be established, although no-one on board the *Endeavour* had any idea why the Guugu Yimithirr had suddenly decided to engage with them. Women and children still kept their distance but came closer than before. At '200 yards', Banks was now able to play the voyeur, using his telescope to observe that the women were 'as naked as the day they were born'. 'Even those parts which I always thought nature would have taught a woman to conceal', he wrote almost longingly, 'were uncovered'.

On the morning of 18 July, after eight days of friendly relations, everything changed. 'Several of the natives' who had now become 'more familiar than ever' came on board the *Endeavour*. Convinced that they had become their 'very good friends', Cook and Banks left the ship for several hours to ascend 'Rocky Mount', about ten kilometres away. Returning yet again with the sombre news that they would have to thread their way through treacherous shoals if they were to reach the open sea, they were told by one of the officers that while they were gone, the 'natives' had 'taken more notice' of the ship's haul of twelve green sea turtles than anything else on board. These were the same turtles that all Cook's men agreed 'tasted' much better than anything 'in England'. Soon after Cook and Banks came back on deck, the men left, already discussing their next move. The following morning almost a dozen Guugu Yimithirr men returned to the ship bringing their spears with them, the largest number of weapons Banks had yet seen them carry. Placing the spears in a tree and leaving a man and boy to guard them, they then came on board the ship. They had come to insist on their fair share of Cook's harvest, immediately demanding 'some' of the turtles on the deck. When Cook refused, they dragged two turtles to the gangway with the intention of throwing them 'over the side' into their canoe. When they were restrained, they showed 'great signs of resentment'. One man, asking Banks directly for turtle and being refused, stamped his foot indignantly and pushed Banks away. Cook watched as they tried to grab anything they could from the deck and throw it overboard. As the conflict escalated, Cook offered them bread, which they 'rejected with scorn'. Turtle was the only thing they wanted. 'All in an instant' they 'leapt into their canoe' and headed for the shore where Cook had left the 'forge and a sow and a litter of young pigs'. Although Cook and Banks got there before them, they were surprised by the swiftness of the attack that followed.

'Taking fire from under a pitch kettle which was boiling' the Guugu Yimithirr quickly set fire to the grass, which was '4 or 5 feet high' and 'to windward' of the few things they had left ashore. As 'dry as a stubble', the grass burnt 'with vast fury'. Banks realised that his tent would soon go up in flames, only just managing to save it in time. One of the 'young pigs', however, was 'scorched to death in the fire'. Before they had time to regroup, several Guugu Yimithirr men ran to a point on the beach where Cook's crew were doing their washing. Fishing nets and 'linen' lay drying on the sand. Cook pursued them. Once again, he was unable to stop them from setting fire to the grass. Threats and pleas went unheeded. Without any firearms, Cook ran back to their campsite and retrieved his musket. Banks already had his musket 'loaded with shot' and together they raced along the beach to the washing place to find the flames 'spreading like wild fire'. At 40 yards (35 metres) distance, Cook fired his musket, hitting one man who immediately dropped his firestick and ran away, along with the rest of his comrades. Determined to intimidate them, Cook reloaded his musket and fired again, this time in the direction of the mangroves where they had run. They were soon out of sight. On the beach, Cook noticed 'a few drops of blood' on the linen, presuming that the man he had shot must have been 'a little hurt'.

After struggling to put the fires out, Banks was dismayed to 'hear their voices returning'. Fearing that they would employ the same tactics, and 'anxious' for the handful of people still washing on the shore, he ran back with Cook. As soon as the Guugu Yimithirr saw Cook, Banks and '3 or 4' others with their muskets raised and brandishing six or seven spears that Cook had 'seized', they became extremely 'alarmed' and 'all made off', but not before an 'old man' came towards them and said something they 'could not understand'. Eager to resolve the conflict, Banks and Cook decided to follow them for about a mile, finally resting on some high rocks on the southern shores of the harbour where they hoped to be able to monitor their movements. Hearing them calling out, the Guugu Yimithirr men sat down a little less than 100 metres away, each party cautiously observing the other. Then, without being prompted, a 'little old man … came forward' carrying a spear 'without a point'. As he walked towards them, he halted several times, 'collecting moisture from under his armpit with his finger' and drawing it 'through his mouth'. Cook and Banks 'beckoned him' to come closer. At this point, the old man turned to his comrades who 'laid their lances against a tree'. Then, slowly, they all came forward to meet them. Both Banks and Cook noticed that their party consisted of three or four men who they had not seen before. One by one, the men they already knew introduced the strangers 'by name'. After giving them some 'trinkets' and returning their spears, which Cook claimed 'reconciled everything', they all walked together back towards the ship, which was only a few hundred metres away, the Guugu Yimithirr 'making signs as they came along that they would not set fire to the grass again', Banks and Cook handing them musket balls and 'by our signs explaining their effect'. For all of this time, as they made their signs to one another, both parties continued to speak. Cook remarked on the 'unintelligible *conversation*', each person compelled to speak in their own tongue despite the fact that most of the words they uttered could not be understood. When they arrived at the ship, the Guugu Yimithirr declined to come on board, staying on the beach for a couple of hours before they were gone. Perhaps they did not want to face seeing the turtles again.

Reflecting on the experience, Banks was surprised at the 'fury' of the grass fires they had lit and how hard they had been to extinguish. Only hours after the Guugu Yimithirr had left, Banks and Cook watched as the country around them, about two miles away, was again set ablaze. From that moment until their departure a few weeks later, they would have no further meaningful contact with the Guugu Yimithirr. The memory of the fires that day stayed with them forever. Banks determined that he would never again pitch a tent in 'such a hot climate' without first burning the surrounding grass. In 1819, when Phillip Parker King landed in the same place at precisely the same time of year, the first thing he did was to set fire to the grass around his campsite. It was necessary, he explained, 'to avoid a repetition of the revengeful and mischievous trick which the natives formerly played [on] Captain Cook'. King did not have to wait as long as Cook to make contact with the Guugu Yimithirr. Only one day after he arrived, he met a group of men in the bush. Persuading 'an old man' to lead his friends towards his tent on the beach, King walked with them. But 'the moment they saw the cutter's mast through the trees they stopped'. As hard as King tried, they 'could not be prevailed upon to advance a step further; and, after devoting some time in watching us from the hills, walked away'.

The old man who stopped at the first sight of King's vessel may well have met Cook and Banks forty-nine years earlier. The story the Guugu Yimithirr had kept alive in their oral tradition of their meeting with the strange visitors contained traces of apprehension, curiosity and the possibility of friendship. But this was all in the knowledge that the visitors would ultimately leave their Country. Uncannily, aspects of King's encounter with the Guugu Yimithirr echoed those of Cook. As some of his crew were washing their clothes, about a dozen men approached them. Tentatively, they exchanged greetings, but when one of the sailors attempted to comb the hair of a young Aboriginal boy, an old man became 'violently enraged' and the others 'armed themselves with stones'. Finally, the old man was led away and 'peace was thus restored'. The following day, 2 July, spears and musket fire were exchanged after some of King's men had refused to take off all of their clothes in front of the Guugu Yimithirr. What began hopefully had ended in mistrust. King placed sentries on night watch and a 'masthead watch' by day. When he returned in 1820, finding the carpenter's bench that had been used to build his boat standing on the beach just as he had left it one year earlier, he noticed 'five natives standing about forty or fifty yards off among the high grass'. As soon as they realised King's party had spotted them, 'they began to repeat the word *itchew* (friend) and to pat their breasts, thereby intimating that their visit had no hostile motive'. Exchanging their 'throwing sticks' for 'Indian Corn', the Guugu Yimithirr beckoned King to walk inland with them but he was 'unwilling to trust' his small party to 'their power'. Shortly after King sailed away, the 'country towards the back of the harbour' was 'set on fire', almost as if, in some kind of ritual cleansing, the presence of those who came from the sea in the white birds would be eternally erased from the land. Exactly how the Guugu Yimithirr connected King with Cook will probably never be known. Perhaps they became one. In the years ahead, few would remember

King's landings in 1819 and 1820. The tree in which he had carved the *Mermaid*'s name went unremembered. All the attention would fall on the *Endeavour*, the 'founding' story that remained largely unchanged, read from the journals of Banks and Cook like holy script.[96]

———————

When Cooktown was mentioned in the southern press in the twentieth century, it was usually seen as an exotic, out-of-the-way destination, a place on the edge of civilisation: the town at the 'end of the road'.[97] As the potential for tourism emerged, Cooktown and the entire Cape York Peninsula were spoken of as a region of 'savage emptiness'—an area 'the size of England and Scotland combined'—in which only a handful of 'white people' lived. 'Nobody seems to know much about it', exclaimed one journalist in 1954, 'even school teachers are vague'.[98] Nature lovers enthused about 'Birds of Paradise', 'brilliant but microscopic sun birds', giant moths and climbing kangaroos. The peninsula was seen as a 'lost world', a 'land of mystery' where 'little [had] changed since the Aboriginal dreamtime'.[99] Many of the first

195

Cooktown memorial erected in 1988 to 'Captain James Cook', 2016, close to where he beached the *Endeavour*

advocates of Cape York's wilderness unintentionally found new ways to remove Aboriginal people from the land. For those who made the trek, the town's origins were palpable. As late as 1990, visitors remarked that Cooktown retained 'the air of a frontier town'.[100]

In 1959, spurred by the knowledge that the Cooktown to Palmer River railway line, which had operated for nearly eighty years, would soon close, the new Cooktown Tourist Development League turned to history in a bid to boost the economy and save the town from a slow but certain death. The publication of the league's tourist booklet, 'Cooktown, Queensland's Most Historic Town', which was distributed all along Queensland's coast, saw the beginning of organised 'tours'. One history in particular, it seemed, had the potential to attract visitors to the town: the story of James Cook and the *Endeavour*. It was decided that an annual re-enactment of Cook's landing would take place, 'not only for the benefit of the community, but also to encourage Australians generally, to reflect upon their heritage'. Although Cook's story had been commemorated in earlier years with parades and 'procession floats', no formal commemoration had occurred since the 1920s.[101] The first re-enactments of the landing in the 1960s were well received, but one occasion—the 1970 visit of Queen Elizabeth II, Prince Philip and Princess Anne for the bicentenary of Cook's 'discovery' of Australia—elevated the significance of the story and proved a boon for Cooktown's heritage and tourist industry.

The publicity surrounding the royal visit placed Cooktown on the map. Hearing of the discovery of the *Endeavour*'s cannons, states competed for their share of 'relics', eager to have a tangible connection to the story in time for the bicentenary, although not every politician was excited by the impending celebrations. When Prime Minister John Gorton excluded Victoria from the list of six recipients of the *Endeavour*'s cannons, the Royal Historical Society of Victoria protested vigorously. They had little support from the state's Premier, Sir Henry Bolte, who declared that he would rather have 'an extra cash handout from Canberra than a cannon from Cooktown'.[102] Money that had long been hard to extract from federal and Queensland governments to develop the far north suddenly became available. In preparation for the royal visit, the town was 'tidied up', which included the destruction of the old Chinese joss house. Even today, many of Cooktown's vacant blocks that can be seen from Grassy Hill are memorials to the enthusiastic bulldozing of 'untidy' old buildings in 1969. Fortunately, other heritage buildings were saved that year. With the support of the Catholic Church and the National Trust, Cooktown's residents rescued the old St Mary's Convent from demolition and secured the necessary funds from the Queensland government for its restoration and establishment as the 'James Cook Museum', which was opened by the Queen in April 1970.[103]

Queen Elizabeth was already well practised in Cook speech-making before she arrived in Cooktown. Cook and Banks featured in almost every public address she delivered en route. At Botany Bay, for the re-enactment of Cook's landing at Kurnell, she lauded their enterprise and courage without once mentioning their interaction with the Gweagal. At Mount Isa she praised the pioneers: 'gradually they tamed the land and built permanent homes'. In what became almost a ritual reclaiming of the continent, the royal yacht *Britannia* followed the *Endeavour*'s course north along the coast, finally dropping anchor just over three kilometres from the mouth of the Endeavour River on the morning of 22 April 1970. The annual re-enactment, normally performed in June to coincide with the time of Cook's arrival, was brought forward especially for the occasion. After arriving on the 'royal barge', the 'royal party' watched the re-enactment of the landing performed by actors in 'full-period costume' from a dais on the beach close to where Cook had landed almost two hundred years earlier. Forty-one Torres Strait Islanders sang and performed a 'mock battle and war dance' to complete the ceremony. There were few residents of the town or the surrounding region who were not there to see 'the royals'. Over fifty trucks brought people from Hope Vale alone.[104]

After a brisk 'motor tour of the town' and opening the James Cook Museum and the Sir Joseph Banks Garden, the Queen was back on the royal yacht within little more than two hours, telling Queensland's Minister for Tourism that she had had an 'absolutely fascinating morning ... one of the most exciting' she had spent in the country so far—Cooktown was 'so different', she exclaimed.[105] Although she had

197

Queen Elizabeth II on the steps of the new James Cook Museum, April 1970

earlier told the Melbourne media that Princess Anne was 'beginning to feel the spell of this vigorous country', her daughter seemed slightly enervated by the tropical north.[106] Ettie, Lady Morris, wife of Queensland's Deputy Premier Sir Kenneth Morris, who 'looked after' the princess in Cooktown that morning, remembered how she had curtly asked: 'Whose house was that before it was a Museum?' Morris politely explained that it had not been someone's 'house' but was instead a convent. 'She wasn't a very happy girl', Morris recalled in 1983, but 'she looks much better now'.[107] The frenzy of activity to prepare Cooktown for two crowded hours of royalty's presence had almost exhausted its citizens. Cooktown was 'getting over the Queen' but it was not yet over Cook.[108]

By the late 1970s, the re-enactment had become a catalyst for the much larger Discovery Festival held at the same time each June. Every year, the matron from Cooktown Hospital drove out to Hope Vale to bring the Aboriginal performers taking part in the re-enactment into town. Although the organisers involved the Aboriginal community from the beginning, and claimed to have a 'close liaison' with them, in the first re-enactments, the story was told of how Cook 'met and overcame an attack by the Aborigines'.[109] Carrying their spears, they retreated before his superior presence. Alberta Hornsby remembered Gertie Deeral telling her husband (Eric's brother) in the 1970s: 'if you take part in the re-enactment our marriage is over'. Some Aboriginal women, she explained, 'objected to their husbands being asked to stand in public in their jocks'.[110] They thought it demeaned them. Remarkably, at a time in the late twentieth century when re-enacting Cook's landing at Kurnell was seen as highly insensitive to Indigenous Australians, the re-enactment in Cooktown continued without serious protest, perhaps because the Discovery Festival became the major event. Activities organised for the festival reflected the general tenor of proceedings: 'Pie eating and Coke drinking', 'Iron Person (physical and gastronomical)', 'spear throwing', the 'goanna pull', 'crab-tying', 'cream cake eating', a 'wet T-Shirt competition' and a prize for the 'best-dressed esky'. It was a carnival atmosphere: mock tournaments, pantomime and copious quantities of booze.[111] The story of James Cook's 7-week stay at Endeavour River was lost somewhere in the haze of festivities. And it would remain that way until the early 2000s, when the re-enactment, and the history of Cooktown's founding, was dramatically transformed through the close collaboration of Eric Deeral, actor John MacDonald, Alberta Hornsby and Loretta Sullivan, president of the Cooktown Re-enactment Association.

In 1998, John MacDonald began 'beavering away' on the journals of Cook and Banks with the intention of translating them into 'dramatic script'. He was in frequent contact with Eric Deeral, who was also re-reading the journals.[112] When the James Cook Museum received a 2.3-million-dollar federation grant, the National Trust of Queensland commissioned Eric to write the text that would form part of several panels to be installed in the museum's new wing and opened in 2001. It was a potentially groundbreaking opportunity. Eric was asked to explain the Guugu Yimithirr perspective on Cook's landing in 1770.[113] From the late 1990s until Deeral's death in 2012, MacDonald and Deeral shared a close relationship, poring over every detail in the journals and working hard to introduce the untold story of Cook's visit into the re-enactment, which they succeeded in doing from 2009. Deeral also encouraged his niece, Alberta Hornsby, to read Cook's and Banks's journals, which she did, somewhat reluctantly. 'I was never that impressed with Cook', said Alberta. 'I didn't talk about Cook growing up. It wasn't part of our history. My grandfather said Cook was responsible for raping our women and everything that happened to us.' Alberta recalled only a few of the older women at Hope Vale speaking of Cook in verse: 'Captain Cook swallowed a hook and found himself in the history book'.[114]

Eric Deeral discovered Cook through the journals. As a young boy at school in Woorabinda, Eric was told by a teacher that he showed signs of leadership. He also encouraged him to read history, a passion he would retain for the rest of his life.[115] Working on the Guugu Yimithirr's perspective on Cook's landing for the new museum wing, Eric immediately saw the importance and value of the story to the Cooktown and Hope Vale communities. As both Alberta and Loretta later explained, 'he was like the "old man" in the story, who in a gesture of peace, came forward to meet Cook and Banks and ordered his men to lay down their weapons'.[116] In the last decade of his life, Eric paved the way for an Indigenous-centred interpretation of Cook's time at the Endeavour River. After his death in 2012, both Alberta and Loretta felt they had to carry on with Eric's work, especially by incorporating the Guugu Yimithirr's story into the annual re-enactment of Cook's landing. Alberta, who proudly describes herself as an

Eric Deeral, 2009

'unlettered, self-proclaimed historian', has continued to research both her Indigenous heritage—including a Guugu Yimithirr dictionary started by Eric and his wife Ellen White that currently has over 4700 entries—and European historical records. The story has grown richer over time, allowing us to see what took place at Gangaar in 1770 in an entirely different light. Alberta recently recorded her account of Cook's meeting with the Guugu Yimithirr, complementing Eric's text which has been displayed in the James Cook Museum since 2001. Like Cooktown's Milbi Wall, we now have a remarkable account to place beside those of Cook and Banks, one created by applying Eric and Alberta's knowledge of traditional Guugu Yimithirr law and culture to British documents.[117]

Eric Deeral: *Ngarrbal-ngay wanhu? Nguba ngaadaal wuwu-thirr*, 'visitors who may need help'.

Prior to the 10th June, 1770 We the Kuku Yalanji and Guugu Yimithirr Bama-ngay who lived along the eastern seaboard, between what we now know as Mossman and the Starcke, north and south of Cooktown were open to the concept of others. We would observe strange sailing vessels going by and we were usually aware of their purpose. They would be looking for fish, dugong, beche de mer, trochus or shells. Sometimes they would visit to replenish their water supplies, repair canoes, or look for women. But they were transients. They did not intend to stay. Often they were islanders who knew and respected our territories. On the morning of the 11th June, 1770 a strange large canoe which the coastal people had kept under observation was seen just east of Kulki (in Kuku Yalandji) which is now known as Cape Tribulation. It appeared that something was not right. Then it started moving along the coast again. At times our Bama [people] lit small fires to inform other clan members regarding the whereabouts of this strange canoe. Two days later our Bama saw it drop anchor at the mouth of the Wahalumbaal Birri, which Captain Cook later named the Endeavour River. Our Guugu Yimithirr ancestors considered that these boat people like others who came and went would not cause problems. After these strange beings beached their large canoe our Bama decided not to make contact but to observe. They decided to do what they normally did. Bama got into their canoes; they speared fish; women and children collected wood and other things from the beach, two Bama even paddled close to the visitors' boat.

Alberta Hornsby: Guugu Yimithirr Country [which comprises thirty-two clan lands] extends from the Annan River (Yuku Baja) in the south, north to the Jeannie River and west to Normanby River. Waymburr [where Cook landed] was a neutral zone where no blood was to be deliberately spilt. This Country was a free zone, a place for the surrounding clans to come together, a place of mediation and ceremony. It is possible that Cook could have been speared if he had landed on the other side of the Endeavour River, however, I believe that the spiritual belief of the Guugu Yimithirr people also prevented harm to the *Endeavour*'s crew. Their belief is based on the principle of '*wawu*', which is the inner spirit of Bama, at death the *wawu* travelled to the east. When the *wawu* returned back to their homelands, they would return white skinned and would not return empty-handed. At that time our ancestors were awaiting the return of their ancestors Milganduur (masked plover) and Galgarungal (wallaroo). It was believed that these two ancestors travelled from the west and at their death their *wawu* travelled to the east. The arrival of these visitors would have caused mixed feelings amongst Bama-ngay [our people] and it was a wise decision that they chose to observe them before any contact would be made. If these visitors were indeed their ancestors then they would know the laws.

Eric Deeral: The strangers gave our Bama fish and beads. Next day four of our men went back and gave them fish in return, which is customary. Though our Bama recognized the predicament these visitors were in, they were discreet because they need to make sure the visitors were not reincarnations of 'wawu-ngay', spirits of our ancestors. Every effort was made to be tactful. Women were not allowed to approach the strangers. Then one morning ten of our men were invited to inspect the visitors' boat. To their horror, they saw a number of turtles on board, presumably taken from our waters. When they asked if they could have one it was refused. To our Bama it became an offence. The sharing code was broken. The visitors had trespassed. They should have got permission from us as the owners or custodians. Then things got out of hand. Our Bama were so confused and angry that they set fire to the camp site. Then they heard a loud bang and saw a puff of smoke. One of the men could not believe that something invisible punctured his leg and blood started to flow. They all ran away. Before going back to their camp our Bama lit more fires to warn other clans that something had gone wrong.

Alberta Hornsby: On the ninth of July two men came by canoe from across the other side of the river. The *Endeavour* Journals describe this time of contact. They paddle the canoe right up to the *Endeavour*. Gifts of cloth, beads and nails are thrown into the canoe, the men are not impressed or interested in the gifts, however, a small fish is accidently thrown over to them and this gift pleased the men. They soon leave and return with two other men.

This was the first of six visits to the *Endeavour* by Bamangay. No women visit, only men. Parkinson recorded what he believed to be the names of nine men. The names he records are names of where these men came from and some are kinship names. Parkinson also records a wordlist of 150 words, which is a great achievement, most of these words are recognisable today. The Guugu Yimithirr Bama could fluently repeat any words the British said to them but the British had great difficulty speaking Guugu Yimithirr.

On the second last visit by Bama they are invited on board the *Endeavour*. On deck there are twelve turtles weighing between two hundred and three hundred pounds. They are not pleased to see this many turtles on the ship and they quickly leave. The next day ten men arrive, they leave their spears with a young boy before boarding the ship and attempt to take one turtle, they are stopped from taking a turtle and soon leave the ship, one of the men grabs a firestick from a nearby fire and sets the grass on fire, which quickly spreads. They run to the nearby stream, where the crew are washing and nets and other items are drying on the grass. The man with the firestick attempts to set this area on fire too. Cook shoots the man with a small shot and apparently wounds him in the leg, spilling blood on Waymburr. The man is rescued by his friends and they behave aggressively towards the *Endeavour* mob. However, when they see the muskets raised, they calm down. Their spears are seized by the British and they take off into the bush and mangroves.

Eric Deeral: Ngamu Yarrbarigu an elder of the clans called all the members together to discuss the day's events. A strategy was agreed on. Ngamu Yarrbarigu and a number of men would visit the stranger's camp the next day and every effort would be made to make peace, because our Bama now knew that the visitors possessed a spirit which was more powerful than they had experienced. Next morning before our Bama left camp, a customary ritual was performed by the Elders. Each man was wiped with sweat from the armpit of the Elders—'ngaalaan thuulngal' and our women chanted—'ganhil gunday'. This was for them to be protected, to practice self-control and to leave camp with a blessing. When our Bama confronted the strangers, each had four spears. The Elder Ngamu Yarrbarigu carried one spear which had no barb. Our elders were afraid to do anything that might result in the spirits of our departed ancestors being upset, in case Cook's mob were indeed Wangaar or reincarnations of our ancestors. And so, with this doubt and fear in their minds, they used discretion, deciding against any rash actions. Ngamu Yarrbarigu said to Cook's men: Ngahthaan gadaai thawun maa naa thi hu 'We come to make friends'. Sensing that the strangers were not sure of their intention and did not understand what their leader, Ngamu Yarrbarigu, said, our Bama then put their plan into action. They withdrew to an outcrop of rocks, where it is possible that more Bama were positioned. There they placed their spears on the ground and sat down. At this point, Cook may have become aware that his life was in danger. However, diplomacy was used by both sides. It may be that the caution on the part of the Guugu Yimithirr saved Cook's life. A cautious agreement was reached.

Alberta Hornsby: Cook and his mob can hear them and they follow them for about a mile. Cook and his mob rest on a rocky outcrop, the Bama men sit about one hundred yards from them. Then a 'little old man' comes forward, he performs a ritual called 'ngalangundaama' where he draws sweat from under his armpits, and blowing the sweat on his hands into the air, this is to call for protection and calm. He carries a spear with a snapped spearhead. He approaches Cook and speaks, Cook gives back the spears they had taken earlier and he takes this action as a sign of Reconciliation, which he records in his journal. The men return to the ship with Cook and his mob but they don't go on board. The *Endeavour* Journals say that they sit for about an hour and then leave, never to return to the site. By now, our Bama would have realised that this mob were not their ancestors. The gifts that were given to Bama were found 'carelessly' thrown around, which suggested that they had no use for them. In Cook's Journal

205

Alberta Hornsby, at home with her grandchildren, Cooktown, 2016

he writes that their gifts were not wanted and they would not part with any of their articles.

Banks writes in his journal that on leaving the river all the hills are set on fire. This was the way that Bama cleansed the area from any bad spirits that may have been left behind and cleansed the area of the British presence.

> Eric Deeral: Then Ngamu Yarrbarigu told his men to leave their spears and follow the strangers towards their camp-site. There were some men who wanted to have a close look at the boat but they agreed to be more cautious. They stayed for a while and then left. Before leaving to board their canoes, our Bama agreed between themselves that the things that the strangers gave were to be got rid of and that no further contact was to be made and that the visitors should have freedom of movement. Then, finally, one day they watched the ship sail out of the Wahalumbaal Birri and away from our Guugu Yimithirr land. Although contact had been limited, it had for the most part been surprisingly friendly. These strangers showed respect for us and our families and it was very sad to see them go. We called them Wangaar, spirits of our dead ancestors. And that name is still used today.

> Alberta Hornsby: This is a really outstanding story of the extent that Aboriginal people go through today to extend that peace to others they share this country with. This visit of Cook is a very important part of our community history. It paved the way for this nation we now call Australia. It's good that we celebrate this history because there's such a lot in the story that we can learn from. The interaction between Cook and our Bama, we're still having that interaction today.[118]

To have both the British and Guugu Yimithirr interpretations of this extended moment side-by-side dramatically alters our view of what occurred. In the Guugu Yimithirr telling, except for the shooting incident, they are in control. In both Cook's and Banks's journals, it is British strategy that largely determines what happens. But in Eric's and Alberta's telling it is the Guugu Yimithirr's law, cautious diplomacy and strategic thinking that guide the course of events. They are not *acted upon*. They are initiators. While Cook and Banks thought the Guugu Yimithirr timid for running away, we now see that this too was part of their initial strategy of observing their ancestors from a distance, just as it was some weeks later, on Possession Island, when the Kaurareg took flight and Cook claimed possession of the entire east coast of the continent for the Crown. The Guugu Yimithirr's spiritual beliefs explain the *Endeavour's* presence and largely determine their response. In Eric's and Alberta's rendition we see the complexity of Indigenous Country. The country Cook saw as a wilderness inhabited by wandering natives—'diversified with hills and plains and these with woods and lawns'—becomes the intimately interconnected territories of thirty-two different Guugu Yimithirr clans.[119]

Almost two hundred and fifty years after Cook set foot on the shores of the Endeavour River, we see everything that he could not see. We see the Country through the eyes of Guugu Yimithirr law, the 'sharing code' broken with the taking of the turtles and the place where Cook landed part of a neutral zone where blood should not be spilt, an insight that radically shifts our understanding of events. We see the old man's deeply personal gesture of offering the sweat from under his arms as a means of guiding Cook to act according to his law. And in Eric's telling, we also witness the strategic and political expedience of his decision to make peace: 'the visitors possessed a spirit which was more powerful than they had experienced'.[120] The reconciliation scene is transfigured because we see and *hear* every aspect of the drama differently. The actions of the Guugu Yimithirr are named. We have two languages. And we can sound at least some of the words that were uttered by the Guugu Yimithirr in 1770. The story suddenly opens out. The document reveals more than it was thought to reveal. As with the journals of Cook and Banks, the details in Eric's and Alberta's interpretation both concur and vary, with different points of emphasis between them. Eric conflates the two days of the turtle conflict and he makes no mention of neutral ground. His conclusion that the Guugu Yimithirr were 'sad to see [Cook] go' differs from Alberta's observation that they cleansed the country after his departure, and appears to gesture towards the contemporary politics of reconciliation, a movement which was then drawing awkwardly to a formal conclusion in 2001 when the text was unveiled in the James Cook Museum. But gesturing towards the present in the telling of history is inherent to its resonance. The past matters not only for itself. It matters because we give it life, because we seek to understand both its difference from the present and the traces of commonality that bind us to the lives of those who have gone before us. Alberta explicitly equates the interaction between Cook and the Guugu Yimithirr with her people's interaction with non-Indigenous society today: everything that happened between them in 1770 remains perpetually present.

For both the Guugu Yimithirr and Cooktown's non-Indigenous community, the shared history of Cook's visit is one bridge to reconciliation, not only locally but for Australia as well. In the eyes of Alberta and Loretta, Cooktown's founding moment is not the arrival of thousands of miners in the 1870s but the moment of reconciliation between Cook and the Guugu Yimithirr elder in 1770. 'They managed to communicate somehow', said Loretta, 'and Cook wrote in his journal: "I handed the spears back to him, which reconciled everything". And we believe that was the first recorded reconciliation in Australia's history, and that occurred here, on the Endeavour River'.[121] John MacDonald, who worked for several years on the script for the new re-enactment, admitted that he had faced opposition: some locals felt we 'took the jolly out of it', he said, 'but I saw the healing possibilities and therapeutic value of the drama. The re-enactment gave people a chance to meet on neutral ground. Doctors who performed met Aboriginal people in a completely different context'.[122] For Alberta, it was this spirit of peace and accommodation that ultimately 'paved the way' for the Australian nation and which will continue to sustain it in the future. As she explained, the reconciliation story also has a direct cultural relevance for Guugu Yimithirr people today.

It's not an easy thing to do because most of the kids today still want to spear Cook. It's an expected behavior that there was a confrontation and that it had to be hostile. Our mob struggle with the thought of the reconciliation, they're good at being hostile … but we need more reverence for our culture. We need more cultural grounding. They acted according to their own law and Aboriginal people have behaved with those characteristics since dispossession.[123]

The moment when peace is established between Cook and the Guugu Yimithirr is not only an allegory of reconciliation. It is also a parable of cultural integrity. At the same time as the story challenges non-Indigenous Australians to see their history from the Indigenous perspective, it also asks the Guugu Yimithirr to forsake some of their most deeply ingrained beliefs about Cook and the arrival of the British in Australia. Cook becomes more than the embodiment of invasion and dispossession; he is also the promise of peace and reconciliation. He plants the seeds and is gone. He claims possession without consent yet he also brings with him the law that will belatedly recognise native title more than two centuries later. He is at once the agent of destruction and the agent of redemption. A man who becomes a story that remains forever open-ended; a story that continually draws us back despite the fact that we know the whole tale will always elude us. Few have explained the significance of this transformation in the telling of Cooktown's founding moment better than historian Iain McCalman.

Cooktown is the Great Barrier Reef's Ur or foundational place of modern European–Australian and Aboriginal meeting, engage-ment and struggle. As such, it carries both tragic and hopeful traces of the past, which are being actively rethought in the present by Guugu Yimithirr elders like the late Eric Deeral and his historian niece, Alberta Hornsby. The surrounding countryside is austere and tough but achingly beautiful; it stands on a type of borderland between the temperate south and the tropical north. For me it thus represents both our past tragedy and our future possibility.[124]

Eric Deeral glimpsed some of this 'future possibility' before his death in 2012. Speaking of the 'culture shock', sickness and death that accompanied his community's evacuation to Woorabinda in 1942, he recalled how his people had no time to 'register' their sorrows. They had to cling to one another in order to survive. Instead of 'going down with it', they built their community anew from 'the remnants of that disaster'. Eric then cast his eye over the Guugu Yimithirr's entire history since the arrival of Europeans:

> When I look back at the whole history of the invasion of the Cookian people and establishment of the first missions … [there] is that strong concept that our people have—we are not going to bow down, we're just going to build the demolished Cookian nation again, and I believe that that strength is still there … we're coming back again like the proverbial kangaroo leaping back again.[125]

Survival, strength and cultural integrity were the histories Eric chose to tell. He remembered invasion, dispossession and displacement, but he did not allow this bleak legacy to cripple him. Instead he spoke of the future possibilities of the society that was *created* from that experience, a society in which Noel Pearson grew up with 'layered identities' and Alberta Hornsby spoke of having lived most of her life 'on the border'—a society of European, Chinese and Indigenous ancestry, one that was built on the back of generations of Aboriginal labour that made the settler economy viable, and one in which Eric's Christian faith merged with his Guugu Yimithirr spiritual beliefs, the 'whole concept of religion' being shared by white and black alike.[126]

For any of us to develop a truly honest and informed historical consciousness in Australia requires a double-act: to hold both the violent dispossession of Indigenous Australians and the steady emergence of a society built on equality, democracy and freedom from racial discrimination in our imagination at the same time, and to do so by hearing both the Indigenous and non-Indigenous perspectives. The shared telling of Cooktown's founding moment is one guiding light. The Guugu Yimithirr's decision to reconcile with

Cook transcends time and place. Both local and national in resonance, it changes Cooktown from a frontier town to a place of community and national rebirth.

––––––––––

On my last day in Cooktown, I climb Grassy Hill for the final time. Nearly two hundred and fifty years later, the outlook remains much the same as the one that greeted James Cook in 1770. Despite the road that rings the hill, the ubiquitous tourist viewing platform that crowns its crest and the dense vegetation that has long since replaced the open grasslands created by the Guugu Yimithirr's burning, the landscape Cook encountered still stretches away before you, the river's curl drawing your eyes deeper into the country beyond. Like the

Endeavour River from Grassy Hill at dusk, 2016

beaches of southern New South Wales and Victoria, the islands of Bass Strait, and the shores of Port Essington and Murujuga, it now seems impossible to separate the landscape from the stories that inhabit it. Lying at opposite ends of the country, their histories barely register in the nation's consciousness, yet if we choose to see them, they interconnect and resound across the thousands of kilometres that separate them, informing and enriching the continent.

Notes

Eyeing the Country

1   'Emotions of pleasure …', George B Worgan, 'Journal of a First Fleet Surgeon', 20 January – 11 July 1788, http://www.sl.nsw.gov.au/collection-items/collection-10-george-bouchier-worgan-letter-written-his-brother-richard-worgan-12-3; Banks observing the 'moving lights' on Botany Bay, 29 April 1770, in Ray Parkin (ed.), *H.M. Bark Endeavour*, Miegunyah, Melbourne 2006 (1997), p. 185.

2   ibid., Parkin (ed.), pp. 182–6; Banks wondering if he had left England 'for Ever', in his 'Endeavour Journal', 10 September 1768, http://www2.sl.nsw.gov.au/banks/series_03/03_016.cfm

3   Banks, 22 April 1770, in Parkin (ed.), p. 168.

4   Banks, 'Some Account of that Part of New Holland Now Called New South Wales', follows his journal entry for 26 August 1770; available online, http://gutenberg.net.au/ebooks05/0501141h.html#nsw

5   Richard Dunn, *The Telescope: A Short History*, Conway Publishing, Royal Observatory Greenwich, London, 2006, p. 8.

6   ibid., pp. 84–5.

7   Biddy Coolman's account in Keith Vincent Smith, 'Voices on the Beach', in Ace Bourke (curator), *Lines in the Sand: Botany Bay Stories from 1770*, Hazlehurst Regional Gallery, 2008, pp. 13, 15–16; available online, http://www.dnacreative.net.au/new/dna_creative___Hazelhurst_Regional_Gallery_files/LITS_96pp(FIN_REVREV)11-4-08.pdf; on possums, religious belief and the devil, see the evidence of Mahroot, the Aboriginal man from 'Botany Bay', taken before the 1845 'Select Committee on Aborigines', 8 September 1845, Government Printer, Sydney, p. 2; and interpretive panels at Kamay Botany Bay National Park Visitors' Centre.

8   Banks at the opera; see Patrick O'Brian, *Joseph Banks: A Life*, The Harvill Press, London, 1987, p. 65.

9   Watkin Tench, 1790, 'A Complete Account of the Settlement of Port Jackson', in L Fitzhardinge (ed.), *Sydney's First Four Years*, Library of Australian History, Sydney, 1979, pp. 162–3.

10 Banks, 'Some Account of that Part of New Holland Now Called New South Wales' (see note 4).

11 ibid.

12 Tim Winton, *Island Home: A Landscape Memoir*, Hamish Hamilton, Melbourne, 2015, p. 10; on the demise of Britishness in Australia, see James Curran and Stuart Ward, *The Unknown Nation: Australia after Empire*, Melbourne University Publishing, Carlton, 2010.

13 See, for example, Ann McGrath and Mary Anne Jebb (eds), *Long History Deep Time: Deepening Histories of Place*, ANU Press, Canberra, 2015; many Australian historians (including Keith Hancock, Alan Atkinson, Bill Gammage, Janet McCalman, Grace Karskens, Tom Griffiths, Peter Read and many others) have written intimate histories of place, yet in popular consciousness, national histories, particularly those drawing on war and military experience, have recently been far more prominent.

14 Robert Macfarlane, *The Old Ways: A Journey on Foot*, Hamish Hamilton, London, 2012, p. 323.

15 Kylie Northover, '"Australian Cities Don't Interest Me," Says British Author Will Self', *The Sydney Morning Herald*, 29 August 2015, http://www.smh.com.au/entertainment/books/australian-cities-dont-interest-me-says-british-author-will-self-20150828-gj9e9w.html

16 Greg Dening, 'Reflections', in *The Death of William Gooch: A History's Anthropology*, Melbourne University Press, Carlton, 1995, p. 157.

17 The best overview of this vast body of scholarship and the rise of Aboriginal history can be found in Bain Attwood, *Telling the Truth about Aboriginal History*, Allen & Unwin, Sydney, 2005, pp. 42–8.

18 Noel Pearson, 'A Rightful Place: Race, Recognition and a More Complete Commonwealth', *Quarterly Essay*, 55, 2014, p. 36.

19 I owe much here to Nicolas Rothwell's Eric Rolls Memorial Lecture, 'What Lies Beyond Us', delivered in Canberra, October 2014. 'Attention to the Australian landscape', writes Rothwell, 'itself dictates the best way of describing Australian experience'.

Chapter 1 Walking the Edge: South-East Australia, 1797

1   The outstanding scholarly work on the wreck of the *Sydney Cove* is Mike Nash, *Sydney Cove: The History and Archaeology of an Eighteenth Century Shipwreck*, Navarine Publishing, Hobart, 2009; Nash's work is indispensable and as a maritime archaeologist he understandably devotes comparatively little space to the walk of the survivors, focusing instead on the history and archaeology of the wreck.

2 For the identification of Aboriginal language groups I have relied on Bunjilaka, Melbourne Museum (http://museumvictoria.com.au/bunjilaka/visiting/first-peoples/victorian-languages), and the most recent scholarly work on New South Wales: Jutta Besold, 'Language Recovery of the New South Wales South Coast Aboriginal Languages', PhD, Australian National University 2013, pp. 1–5, Besold reproduces Tindale's map p. 63; From Ninety-Mile Beach, Victoria, to the Royal National Park just south of Sydney, the language groups are as follows: Tatungalung and Krauatungulung (both part of the Gunai-Kurnai language family), Bidwell Maap, Thaua (also spelt Dhawa or Thawa), Djirringanj, Dhurga, Dharumba, Wodi Wodi and Dharrawal; also see http://www.vaclang.org.au/Resources/maps.html

3 For the benefit of the reader and to avoid repetition, I have used contemporary place names throughout this chapter to mark the walkers' progress.

4 Including those places mentioned in the text, Cook named Ram Head, Cape Dromedary, Point Upright, Cape St. George, Red Point, Long Nose, Point Solander, Cape Banks and Point Sutherland.

5 Clark's name sometimes appears mistakenly in the historical record as 'Clarke'. To date, the details of William Clark's birth and death have not been known. But after discovering his death in Calcutta and the will of his brother John, I have been able to identify his place and date of birth after extensive searching of the Scottish government genealogy website www.scotlandspeople.gov.uk; a facsimile of William Clark's birth certificate can be found on the same site (26/2/1769 Clark, William [O.P.R. Births 507/0000110369 Campbeltown]); his parents were William Clark, merchant, Campbeltown, Argyll, Scotland (died 12 December 1778), married to Margaret Kilpatrick. Their children, all born in Campbeltown, County Argyll, were: James, born 19 November 1765 (no date of death); John (who was with William in Calcutta and arrived before him), born 14 June 1767, died 21 June 1804, buried in Campbeltown; William, 26 February 1769, (died 30 April 1800 in Calcutta although his death is of course not listed in the Scottish records, only in India); Kilpatrick, born 16 December 1770, died 1 November 1774; Charles, born 19 January 1773, died January 1791; Kilpatrick Clark, born 18 December 1774, died 25 December 1774; Ann, born 10 December 1775, (she is still alive in 1804 as John Clark refers to her in his will); Janet Clark, born 8 May 1778 (date of death unknown, most likely dead by 1804). William's mother, Margaret Kilpatrick, remarried after William Clark senior died in 1788, to James Pollock, 'writer' (lawyer), also of Campbeltown, to whom she had at least three more children, all of whom died in their first few years. She also gave birth to other children who were alive in 1804, because John Clark left his two 'half-sisters' 1500 pounds in his will. Margaret Kilpatrick died in 1788, while James Pollock died in 1819 in Campbeltown.

On the history of Campbeltown, Scotland, see Carol McNeill, *Old Campbeltown and Machrihanish*, Stenlake Publishing, 2004; William Smith, *Views of Campbeltown & Neighbourhood*, Edinburgh, 1835; Frank Bigwood, 'Campbeltown—A New Royal Burgh in the Eighteenth Century', in *The Campbeltown Book*, Kintyre Civic Society, Campbeltown, 2003; *The Statistical Account of Scotland 1791–1799*, edited by Sir John Sinclair, Vol. VIII, Argyll, in which Reverend John Smith writes on the Parish of Campbeltown; on Scottish emigration and life expectancy, TM Devine, *To the Ends of the Earth: Scotland's Global Diaspora, 1750–2010*, Allen Lane, London, 2011; also Andrew Blaikie, 'Rituals Transitions and Life Courses', in Trevor Griffiths and Graeme Morton (eds), *A History of Everyday Life in Scotland 1800 to 1900*, Edinburgh University Press, 2010, pp. 89–114, 98; Campbell and Clark are both listed as 'ship or boat owners' in Campbeltown 'from 1700–1800'; see *Campbeltown Custom House Reports and Extracts from the Records Preserved in the Office of the Collector at Campbeltown 1738–1848*, McEachran Collection No. 146, p. 56; 'Clark, Campbell & Co. of Campbeltown' were operating as merchants in Campbeltown in 1793; see *Kintyre Instructions: The 5th Duke of Argyll's Instructions to his Kintyre Chamberlain, 1785–1805*, Commentaries by Angus Martin, The Grimsay Press, Glasgow, 2011, p. 157.

6   For descriptions of Calcutta in the late eighteenth century, see Amasa Delano, *A Narrative of Voyages and Travels in the Northern and Southern Hemispheres*, Prager, New York, 1970 (first published 1817), pp. 237–49; and JP Losty, *Calcutta City of Palaces: A Survey of the City in the Days of the East India Company 1690–1858*, The British Library, London, 1990, pp. 37–8, 44–5; also see Krishna Dutta, *Calcutta: A Cultural and Literary History*, Signal Books, Oxford, 2003, pp. 22–7; and Suzanne Rickard, 'Lifelines from Calcutta' in James Broadbent, Suzanne Rickard & Margaret Steven, *India, China, Australia: Trade and Society 1788–1850*, Historic Houses Trust of NSW, Sydney, 2003, pp. 65–93.

7   Descriptions of 'the Course' in Losty, *Calcutta: City of Palaces*, p. 43; details of theatre in Dutta, p. 221; location of Campbell & Clark's agency in Theatre Street, in Margaret Steven, *Merchant Campbell 1769–1846: A Study of Colonial Trade*, Oxford University Press, Melbourne, 1965, p. 19; also see Janette Holcomb, *Early Merchant Families of Sydney*, Australian Scholarly Publishing, North Melbourne, 2013, pp. 16–21; advertisement in *Calcutta Gazette*, 27 October 1796, and see Mike Nash, pp. 21–4.

8   On the country traders, see ibid., Nash, pp. 25–8; on Storey and Campbell, see ibid., Holcomb, p. 21; names of ships from India to Sydney in David Collins, *An Account of the English Colony in New South Wales, Vol. 2*, edited by Brian Fletcher, AH Reed, Sydney, 1975, pp. 228–9.

9   Description of ship, Nash, p. 35; Hamilton was born on Arran, 1 March 1759 (birth certificate no. 553/0000100094); details on Hamilton in note 46;

although his Christian name sometimes appears as Guy (the name he often went by), Gavin is the name that I have used.

10 Description of Lascars in Delano, p. 242; on their origin, see http://www.banglastories.org/the-bengal-diaspora/history/ayahs-lascars-and-princes.html and Janet J Ewald, 'Crosses of the Sea: Slaves, Freedmen, and Other Migrants in the Northwest Indian Ocean, c. 1750–1914', *American Historical Review*, February 2000, pp. 69–91, 75–6; cargo of ship and details of crew in Gavin Hamilton, Ships' Protests of Bills 1792–1815, Judge Advocate's Office, Archives Office of New South Wales, Ref. 5/1162: pp. 64–73; also Nash, p. 39.

11 Details of Hamilton's instruments drawn from *Sydney Cove* exhibition panels at the Queen Victoria Museum, Launceston, Tasmania.

12 All details of the wreck are drawn from Gavin Hamilton, Ships' Protests of Bills 1792–1815, pp. 64–73.

13 RM Fowler, *The Furneaux Group, Bass Strait: A History*, Roebuck, Canberra, 1980, pp. 8–9.

14 Details of the survivors' first days on Preservation Island are also drawn from Hamilton's 'Protest'; from this point on, the story of the walk is related in Clark's journal, published as 'Narrative of the Shipwreck of Captain Hamilton and the Crew of the *Sydney Cove*', *Historical Records of New South Wales*, Vol. 3, pp. 760–8; Clark's account first appeared in the *Asiatic Mirror*, 27 December 1797 & 10 January 1798, followed closely by the *Calcutta Gazette*, Thursday 28 December 1797, pp. 1, 4, January 1798, p. 1 & 11 January 1798, p. 1.

15 A comparable journey was undertaken fifteen years earlier by the survivors of the *Grosvenor*, which departed from Calcutta and was wrecked on the coast of south-east Africa in 1782; see Stephen Taylor, *The Caliban Shore: The Fate of the* Grosvenor *Castaways*, Faber & Faber, London, 2004.

16 On shoes, see Broadbent, Rickard & Steven, p. 156 and exhibition panels, Queen Victoria Museum, Launceston.

17 Clark, 'Narrative of the Shipwreck of Captain Hamilton and the Crew of the *Sydney Cove*'.

18 Old Aboriginal man speaking via his son, Budginbro, quoted in Oswald Brierly, 'Wanderer' Journal, voyage from Plymouth to NSW 1841–1843, p. 6, Mitchell Library Microfilm 154530(0) (continued from 153510).

19 The names of Aboriginal territorial groups do not necessarily correspond with those of language groups. Territorial boundaries, language groups, tribal names and many cultural details remain contested due to insufficient evidence. See http://archives.samuseum.sa.gov.au/tribalmap/images/maps/level_3/images/E5.jpg (Tindale), also Jutta Besold, 'Language Recovery of the New South Wales South Coast Aboriginal Languages', ANU PhD, May 2013, Part A, p. 63; and on Tharawal, http://www.tharawal.com.au/who-we-are; details on Wallaga Lake see http://www.eurobodalla.com.au/indigenous

20 Bundarwa, see Besold, ibid., Part B, p. 112.

21 We know that Clark was speared in his hands not from his journal but from Hamilton's 'Protest'.

22 This portrayal of the carpenter can be found in Reverend TF Palmer to Reverend Dr Disney, 14 August 1797; published in *The Monthly Repository of Theology and General Literature*, Vol. 12, 1817, pp. 264–6; Palmer had talked with Clark after he arrived in Sydney.

23 Clark's thoughts on Thompson, see Palmer, ibid.

24 Account of the rescue, Governor Hunter to Sir Joseph Banks, 1 August 1797, A1787, CY 866, pp. 33–7, Mitchell Library.

25 Hunter to Duke of Portland, 6 July 1797, *Historical Records of New South Wales,* Vol. III, pp. 277–8.

26 Clark's arrival in Sydney, Hunter to Sir Joseph Banks, 15 August 1797, letters of Governor Hunter 1795–1802, Mitchell Library, A1787, CY866, pp. 33–7; journalist's account of his voyage in *Calcutta Gazette*, 14 December 1797; on early Sydney: signal mast at South Head, see http://www.woollahra.nsw.gov.au/__data/assets/pdf_file/0009/16488/South_Head_signal_st_sheet_2_-_layout.pdf; first church, see http://www.sl.nsw.gov.au/discover_collections/history_nation/religion/places/; Government House, see http://www.environment.gov.au/heritage/places/national/first-government-house; wooden bridge over the Tank Stream, see MF Peron, *Account of Port Jackson and Sydney Town, New South Wales*, reproduced in the *Bombay Courier*, Vol. 20, Issue 940, 8 September 1810; the polluted state of the stream, see Collins, p. 28.

27 Reverend TF Palmer to Reverend Dr Disney, 14 August 1797; Palmer had reportedly lived for a while with the Eora, see his biographical entry, http://adb.anu.edu.au/biography/palmer-thomas-fyshe-2535; 'extremity of the globe', Matthew Flinders, Tom Thumb Journal, in Tim Flannery (ed.), *Terra Australis*, Text, Melbourne, 2000, p. 3; 'unsettled part', Collins, pp. 27–8.

28 Hunter's account can be found in his letters to Banks, 1 & 15 August 1797; also see Hunter to Duke of Portland, pp. 277–8; Collins, pp. 27–33; Flinders's account in Matthew Flinders, *A Voyage to Terra Australis Vol. 1*, W Bulmer & Co, London, 1814, p. civ.

29 Hamilton's 'Protest'.

30 ibid.

31 Hunter to Banks, 1 August 1797; if, as Hunter claimed, Hamilton was the last European left on the island, then Thomas Valence, who signed Hamilton's 'Protest' (together with Hamilton and William Clark), was not a member of the *Sydney Cove*'s crew, as is often claimed.

32 ibid.; also see Hamilton's 'Protest'; I am indebted to James Luddington for his advice on the flora and fauna of Preservation Island; on mutton-birds, see Flinders, p. cxxxiv; and Charles Begg & Neil C Begg, *The World of*

John Boultbee: Including an Account of Sealing in Australia and New Zealand, Whitcoulls Publishers, Christchurch, 1979, p. 61.

33 ibid., Hamilton's 'Protest'.

34 ibid.

35 ibid.; storm in Sydney and account of the rescue, see Collins, p. 32; also Captain Kent to Secretary Nepean, 19 November 1797, http://gutenberg. net.au/ebooks13/1300541h.html; and Hunter to Banks, 1 August 1797.

36 Hamilton's 'Protest'; Hunter to Banks, 15 August 1797; also Reverend TF Palmer to Reverend Dr Disney, 14 August 1797; *Bombay Courier,* Vol. 7, No. 275, 1798, 6 January 1798 ('By the *Britannia,* accounts are received of the loss of the ship Sidney [*sic*] Cove, Captain Hamilton, which sailed from hence on the 10th of November, 1796 for Port Jackson').

37 On spirits, see Hunter, 12 December 1796, *Historical Records of Australia,* p. 70 and Collins, p. 57; on Irish convicts and Bass, see Hunter to Portland, 1 March 1798, http://gutenberg.net.au/ebooks13/1300541h.html

38 ibid., Hunter to Portland, 1 March 1798, and Collins, p. 68; also see Lieutenant James Grant in his account of the voyage of the *Lady Nelson, Historical Records of New South Wales, Vol. IV.—Hunter and King. 1800–02,* FM Bladen (ed.), NSW Government, 1896, pp. 478–9.

39 'Narrative of the Shipwreck of Captain Hamilton and the Crew of the *Sydney Cove', Historical Records of New South Wales,* Vol. 3, pp. 760–8; on Hamilton's return to Preservation Island, see Collins, p. 58; on Clark in Calcutta, see *Calcutta Gazette,* 4 January 1798 ('Messrs Campbell & Clark beg to inform their friends and the public, that Mr. William Clark and Mr. Robert Campbell, Junior, are this day admitted partners in their house, and the business will for the future be carried on, under the Firm of Campbell and Clark'); examples of articles in England and Scotland, *London Packet or New Lloyd's Evening Post,* 28 September – 1 October, 1798, Issue 4540; *Morning Post and Gazetteer,* 28 September 1798, Issue 9275*; Star,* 3 October 1798, Issue 3132; *Caledonian Mercury,* Midlothian, Scotland, 24 September 1798.

40 Flinders and Hamilton on Preservation Island, see Dan Sprod (ed.), *Van Diemen's Land Revealed: Flinders and Bass and Their Circumnavigation of the Island in the Colonial Sloop* Norfolk *1798–1799,* Blubber Head Press, Hobart, 2009, pp. 17–22; also Flinders, pp. cxxxiv–xxxv; on Hunter and the wombat, see Hunter to Banks, 5 August 1797 and Henry Nicholls, 'The Tale of a Wombat: A Journey from Australia to Newcastle upon Tyne', *Guardian Australia,* 30 December 2013, http://www.theguardian.com/science/ animal-magic/2013/dec/30/wombat-australia-to-newcastle-upon-tyne

41 On sealers, see Charles Begg & Neil C Begg, pp. 58–60; on sealers and Baudin, see Tim Jetson, *An Island of Contentment?: A History of Preservation Island,* Garrots Pty. Ltd., Launceston, 1994, pp. 7–10.

42   On Campbell's arrival and Hamilton's death, see Collins, p. 84; inscription on Hamilton's grave, JH Watson's article on the wreck of the *Sydney Cove*, *The McIvor Times and Rodney Advertiser* (Heathcote, Victoria), 11 July 1907, p. 3.

43   Clark trading in Calcutta, *Calcutta Gazette*, 8 August 1799 ('Messrs John & Wm. Clark, Having relinquished their shares and Interest in the House of Campbell, Clark & Co. beg leave to advise their friends at a distance from the Presidency, that it is their intention to continue to act as agents and to supply wines and goods of every description, that may be required from Calcutta ... 13th July 1799'; shortly after this, John and William Clark took up in partnership with Allan Maclean); also see Margaret Steven, *Merchant Campbell 1769–1846: A Study of Colonial Trade*, p. 100; Clark's death reported in *Calcutta Gazette*, 8 May 1800, p. 1, also in *Bombay Courier*, Vol. 9, 31 May 1800, and *The Bengal Obituary*, Holmes & Co., Calcutta, 1851, p. 84; conclusive proof that this is indeed our William Clark came in an advertisement placed by his brother, John, in the *Calcutta Gazette*, 8 May 1800 ('Notice is hereby given, that in consequence of the death of Mr. William Clark, the Co-partnership of Clarks and Maclean, is this day dissolved, and the Business will, in future, be carried on by John Clark and Allan Maclean, under the firm of Clark and Maclean. Calcutta, April 30 1800'); on Campbell, see Holcomb, pp. 21–8.

44   Dutta, p. 80.

45   'Will of John Clark, Merchant of Calcutta, East Indies', 27 August 1804, Public Record Office, The National Archives, Kew, catalogue reference: prob 11/1412/291; a PDF can be found online http://discovery. nationalarchives.gov.uk/details/r/D339542; his death on 21 June 1804 is recorded in Scotland's record of births, deaths and marriages ('OPR. Deaths 5070000200182 Campbeltown'); John Clark's death is also noted in *The Scots Magazine*, 1 July 1804, p. 88 (Deaths: '21. [June] At Campbeltown, John Clark, Esq. late of Bengal'); same also noted in *Caledonian Mercury*, 30 June 1804, p. 3.

46   John Hamilton of 'The Pound', Heathcote, Victoria, to Captain JH Watson, vice-president, Australian Historical Society, 18 April 1910, in 'Collection of Pamphlets Consisting Mainly of Australian Biographies', Mitchell Library, Pam file/Q921-QA920; the discovery of this letter had significant implications. It was evidence that Peter Hamilton (born in Arran) was Gavin Hamilton's nephew, which of course meant that Peter's father and Gavin were brothers. With the help of Jean Glen on Arran, I was then able to trace Gavin's birth on Arran (1 March 1759). Gavin's father, James, also fathered a son William, who later became the father of Peter Hamilton (mentioned in the letter above by his son, John Hamilton). Further proof of the Heathcote Hamilton family's connection to Gavin can be found in

The McIvor Times and Rodney Advertiser (Heathcote, Victoria), 24 July 1913, p. 2 ('Death. Hamilton. On the 20th July, at the residence of his nephew, Harry Hamilton, Heathcote, McIvor, James Thomas Gunn Hamilton, farmer, Cornelia, youngest son of the late Captain Peter Hamilton, mariner and shipowner, Port Glasgow, 1840, and grand nephew of Captain Gavin Hamilton, commander of the ship *Sydney Cove*, which was wrecked on 8th Feby [*sic*], 1797, on Preservation Island. Born in Melbourne, 9th March 1842. A resident in the district since 1847').

47 ibid., 12 July 1910.

48 F Campbell, of 'Yarralumla' Queanbeyan, to Watson, 1 June 1910, in same folder above (the letter tells the slightly altered version of the story: 'Captain Hamilton lost the "Sydney Cove" on an island in Bass' Straits [*sic*] & took to a whaleboat with several of the crew, in which they made for the mainland of Australia. They sighted land at the ninety mile Beach, but unfortunately in landing the whaleboat was upset in the surf & all drowned except the Captain & three sailors. All was lost except the clothes in which they stood. Then they started to walk along the seacoast to Sydney. The blacks frequently met them but in no way molested them. After months of painful & slow progress they did manage at last to crawl to Sydney, where the Captain was laid up by his sufferings in the Hospital, from which he died"); on Hamilton's grave, see 'Old Sydney Cemeteries', *The Sydney Morning Herald*, 21 January 1897, p. 3 and *The Sydney Morning Herald*, 30 August 1930, p. 11.

49 ibid., Campbell; and Holcomb, pp. 21–8. Bicentenary of walk and Hamilton family visit, Queen Victoria Museum, Launceston and Verna J Cooper, *The Hamilton Story of Captain Peter Hamilton and His Wife Jane and Their Ancestors in Scotland and Their Descendants in Australia*, self-published, 2006 (kindly sent to me by Jean Glen in Arran); I also spoke with Della Metzke and Peter Hamilton, both descendants of Peter (nephew of Gavin) Hamilton, who perished entering Port Phillip Bay in 1842.

50 MF Peron, *Account of Port Jackson and Sydney Town, New South Wales*; Hunter on Bass, Hunter to Portland, 1 March 1798, *Historical Records of Australia*, pp. 132–3.

51 *The Mercury*, 14 & 15 December 1944, p. 14.

52 'Protest Against Disaster', *The Sydney Morning Herald*, 22 December 1951, p. 7.

53 'Forgotten History', *The Argus*, 16 June 1917, p. 8; *The Mercury*, 14 December 1944, pp. 14 & 15 December 1944, p. 8; 'History of Bass Strait Began with Wreck', *The Mercury*, 14 December 1944, p. 14; and *The Mercury*, 9 October 1937, p. 14; similar first white man stories were published in England; see, for example, *Shields Daily Gazette*, 20 February 1892, p. 5 under 'Facts and Scraps' ('The first European who trod Victorian soil is believed to have

been Mr. Clarke [*sic*], the supercargo, and some of the crew of The Sydney Cove, a vessel wrecked in 1779 [*sic*] on Furneaux').

54 *Gippsland Times*, 20 July 1922, p. 5.

55 '150th Anniversary of Coal Discovery in NSW', *The Sydney Morning Herald*, 2 August 1947; note from Tathra Plaque, from my visit there.

56 Isaac Selby, *The Pilgrims of New Holland or the Wreck of the Sydney Cove, a Drama in Five Acts*, 1956, manuscript, State Library of Victoria.

57 'Forgotten History', *The Argus*, 16 June 1917, p. 8; on 1 June 1804, Governor King wrote to Lieutenant Governor Paterson regarding an 'American Vessel, now said to be lying in Kent's Bay among Cape Barren Islands, where the crew are building [a] Vessel from the remains of the Sydney Cove's Wreck and other Timber which they have collected on different parts of this Coast, and have erected a Dwelling' (*Historical Records of Australia*, Series 3, Vol. 1, p. 589). He instructed Paterson to place the King's mark on any of the timbers he found so as to stop this; Paterson reached the island in November, and this was the last record of the wreck. As Mike Nash points out, it remained undisturbed for 170 years.

58 *The Launceston Examiner*, 4 January 1977, p. 3.

59 Mike Nash's *Sydney Cove* is the authoritative source on the excavation of the wreck and the survivors' camp, and the developing story of its heritage status.

60 http://www.ulladulla.info/sydney-cove-wreck-1797

61 http://thedirton.therocks.com/2010/08/fire-water-sydney-cove-shipwreck.html

Chapter 2 'World's End': Port Essington, Cobourg Peninsula, Western Arnhem Land

1 'World's End' in John McArthur's 'Notebook', Port Essington 1838–1850, rear inside cover, Northern Territory Archives, NTRS3601; the best general historical works on Victoria Settlement are Peter Spillett, *Forsaken Settlement: An Illustrated History of the Settlement of Port Essington North Australia, 1838–1849*, Landsdowne Press, Sydney, 1972; Alan Powell, *Far Country: A Short History of the Northern Territory*, Charles Darwin University Press, 2009 (first published 1982); John Mulvaney, *Encounters in Place: Outsiders and Aboriginal Australians 1606–1985*, University of Queensland Press, 1989, pp. 68–74; Jim Allen, 'Port Essington: The Historical Archaeology of a North Australian Nineteenth-Century Military Outpost', *Studies in Australasian Historical Archaeology*, Vol. 1, Sydney University Press, 2008; and Warwick Anderson, *The Cultivation of Whiteness: Science, Health and Racial Destiny in Australia*, Melbourne University Press, 2002, pp. 76–80.

2 'check-mate', George Windsor Earl to Captain Washington, 16 August 1838, in Earl, *Enterprise in Tropical Australia*, edited by Bob Reece, Northern Territory University Press, Darwin, 2002 (first published 1846), p. 16;

possession 'much debated', J Lort Stokes, *Discoveries in Australia*, T & W Boone, London, 1846, p. 388; 'immense body of light', Henry Ennis, *Remarks on Board His Majesty's Ship* Tamar, facsimile edition, Richard Griffin, Melbourne, 1983 (1825), p. 14.

3   ibid., Ennis, pp. 10–11; Ennis described the ritual of taking possession as a kind of 'magic' while at Fort Dundas.

4   ibid., Ennis; John Septimus Roe, Letters: *The Experienced Navigator Returns to Australian Waters: The Voyage of the* Tamar *15 February 1824–18 July 1825*, http://acms.sl.nsw.gov.au/item/itemdetailpaged.aspx?itemid=910906

5   On Dutch ship, 1705, see http://www.ntlis.nt.gov.au/placenames/view.jsp?id=17911; on King's visit to Port Essington, Phillip Parker King, *Narrative of a Survey of the Inter-Tropical and Western Coasts of Australia Vol. 1*, Friends of the State Library of South Australia (first published 1827), Adelaide, 2012, p. 87; on Bremer at Port Essington, see ibid., Ennis, p. 11.

6   *Sydney Gazette*, 25 August 1838, p. 2.

7   ibid.; on spacious harbour, *The Australian*, 10 March 1825, p. 3; on the future emporium, George Windsor Earl, *Sailing Directions for the Arafura Sea: Compiled from the Narratives of Lieuts Kolff and Modera of the Dutch Navy*, Hydrographic Office, London 1839, http://www.nla.gov.au/apps/doview/nla.aus-f2747-p.pdf

8   George Chaloupka, *Journey in Time: The 50,000-year Story of the Australian Aboriginal Rock Art of Arnhem Land*, Reed New Holland, Sydney, 2010 (1993), pp. 191–4; also see Marshall Clark & Sally K May (eds), *Macassan History and Heritage: Journeys, Encounters and Influences*, ANU Press, Canberra, 2013, especially the chapter by Maggie Brady, 'Drug Substances Used by the Maccassans: The Mystery of the Tobacco Pipe', and her reference to Yolngu informants claiming some of their people had 'lived in Maccassar for many years', p. 257; in addition, see 'Trip of the Flying Cloud to Port Essington', *Northern Territory Times and Gazette*, 20 February 1874, p. 3, in which Jack Davis 'remembered the officers and men of the old settlement; he had been to Singapore and China with a Captain Bisset; and he said he could speak Malay as well as English'.

9   Bruce Birch, 'Confalonieri's Manuscripts', in Stefano Girola and Roland Pizzini, *Nagoyo: The Life of don Angelo Confalonieri among the Aborigines of Australia 1846–1848*, Fondazione Museo Storico Del Trino, pp. 107–54, 108–9.

10   On rock art, see George Chaloupka, *Journey in Time,* pp. 191–92; on Indigenous place names in Cobourg today, see http://www.environment.gov.au/node/35961

11   On church, see Stokes, p. 385; on arrival at Port Essington, see George Augustus Earl, *Enterprise in Tropical Australia*, with an Introduction by RHW Reece, NTU Press, Darwin, 2002, pp. 5, 32–4.

12   ibid., Earl; on Barker, see Mulvaney, *Encounters in Place,* p. 69; on Smyth, see John Connor, *The Australian Frontier Wars 1788–1838*, UNSW Press, 2002, p. 74.

13   'not a soul among us', Earl to Captain John Washington, 16 August 1838, in JM Cameron (ed.), *Letters from Port Essington 1838–1845*, Historical Society of the Northern Territory, Darwin, 1999, p. 15; otherwise, Earl, *Enterprise in Tropical Australia*, pp. 32–40.

14   ibid., Earl, *Enterprise in Tropical Australia*, pp. 59–60; 'venetian blinds' quoted in *Cobourg Peninsular Historic Sites, Gurig National Park Volume 1*, Conservation Plan, Parks and Wildlife Commission of the Northern Territory, November 1999, p. 14; Bremer to Barrow, Secretary of the Admiralty, 9 February 1839, in Cameron (ed.), *Letters from Port Essington 1838–1845*, p. 26; details on Miro and other Aborigines, also 'bringing in honey', see 'Port Essington' in *The Australian*, 20 July 1839, p. 3.

15   McArthur to ED Thomson, 20 September 1842; on architecture at Port Essington, see David Bridgman, *Acclimatization: Architecture at the Top End of Australia*, Royal Australian Institute of Architects, Canberra, 2003, pp. 4, 18–21.

16   Marine journeys inland, Lieutenant Peter Benson Stewart, 16 November 1838, in Cameron (ed.), *Letters from Port Essington*, p. 21; 'charm of novelty', Earl, *Enterprise in Tropical Australia*, p. 38; crocodiles and white ants, Bremer to Captain Francis Beaufort, Hydrographic Office, London, 9 December 1838, in Cameron, *Letters from Port Essington,* pp. 16–17.

17   Earl, *Enterprise in Tropical Australia*, p. 18; missing sailor found, 'Port Essington', *The Australian*, 20 July 1839 p. 3; Aboriginal bushcraft, Lieutenant PB Stewart's journal of an expedition into the interior of the Cobourg Peninsula, May 1839, in Cameron (ed.), *Letters from Port Essington*, pp. 54–8; fish floating to the surface, Alfred Searcy quoted in Philip A Clarke, *Australian Plants as Aboriginal Tools*, Rosenberg, Sydney, 2012, p. 51.

18   French officer quoted in Cameron, introduction to *Letters from Port Essington*, p. 7; bottles found, Allen, 'Port Essington', p. 48; d'Urville's visit, *Cobourg Peninsular Historic Sites Gurig National Park Volume 1*, p. 14; Allen, 'Port Essington', p. 93; and Edward Duyker, *Dumont d'Urville: Explorer and Polymath*, Otago University Press, 2014, pp. 404–11.

19   Earl, *Enterprise in Tropical Australia*, p. 7 (Reece's introduction) and p. 62; McArthur was the nephew of wool pioneer John Macarthur.

20   On the cyclone, McArthur in Allen, 'Port Essington', p. 120; 'Port Essington and the Passage to Timor and Swan River, from the Remarks of Commander Owen Stanley, H.M.S. Britomart', *Nautical Magazine*, September 1840, pp. 583–4.

21   Mulvaney, *Encounters in Place*, p. 69; Bridgman, p. 21.

22 Waiting for letters, see Stokes, p. 384; on McArthur's exasperation, see his letters, especially to ED Thomson, 24 August 1843 and to GW Hope, 28 November 1844, in Cameron (ed.), *Letters from Port Essington*, pp. 131–2, 139–42.

23 Stanley's production of the play, *Cobourg Peninsular Historic Sites Gurig National Park Volume 1*, p. 15; on Reynolds' *Cheap Living*, see Google Books; Hutchings, see Henry Keppel, *A Visit to the Indian Archipelago*, Richard Bentley, London, 1853, pp. 174–5; on games, see McArthur to Gipps, 3 September 1841, in Cameron, *Letters from Port Essington*, p. 96.

24 HJ Firth & JH Calaby (eds), *Fauna Survey of the Port Essington District, Cobourg Peninsula, Northern Territory of Australia*, CSIRO, 1974, pp. 2, 7, 10.

25 Examples include Jim Allen and Peter Corris (eds), *The Journal of John Sweatman: A Nineteenth Century Surveying Voyage in North Australia and Torres Strait*, UQP, 1977; Alexander Sibbald, Diary, Northern Territory Archives, Manuscript; Henry Keppel, *A Visit to the Indian Archipelago*.

26 ibid., Sibbald, Diary.

27 *The Journal of John Sweatman*, pp. xxvii, 146–7.

28 ibid., McArthur to James Stephen, 20 September 1842, in Cameron (ed.), *Letters from Port Essington*, pp. 106–10.

29 On Neinmal, see John MacGillivray, *Narrative of the Voyage of H.M.S. Rattlesnake*, vol. 1, T & W Boone, 1852, pp. 152–6 and Mulvaney, *Encounters in Place*, p. 70.

30 McArthur to Gipps, 2 November 1840, in Cameron (ed.), *Letters from Port Essington*, p. 78; Sibbald, Diary; details on Jack Davis, on-site information, Victoria Settlement.

31 The Notebook of John McArthur, Manuscript, Northern Territory Archives; Gipps to Lord Stanley, 15 December 1845, and McArthur to GW Hope, 28 November 1844, in Cameron (ed.), *Letters from Port Essington*, pp. 139–42, 168; Victoria was never conceived as a convict settlement, although nineteen convicts worked there as stone masons in 1844–45 (*Cobourg Peninsular Historic Sites, Gurig National Park Volume 1: Conservation Plan*, Parks and Wildlife Commission of the Northern Territory, November 1999, p. 23).

32 EM Webster (ed.), *An Explorer at Rest: Ludwig Leichhardt's Journals*, Melbourne University Press, 1986, pp. 19–23.

33 ibid., p. 23.

34 ibid., pp. 23–44, 69; on Leichhardt's return to Sydney, see *South Australian Register*, 29 April 1846, p. 3.

35 Citta del Vaticano, Roma, Archivio Propaganda Fide, Seritt Riferite nei Congressi, Oceania, 1842–1845, T.2 548–1067, Leaf 993, Letter from the Propagation of the Faith, Lyon, 19 July 1845, guaranteeing 'quarante mille francs' for the mission to Australia; Leaf 995–6, another letter from Cardinal

Fransoni, Prefetto della S. Congne de Propaganda Fide, Roma, dated 15 July 1845 includes a guarantee of 100 '*franche*'; also see leaves 1002–03, Angelo Confalonieri (in London) to his superiors in Rome, 12 September 1845; and Rolando Pizzini, 'Angelo Confalonieri in Australia', in Stefano Girola and Rolando Pizzini (eds), *Nagoyo: The Life of don Angelo Confalonieri …*', pp. 31, 44, 47; Archbishop Polding in Sydney believed Catholic missionaries would help to stem the settlers' determination to emulate the Portuguese and Spanish in the Americas by enslaving the natives or hunting them to extinction; see *Nagoyo*, pp. 48–50.

36   The best account of Angelo's shipwreck is in *The Journal of John Sweatman*, pp. 114–16; on his treks in the Alps, Maurizio Dalla Serra, 'A Biographical Profile of Angelo Confalonieri', in Stefano Girola and Rolando Pizzini (eds), *Nagoyo*, p. 28; Angelo writing of his plight, see his letters written in May 1846 and published belatedly in *The Sydney Chronicle*, 6 January 1847, and another letter published in the same paper on 16 January 1847; on his intention to establish a mission before the Protestants, see Angelo's letter to Rome, shortly before his departure from Sydney in April 1846, Citta del Vaticano, Roma, Archivio Propaganda Fide, Seritt Riferite nei Congressi, Oceania, 1846–1847, T.3, leaves 26–7 (my thanks to Nick Eckstein for this translation).

37   *immensa distanza,* see Angelo Confalonieri's letter to Propaganda Fide, 1 October 1847, Citta del Vaticano, Roma, Archivio Propaganda Fide, Seritt Riferite nei Congressi, Oceania, 1846–1847, T.3, leaf 791; also, Angelo's letter in *The Sydney Chronicle*, 16 January 1847, p. 3; details of Angelo's hut, Oswald Brierly Journal, Manuscript only, undated, 1848, H.M. *Rattlesnake, North Australian Coast*, Mitchell Library.

38   *The Journal of John Sweatman*, p. 116.

39   Angelo quoted in Rolando Pizzini, 'Angelo Confalonieri in Australia', in Stefano Girola and Rolando Pizzini (eds), *Nagoyo*, p. 61; his boast at having mastered their language, Angelo Confalonieri's letter to his superiors in Rome, 4 October 1847, Citta del Vaticano, Roma, Archivio Propaganda Fide, Seritt Riferite nei Congressi, Oceania, 1846–1847, T.3, leaf 792; on Jim Crow, *The Journal of John Sweatman*, p. 148; on Angelo at Port Essington, also see Spillett, *Forsaken Settlement*, pp. 146–8.

40   Angelo's map, Bruce Birch, 'Confalonieri's Manuscripts', in Stefano Girola and Roland Pizzini, *Nagoyo*, pp. 147–52.

41   Angelo's beautifully written 'Specimen of the Aboriginal Language or Short Conversation with the Natives of North Australia Port Essington 1847', 'Angel. Confalonieri. Mis. [Missionary]' is attached to his letter to Rome, dated 4 October 1847, Citta del Vaticano, Roma, Archivio Propaganda Fide, Seritt Riferite nei Congressi, Oceania, 1846–1847, T.3, letter and manuscript, leaves 794–807; Confalonieri produced an earlier draft of this

manuscript in 1846, which varied slightly from the 1847 document he sent to Rome. The earlier draft is held in the Sir George Grey Collection of the Auckland City Libraries in New Zealand; Bruce Birch is the authority on both manuscripts. See his 'Confalonieri's Manuscripts' in Stefano Girola and Rolando Pizzini (eds), *Nagoyo*, pp. 107–52.

42   *The Journal of John Sweatman*, p. 116; also see TH Huxley's *Diary of the Voyage of HMS* Rattlesnake, edited from the published Manuscript by Julian Huxley, Doubleday & Co, New York, 1972 (first published 1936), p. 116.

43   ibid., Huxley, p. 117; *The Journal of John Sweatman*, p. 116; on 'closely related' languages and skin name see Bruce Birch, 'Confalonieri's Manuscripts', in Stefano Girola and Roland Pizzini, *Nagoyo*, pp. 108–14, 120–4.

44   'esteemed man', McArthur to Polding, quoted in DF Bourke, *The History of the Catholic Church in Western Australia*, undated, Archdiocese of Perth; denying God, John MacGillivray, *Narrative of the Voyage of H.M.S. Rattlesnake*, Vol. 1, p. 158; McArthur recorded dining with Angelo in his 'Notebook'; the description of Dunbar's visit is in Oswald Brierly, Journal, Manuscript only, *H.M.* Rattlesnake, *North Australian Coast*, undated entry but November 1848.

45   ibid., Brierly, Journal; curtains blowing, Brierly, *Journal with Sketches*, *H.M.* Rattlesnake, *North Australian Coast, Port Essington*, Manuscript, Mitchell Library.

46   ibid., Brierly, *Journal with Sketches*, 9 November 1848.

47   ibid., 11 November 1848.

48   ibid., 15 November 1848.

49   Sibbald, Diary.

50   'great desert', John Beete Jukes, *Narrative of the Voyage of H.M.S. Fly*', T & W Boone, London 1847, p. 363; 'Malay curry', Brierly, *Journal with Sketches*, 15 November; 'beyond keeping the houses', *The Journal of John Sweatman*, p. 140; 'sombre …', Jukes quoted in Alan Powell, *Far Country: A Short History of the Northern Territory*, Charles Darwin University Press, 2009, p. 45; 'barren', *The Colonist*, 14 July 1836, p. 2; McArthur on the 'mimic Babel', in his crucial letter to GW Hope, 28 November 1844, in Cameron, *Letters from Port Essington*, p. 141.

51   'blot …', 'Abandonment of Port Essington', *South Australian Register*, 21 November 1849, p. 3; T Huxley, *Diary of the Voyage of HMS Rattlesnake*, pp. 113–16; McArthur's poems are in his 'Notebook', Manuscript, Northern Territory Archives; 'pent-up', Brierly, *Journal with Sketches*, 11 November 1848; 'nostalgia', Edward Duyker, *Dumont d'Urville: Explorer and Polymath*, p. 411; Huxley's 'ill-managed hole', quoted in Iain McCalman, *Darwin's Armada*, Viking (Penguin), Camberwell, Victoria, 2009, p. 193.

52   Henry Keppel, *A Visit to the Indian Archipelago*, p. 150; Brierly, *Journal with Sketches*, 16 November 1848.

53 ibid., Keppel, p. 154, and on his impressions of Port Essington and Aboriginal people, pp. 153–90.

54 ibid., Keppel, p. 190; death of men while loading in *Cobourg Peninsular Historic Sites Gurig National Park Volume 1*, p. 27.

55 ibid., Keppel, p. 190.

56 'busy pushing capitalists', McArthur to GW Hope, 28 November 1844, in Cameron (ed.), *Letters from Port Essington*, p. 140.

57 Extracts from the private log of T Beckford Simpson, Master of the Barque *General Palmer* when employed by Her Majesty's Colonial Government to make enquiries after Dr Leichhardt and his party, 2 June 1851; 'ring-fence', Sir John Barrow, quoted in Alan Powell, *Far Country*, p. 45; on Australian failed settlements, see Graham Connah, 'It Didn't Always Work: Investigating the Sites of Failed Settlement', Chapter 4 in his *The Archaeology of Australia's History*, Cambridge University Press, 1993; overseas examples of failed colonial settlements are numerous; see Ed Wright, *Ghost Colonies: Failed Utopias, Forgotten Exiles and Abandoned Outposts of Empire*, Millers Point, 2009; and Robert Aldrich, *Greater France: A History of French Overseas Expansion*, London, 1996, pp. 84–5.

58 Cobourg Peninsula today, see National Parks information site, https://nt.gov.au/__data/assets/pdf_file/0017/200069/garig-gunak-barlu-national-park.pdf; on environmental legacy of the settlement, John Mulvaney, *Encounters in Place*, p. 74; on 'Flash Poll', see *Alfred Searcy, In Australian Tropics,* George Robertson & Co., Sydney, 1909, pp. 57–8, and 'A Visit to the Abandoned Settlement of Port Essington', *South Australian Register*, 18 May 1891, p. 6; on Jack Davis, 'Trip of the Flying Cloud to Port Essington', *Northern Territory Times and Gazette*, 20 February 1874, p. 3; on objects collected from Port Essington see 'Encounters' exhibition online, http://www.nma.gov.au/exhibitions/encounters/mapping/port_essington & the exhibition catalogue, *Encounters: Revealing Stories of Aboriginal and Torres Strait Islander Objects from the British Museum*, National Museum of Australia Press, Canberra, 2015, pp. 76–81. Traces of Port Essington's story resurfaced in surprising ways. In 1977, composer Peter Sculthorpe wrote 'Port Essington: for Strings', a 6-movement piece he described as his 'most Australian work'. Borrowing an Aboriginal chant originally recorded by AP Elkin, Sculthorpe transformed it into a 'European idiom', imitating the marines' borrowing of Aboriginal words, movement and dance. See the liner notes to Sculthorpe's 'Port Essington', 1977, ABC Classics ABC454504-2, 1996, originally commissioned for Thomas Keneally's script for the ABC television film on Port Essington in 1974.

59 Kangaroo dance on the deck of the *Meander*, Keppel, *A Visit to the Indian Archipelago*, p. 190.

60 Iwaidja to English, free translation by Bruce Birch.

61 George Chaloupka, *Journey in Time: The 50,000-Year Story of the Australian Aboriginal Rock Art of Arnhem Land*, pp. 45–6, 191–2, 214; the image of Leichhardt became public knowledge in 2009; see http://www.abc.net.au/news/2009-03-08/traditional-owners-unveil-leichhardt-rock-art/1612708.

62 rock art as 'history book', Ronald Lamilami quoted by Sally K May et al., 'Painting History: Indigenous Depictions and Observations of the "Other" in Northwestern Arnhem Land, Australia', *Australian Archaeology*, No. 71, December 2010, pp. 57–65.

Chapter 3 'Hip Bone Sticking Out': Murujuga and the Legacy of the Pilbara Frontier

1 My thanks to Rio Tinto and my guide, Mandy Leeming; information sheet provided by Rio.

2 George Seddon, 'Visions of the Pilbara', in Ann Hamblin (ed.), *Visions of Future Landscapes: Proceedings of the Australian Academy of Science 1999*, Canberra, 1999; Iain Copp, *Geology & Landforms of the Pilbara*, Government of Western Australia, Department of Environment and Conservation, Kensington, 2011, pp. 2, 5.

3 Nichola Garvey, *A Sense of Purpose: Fortescue's 10-Year Journey 2003–2013*, Fortescue Metals, Perth, 2013, p. 123.

4 On the 'Climbing Men', see Mike Donaldson, *Burrup Rock Art: Ancient Aboriginal Rock Art of Burrup Peninsula and Dampier Archipelago*, Wildrocks Publications, Mount Lawley, Western Australia, 2009, pp. 177–85; Ken Mulvaney has documented ninety-three archaic faces in the Dampier Archipelago, with only forty-five known on the Australia mainland, fourteen of which can be found in the hills above Karratha.

5 Nicolas Rothwell, 'A Void Is Peopled Once Again', *The Weekend Australian*, 21 September 2013.

6 Denis Vairasse, 'The History of the Sevarites or Sevarambi (1677–1678)', in Umberto Eco, *The Book of Legendary Lands*, Quercus, London, 2013, p. 339.

7 Phillip Parker King, *Narrative of a Survey of the Inter-Tropical and Western Coasts of Australia, Vol. 1*, Marsden Horden & Friends of the State Library of Adelaide, 2002 (first published 1827), pp. xvi, 31, 37.

8 Today there is West Lewis Island and East Lewis Island. These would have looked as one from a distance.

9 King, pp. 29–49.

10 FT Gregory, Journal, 17 May and 12 October, in Augustus Charles Gregory and Francis Thomas Gregory, *Journals of Australian Explorations*, James C Beal, Government Printer, Brisbane, 1884, http://gutenberg.net.au/ebooks14/1402621h.html

11 ibid., Appendix.

12 Susan Hunt, *Spinifex and Hessian: Women's Lives in North-Western Australia 1860–1900*, UWA Press, Perth, 1986, pp. 14–15.

13 Seddon, p. 161.

14 On Aboriginal population of the north, ibid., p. 11; on Yaburara's population, see TJ Gara, *The Aborigines of the Dampier Archipelago: An Ethno-History of the Yaburara*, n.p., 1990–96, p. 1; on British sovereignty, see Geoffrey Bolton, *Land of Vision and Mirage: Western Australia Since 1826*, UWA Press, 2008, p. 5 & http://www.wanowandthen.com/Edmund-Lockyer.html

15 ibid., Gara, p. 41.

16 Richard Thatcher, 'The Pearl Station on the North West Coast', *The Herald* (Fremantle), 30 October 1869, p. 3 and ibid., Gara, p. 39.

17 Patricia Vinnicombe, *Dampier Archaeological Project: Resource Document, Survey and Salvage of Aboriginal Sites, Burrup Peninsula, Western Australia*, Western Australia Museum, 1987, p. 6.

18 'First Settlement in the North West', Diary of Charles Nairn, May 1863 – March 1864 (Karratha Library); numbers of sheep in the north sourced from information provided by Karijini Visitors' Centre, Karijini National Park, 2015.

19 ibid., Nairn.

20 Guy Wright & Leonie Stella, *Pearling in the Pilbara 1860s – 1890s,* Research Unit, Native Title Tribunal, 2003 (held at National Library of Australia), pp. 11–14.

21 'Swarms' of pearling boats, Alexander McRae, 1868, quoted in ibid., p. 12; pearls in Aboriginal culture, p. 9.

22 Wright & Stella, p. 1.

23 R. Sholl quoted in Gara, *The Aborigines of the Dampier Archipelago*, p. 16.

24 Wright & Stella, pp. 14–17.

25 Quoted in Gara, *The Aborigines of the Dampier Archipelago*, p. 11.

26 *The Inquirer and Commercial News* (Perth), 1 April 1863, p. 3; this includes the evidence of 'Jacky' and in a separate article, Sholl's report, and in another article, the report of Alexander McRae. Gara aside, the best account of the Flying Foam Massacre (and the early history of north-west Australia) is Kay Forrest, *The Challenge and the Chance: The Colonisation and Settlement of North West Australia 1861–1914*, Hesperian Press, Carlisle, Western Australia, 1996.

27 ibid., report of Alexander McRae.

28 Withnell's report is also published in *The Inquirer and Commercial News,* 1 April 1863, p. 3. Sholl's letter is quoted in Forrest, *The Challenge and the Chance*, p. 61.

29 Sholl in *Perth Gazette and WA Times*, 5 June 1868, p. 3.

30 Quoted in Tom Gara, 'The Flying Foam Massacre', in Moya Smith (ed.), *Archaeology at ANZAAS*, Western Australian Museum, 1983, pp. 90–1; Gara's article (pp. 86–94) is the most reliable article on the massacre. He was

the first to point out the fact that Withnell's party carried no chains or handcuffs to apprehend the murderers. He quotes both the Aboriginal evidence and Taylor. Also see Forrest, *The Challenge and the Chance*, p. 63.

31   McRae quoted in Wright & Stella, p. 18.

32   *Mount Alexander Mail*, 20 April 1868, p. 2.

33   Quoted in Noel Olive, *Enough Is Enough: A History of the Pilbara*, Fremantle Arts Centre Press, 2007, p. 55.

34   *Perth Gazette and WA Times*, 14 August 1868, p. 2; Rowland's trial (he received a 12-year sentence) is covered in Forrest, *The Challenge and the Chance*, p. 62; a useful list of the legislation relevant to Aboriginal people in WA in the nineteenth and twentieth centuries can be found at http://www.noongarculture.org.au/list-of-wa-legislation/

35   Charles Nairn, Diary, 28 May 1863.

36   Sholl quoted in Gara, 'The Flying Foam Massacre', p. 89; Parker's comments in court, *Perth Gazette and WA Times*, 14 August 1868, p. 2.

37   Wright & Stella, pp. 34, 38; Lieutenant Colonel Edward Fox Angelo, Government Resident at Roebourne (1883–86), wrote to Governor Broome, 10 April 1886, regarding the local pearling industry: 'I find here in full force a disguised and unquestionable system of slavery carried on under the protection of the British flag which it is impossible for me to battle single handed'.

38   Rev. JB Gribble, *Dark Deeds in a Sunny Land or Blacks and Whites in North-West Australia*, UWA Press, 1987, p. 47; in the appendix, see the essay by Sue-Jane Hunt, 'The Gribble Affair: A Study in Colonial Politics'.

39   AR Richardson to the editor, *The West Australian*, 7 November 1892, p. 3; on debate over Gribble's allegations, see *The West Australian*, 20 September 1886, p. 3; *Western Mail*, 25 September, 1886, p. 24.

40   ibid., Richardson.

41   Charles Harper to the editor, *The West Australian*, 9 November, 1892, p. 3.

42   AR Richardson to the editor, *The West Australian*, 7 November 1892, p. 3.

43   ibid.

44   *The West Australian*, 19 May 1898, p. 4.

45   John Slade Durlacher, *Landlords of the Iron Shore*, Hesperian Press, 2013, pp. 74–5.

46   'Mother of the North West', *The West Australian*, 17 May 1928, p. 17.

47   *The West Australian*, 5 August 1933, p. 5.

48   *WA Natives (Citizenship Rights) Act 1944*.

49   *The West Australian*, 23 November 1946, p. 5.

50   Gara, *The Aborigines of the Dampier Archipelago*, pp. 18–20.

51   Richard Thatcher, 'The Pearl Station on the North West Coast', *The Herald* (Fremantle), 30 October 1869, p. 3; in the 1993 documentary film *Exile and the Kingdom* it was claimed that the Yaburara were 'no more'; Withnell on tattooed figures in Mike Donaldson, *Burrup Rock Art*, p. 498.

52 Charles Court, 'Minister for Industrial Development and the North-West', in *Symposium on Northern Development: Pilbara Prospects in the 1970s*, Institute of Engineers, Perth, UWA, 1968, pp. 1–7.

53 RH Underwood (formerly MLA for the Pilbara), 'Populating the North', *The West Australian*, 5 August 1939, p. 19 and GW Miles, 'Australia's Unexplored Nor' West', *The West Australian*, 22 October 1922, p. 1.

54 Geologist HP Woodward, 1888, quoted in *The Pilbara: A Regional Profile Department of Industrial Development*, Pilbara Regional Office, Karratha, 1983, p. 9.

55 'Iron Export Embargo', *The West Australian*, 25 March 1938, p. 25.

56 Court quoted in *Know the Song, Know the Country: The Ngaardangarli Story of Culture and History in Ngarluma & Yindjibarndi Country*, Juluwarlu Aboriginal Corporation, Roebourne, 2004, p. 16.

57 HE Graham, Minister for Development and Decentralisation, in *Symposium on Northern Development: Pilbara Prospects in the 1970s*, p. 7; 'almost empty', GW Miles, *The West Australian*, 22 October 1922, p. 1.

58 Vinnicombe, p. 1.

59 Warwick Dix, Registrar of Aboriginal Sites at WA Museum, quoted in *Hammersley News*, 8 February 1973, p. 7.

60 WDL Ride & A Norman (eds), *Depuch Island: Report on the Aboriginal Engravings and Flora and Fauna of Depuch Island, Western Australia*, Western Australian Museum, Special Publication No. 2, Government Printer, Perth, 1964, pp. 19, 23.

61 Gara, *The Aborigines of the Dampier Archipelago*, p. 38.

62 Edgar Lewis, 'Foreword' to Ride & Norman (eds).

63 'Natural wealth', ibid.; K Mulvaney & W Hicks, 'Murujuga Madness: World Heritage Values Disregarded', *Proceedings of the First International Conference on Best Practices in World Heritage*, Archaeology Menorca, Spain, 2012, pp. 187–201.

64 *Hammersley News*, 8 February 1973, p. 7; on Bedarnik and Virili, see Nicolas Rothwell, 'Lines in the Sand', *The Weekend Australian*, 25–26 January 2003; on Hallam and others, see Andrew Burrell, 'On the Rocks', *Financial Review Magazine*, 29 February 2008.

65 *Pilbara News*, 7 July 2004; *The West Australian*, July 7 2004.

66 Alice Smith in *Know the Song, Know the Country*, p. 16.

67 Two of the best sources on local Indigenous history include *Know the Song, Know the Country* and the historical overview in the Shire of Roebourne's Local Government Heritage Inventory, Vol. 1, September 2013; also see the 1993 documentary film *Exile and the Kingdom* and Noel Olive's *Enough Is Enough: A History of the Pilbara Mob*, which contains several recollections and testaments from local Aboriginal people regarding the European invasion.

68 ibid., *Exile and the Kingdom*.

69 *Fred Williams' Pilbara: Images from the North West*, Rio Tinto, Hamersley Iron and UWA, 1998 (exhibition catalogue Lawrence Wilson Art Gallery, UWA, 6 November 1998), p. 16; Williams produced two paintings of Mount Nameless, one 'Morning', the other, 'Afternoon'.

70 Quote sourced from display at Karijini Visitors' Centre, November 2015.

71 http://www.namelessfestival.com.au/behind-the-scenes/history-of-the-festival.aspx

72 *Exile and the Kingdom.*

73 On the new Indigenous mining entrepreneurs, see Russell Skelton, 'Dreamtime, Boomtime', *The Sydney Morning Herald*, 6 March 2013, pp. 22–3.

74 Hicks quoted in Andrew Burrell, 'On the Rocks', *Financial Review Magazine*, 29 February 2008.

75 ibid.; also see Ken Mulvaney, *Murujuga Marni: Rock Art of the Macropod Hunters and Mollusc Harvesters*, UWAP, 2015, pp. xi, 17–18.

76 *The West Australian*, 4 May 2007, p. 5.

77 WA Premier Alan Carpenter in *The West Australian*, 31 August 2006.

78 Ken Mulvaney quoted in Andrew Burrell, 'Pressure on Woodside over Threat to Ancient Art', *Financial Review*, 8 September 2006.

79 On vandalism of sites, see *Pilbara News*, 13 September 2006; *The West Australian*, 3 October 2007; *The West Australian*, 13 January 2009; the latter two feature WA Greens MP Robin Chappie, a long-time champion of Murujuga's rock art and the campaign for World Heritage listing.

80 Robert Bedarnik, 'Dampier Report', in *AURA, Newsletter of the Australian Rock Art Research Association*, Vol. 21, No. 2, 2004, pp. 14–15.

81 Hicks quoted in Gerry Georgatos, 'Pilbara's Yaburara People Remember One of Australia's Largest Massacres', *The Stringer: Independent News*, 1 March 2014, http://thestringer.com.au/pilbaras-yaburara-people-remember-one-of-australias-largest-massacres-6749#.VrgOV84eXdk

82 ibid., Georgatos; also see *Pilbara Echo*, 22 February 2013, http://www.pilbaraecho.com.au/2013/02/22/the-flying-foam-massacre-remembered/

83 Ken Mulvaney, *Murujuga Marni*, p. 349.

84 Barnett pleading he wasn't told of the area's significance, in Burrell, 'Pressure on Woodside over Threat to Ancient Art'; Barnett on the 'greatest cultural heritage site', in Griffin Longley, 'Gas v Art: Civilisations Collide in WA's North-West', Weekend Extra, *The West Australian*, 30 September 2006; also see Carmen Lawrence, 'The Limits of Dominion: Custodians on the Edge', in Looking West, *Griffith Review*, 47, 2015, pp. 32–46; and in the same issue, Ken Mulvaney, 'Ancient Treasures: Past and Present on the Dampier Archipelago', pp. 233–50; Anna Haebich, 'From the Edge of the Edge', pp. 11–17; and Rebecca Giggs, 'Open Ground: Trespassing on the Mining Boom', pp. 18–31; also see Nicolas Rothwell, 'Soundings', in *Journey to the Interior*, Black Inc., Melbourne, 2010, pp. 216–25.

Chapter 4 On Grassy Hill: Gangaar (Cooktown), North Queensland

1   Raymond Evans, *A History of Queensland*, Cambridge University Press, 2007, p. 19; for the crab analogy, see 'Badtjala Song', translated by Gemma Cronin, in Lisa Chandler (ed.), *East Coast Encounter: Re-imagining 1770*, One Day Hill, Collingwood, Victoria, 2014, p. 10.

2   From Eric Deeral's text, panel, James Cook Museum, Cooktown, 2016; Cook, 17 June 1770, in Ray Parkin (ed.), *H.M. Bark Endeavour*, Miegunyah, Melbourne 2006 (1997), pp. 329–30.

3   George Dalrymple, October 1873, in *The Best Life I Ever Had: Droving around Cooktown*, Cooktown Shire Council, 2003, pp. 1–2.

4   'Cooktown: A Historical Spot', *The Queenslander*, 26 June 1897, p. 28.

5   Whalers, *The Western Champion*, 11 March 1922, p. 16; steamers, *Cairns Post*, 23 November 1938, p. 13.

6   Cook, 30 June 1770, in Parkin (ed.), p. 344.

7   Nancy Francis, 'Captain Cook and Cooktown', *Cairns Post*, 3 October 1933, p. 3 and 'Cooktown, a Historical Spot', *The Queenslander*, 26 June 1897, p. 28.

8   I am indebted to Alberta Hornsby for traditional Guugu Yimithirr names; Alberta to me, Cooktown, April 2016; also see http://www.fatsilc.org.au/languages/language-of-the-month/lotm-1996-to-2000/1997-jul---alberta-hornsby-

9   'Life in Cape York Peninsula', *The Age*, 18 December 1954, p. 13.

10 Phillip Parker King, *Narrative of a Survey of the Inter-Tropical and Western Coasts of Australia Vol. 1*, Friends of the State Library of South Australia (first published 1827), Adelaide, 2012, pp. 223–4.

11 Parkin (ed.), p. 317.

12 Francis, p. 3; the log resides today in the James Cook Museum in Cooktown.

13 ibid.

14 Frank Reid, 'Historic Relics', *The Sunday Mail*, 27 December 1931.

15 *The New York Times*, 13 January 1969, p. 1.

16 SE Stephens & Sir Raphael Cilento, Introduction to *Cooktown and Its Museum*, National Trust of Queensland, The James Cook Historical Museum and Joseph Banks Garden, 1976, p. 1.

17 Deeral's reflection, Alberta Hornsby to me, Cooktown, April 2016; Noel Pearson, *Up from the Mission: Selected Writings*, Black Inc., Melbourne 2009, p. 12.

18 George Dalrymple, in SE Stephens, 'The Endeavour River and Cooktown', *Queensland Heritage*, Vol. 2, No. 2, 1970, p. 23, https://espace.library.uq.edu.au/view/UQ:246239/Qld_heritage_v2_no2_1970_p23_p30.pdf

19 First edition of the *Cooktown Independent*, Friday 6 June 1884; also see Suzanne Falkiner & Alan Oldfield, *Lizard Island: The Journey of Mary Watson*, Allen & Unwin, Sydney, p. 33.

20   ibid., Falkiner & Oldfield; 'next capital', Geoff Weingarth, in Gretchen Miller (producer), 'Cook in Cooktown', RN 'Earshot', 15 September 2015, http://www.abc.net.au/radionational/programs/earshot/captain-cook-and-endeavour-in-cooktown/6723770; 'Canton of the South', Stephens & Cilento, p. 9.

21   'Sketches at Cooktown', *The Illustrated Sydney News*, 30 May 1874, p. 18.

22   ibid.; also see *Cooktown Independent*, Friday 6 June 1884.

23   *The Sydney Morning Herald*, 9 May 1936, p. 13.

24   Quoted in Belinda McKay, 'Constructing a Life on the Northern Frontier: E. A. C. Olive of Cooktown', *Queensland Review*, Vol. 7, No. 2, 2000, online version p. 3; also see her general discussion of the frontier, pp. 1–3, http://www98.griffith.edu.au/dspace/bitstream/handle/10072/3231/E?sequence=1

25   *Brisbane Courier*, 12 May 1876, p. 2.

26   *The Cooktown Courier*, 5 December 1874.

27   James V Mulligan, *Guide to the Palmer River and Normandy Goldfields, North Queensland*, George Slater, Brisbane, 1875, p. 8.

28   'race war', *Brisbane Courier*, 26 November 1880, p. 2.

29   Quoted in Falkiner & Oldfield, p. 31.

30   'The Northern Blacks and Our Native Police Force', *The Queensland Figaro*, 22 November 1884, p. 15; also see Robert Ormston, The Rise and Fall of a Frontier Mining Town, PhD, University of Queensland, May 1996, p. 111, http://espace.library.uq.edu.au/view/UQ:189317; & 'pay dearly', *Goulburn Herald*, 7 March 1874, p. 2.

31   *The Cooktown Courier*, 3 October 1874, syndicated in *Northern Argus*, 20 October 1874, p. 3.

32   Raymond Evans, 'Across the Queensland Frontier', in Bain Attwood & Stephen Foster (eds), *Frontier Conflict: The Australian Experience*, National Museum of Australia, 2003, p. 66.

33   *The Cooktown Courier*, 28 February 1877, in Raymond Evans, 'Plenty Shoot 'Em': The Destruction of Aboriginal Societies along the Queensland Frontier', in A Dirk Moses (ed.), *Genocide and Settler Society: Frontier Violence and Stolen Indigenous Children in Australian History*, Berghan, 2004, p. 157.

34   On Chinese, see John Shay (ed.), *Cooktown through the Years*, Cooktown and District Historical Society, 2009, pp. 48–52.

35   *Cooktown Herald*, 8 December 1875, p. 2; 'murderously hostile', *Goulburn Herald*, 7 March 1874, p. 2.

36   'The Northern Blacks and Our Native Police Force', *The Queensland Figaro*, 22 November 1884, p. 15.

37   *Brisbane Courier*, 26 November 1880, p. 2.

38   ibid.

39   *The Cooktown Courier*, editorial, 28 February 1877.

40   Quoted in Falkiner & Oldfield, p. 34.

41   William J Sowden, *The Northern Territory as It Is: A Narrative of the South Australian Parliamentary Party's Trip and Full Description of the Northern Territory; Its Settlements and Industries*, WK Thomas & Co., Adelaide, 1882; https://archive.org/stream/northernterritor00sowd/northernterritor00sowd_djvu.txt

42   CH Tongue, memoir, December 1884 – February 1885, transcribed by S Tongue in May 2010, John Oxley Library, Brisbane.

43   ibid.

44   John and Leslie Haviland, 'How Much Food Will There Be in Heaven? Lutherans and Aborigines around Cooktown to 1900', *Aboriginal History*, Vol. 4, No. 2, 1980, p. 126, http://press.anu.edu.au/wp-content/uploads/2016/01/article07.pdf

45   'The Cooktown Blacks', *The Queenslander*, 16 February 1889, p. 302.

46   One of the best examples of this humanitarian concern can be found in *The Queenslander*, 20 November 1880, p. 656.

47   Noel Pearson, *Up from the Mission*, p. 12.

48   Noel Pearson, 'A Rightful Place: Race, Recognition and a More Complete Commonwealth', *Quarterly Essay*, 55, 2014, p. 28.

49   Noel Loos, *Invasion and Resistance: Aboriginal European Relations on the North Queensland Frontier 1861–1897*, ANU Press, Canberra, 1982, pp. 82–4.

50   'Blacks Troublesome, Cape York to Jardine River', *The Telegraph* [Brisbane], 3 April 1905, p. 7; on the extent of the conflict in the Cooktown area, also see I Hughes, 'A State of Open Warfare: Frontier Conflict in the Cooktown Area', Chapter Three in Lectures in North Queensland History, Second Series, James Cook University, 1975, pp. 31–46, http://www.textqueensland.com.au/item/chapter/6b11274f2d6059029f9f29b66d6d9e34

51   MJ Morwood & DR Hobbs (eds), 'Quinkan Prehistory: The Archaeology of Aboriginal Art in Southeast Cape York Peninsula', Australia, *Tempus*, Vol. 3, 1995, p. 65.

52   Kim McKenzie & Carol Cooper, 'Eyewitness? Drawings by Oscar of Cooktown, in *Gold: Forgotten Histories and Lost Objects of Australia*, edited by Iain McCalman, Alexander Cook and Andrew Reeves, Cambridge University Press, 2001, pp. 157–63.

53   WGF Poland, *Loose Leaves: Reminiscences of a Pioneer North Queensland Missionary*, Lutheran Publishing, Adelaide, 1988, p. 38.

54   Text from Panel, James Cook Museum, Cooktown, 2016.

55   Noel Pearson, 1994 Hancock Lecture, p. 117, http://www.humanities.org.au/Portals/0/documents/Events/Lectures/Hancock/txt/Hancock1994.pdf

56   *Queensland Times, Ipswich Herald and General Advertiser*, 16 September 1890, p. 6.

57   *The Cooktown Courier*, 3 October 1874, syndicated in *Northern Argus*, 20 October 1874, p. 3; *The Maitland Mercury*, 21 November 1874, p. 4;

and 'Constructing National Histories: Perpetrator Narration and the Desire for Victimhood', in Bain Attwood and Stephen Foster (eds), *Frontier Conflict: The Australian Experience*, National Museum of Australia, Canberra, 2003, pp. 185–200.

58 ibid., *The Cooktown Courier*; and *Cooktown Herald Palmer River Advertiser*, 1 July 1874, p. 2.

59 Droughts and lives in jeopardy, 'The Northern Blacks and Our Native Police Force', *The Queensland Figaro*, 22 November 1884, p. 15; floods, *Goulburn Herald*, 7 March 1874, p. 2; 'pathless forest' and 'Anglo-Saxon energy', *The Cooktown Courier*, editorial, 23 May 1874.

60 *Goulburn Herald*, 7 March 1874; also see I Hughes, 'A State of Open Warfare: Frontier Conflict in the Cooktown Area', p. 38, where he quotes *The Cooktown Courier* arguing that 'a hardworking man' cannot be to 'blame' for 'an indiscriminate act of slaughter' against the Aborigines.

61 *The Cooktown Courier*, 5 June 1874.

62 ibid.

63 On annexation, see Denver Beanland, *The Queensland Caesar*, Brisbane, 2013, p. 167.

64 *Cooktown Independent*, 6 June 1884.

65 *Cooktown Independent*, syndicated in *The Queenslander*, 16 February 1889, p. 302.

66 *Cooktown Herald*, 3 February 1877.

67 McKay, p. 2.

68 'The Blacks at Cooktown', *Northern Star* (Lismore), 17 March 1877, p. 3.

69 Falkiner & Oldfield, pp. 80–3.

70 *The Sydney Morning Herald*, 8 December 1881, p. 5.

71 Willie Gordon with Judy Bennett, *Guurrbi: My Family & Other Stories*, Guurrbi Tours, Cooktown, 2012, p. 30.

72 A brief summary of the Watson story can be found in Ivana McAlpine, *Mary Watson*, Imdesign, Sydney, 2004; the best account is Falkiner & Oldfield, *Lizard Island*.

73 ibid., McAlpine, 'Death'.

74 *The Queensland Figaro*, 22 November 1884, p. 15.

75 Watson's diary, reproduced in *The Argus*, 8 August 1953, p. 8; alternatively, see McIver.

76 *The Queensland Figaro*, 22 November 1884, p. 15; *Barrier Miner*, 5 June 1935, p. 5; *Darling Downs Gazette*, 10 February 1882, p. 5.

77 Phillip Parker King, 2 August 1820, in *Narrative of a Survey of the Inter-Tropical and Western Coasts of Australia Vol. 1*, p. 375.

78 Stephens & Cilento, p. 12.

79 *Barrier Miner*, 5 June 1935, p. 5.

80 Examples of the Watson story: 'An Australian Heroine', *The Dawn*, 1 June 1893, p. 8; 'Lizard Island Tragedy: The 28th Anniversary of the Death of Mrs. Watson and Infant', *Gympie Times and Mary River Mining Gazette*, 23 October 1909, p. 5; 'Heroine of Lizard Island: Epic Story of Mary Watson Fought off Cannibals only to Die a Tortuous Death from Thirst on a Lonely Coral Isle', *Truth* (Brisbane), 10 April 1927, p. 15; *The Worker* (Brisbane), 23 September 1931, p. 5; *The Telegraph* (Brisbane), 23 January 1932, p. 11; and *The Argus*, 15 October 1955, p. 6.

81 http://www.janesoceania.com/australia_aboriginal_history/index1.htm

82 *Brisbane Courier*, 26 November 1880, p. 2.

83 'Oral history of Cape York', compiled by Duncan Jackson, Cooktown Shire Council, 1989, Cooktown Library.

84 *The Queenslander*, 26 June 1897, p. 28.

85 John Shay (ed.), *Cooktown through the Years*, p. 72.

86 Hugh Henry, 'Cooktown Then and Now', *The Sydney Morning Herald*, 1 November 1941, p. 11.

87 'Palmer Gold Diggings: J. A. Binnie's Memoirs', *Townsville Daily Bulletin*, 11 June 1953, p. 7; 'Cooktown: Spencer Browne's Memoirs', *Townsville Daily Bulletin*, 11 December 1952, p. 6.

88 'non-Aboriginal space', in McKay, p. 13; 'all these people gone', the words of Roger Hart, in John B Haviland with Roger Hart, *Old Man Fog and the Last Aborigines of Barrow Point*, Crawford House, Bathurst (Smithsonian Institute, 1998), p. 161.

89 ibid., Haviland & Hart, p. 162.

90 John Shay (ed.), *Cooktown through the Years*, p. 59.

91 Eric Deeral's remarks appear on a panel in the James Cook Museum, Cooktown; Noel Pearson, *A Rightful Place*, pp. 24–7, and *Up from the Mission*, pp. 14–16, 26–7, 32–4.

92 Eric Deeral, interviewed by Phillip Connors, 28 September 1999, held at National Library of Australia, TRC 5000/58; also see Haviland & Hart, pp. 133–4.

93 Alberta Hornsby to me, Cooktown, April 2016; Noel Pearson, *A Rightful Place*, p. 27; on white victimhood in Australian history, see the two key works by Ann Curthoys, 'Whose Home? Expulsion, Exodus, and Exile in White Australian Historical Mythology', *Journal of Australian Studies*, No. 61, 1999, 1–18.

94 Geoff Weingarth, in Gretchen Miller (producer), 'Cook in Cooktown', Radio National, 'Earshot', 15 September 2015.

95 Alberta Hornsby explained to me that Yaparico was not in fact his name, but meant 'older brother'.

96 All of this section is drawn from Cook's and Banks's journals, 16 June – 19 July 1770, in Parkin (ed.), pp. 328–70; also, Phillip Parker King, p. 212–26,

364–74; one of the best sources on Cook is Nicholas Thomas, *Discoveries: The Voyages of Captain Cook*, Allen Lane, Penguin, London, 2003.

97   *The Canberra Times*, 14 July 1973, p. 11.

98   'Life in the Cape York Peninsula', *The Age*, 18 December 1954, p. 13.

99   'Australia's Land of Mystery: Cape York Peninsula', *Chronicle* (Adelaide), 27 December 1934, p. 44; *The Australian Women's Weekly*, 16 September 1981, p. 14.

100 *The Canberra Times*, 20 March 1990, p. 6.

101 Gordon Grimwade & Anne Meiklejohn, *Cooktown Heritage Study Volume 1*, Resource Consultancy Services, Cairns, 1993, p. 20; Bev Shay (ed.), *50 Years of Discovery Festival and Re-enactment at Cooktown*, Cooktown Historical Society, 2009, p. 1.

102 *The Canberra Times*, 14 January 1970, p. 8.

103 The Cooktown Historical Society has a permanent exhibition in Cooktown, which includes text on the 1970 royal visit; also see John Shay (ed.), *Cooktown through the Years*, pp. 78–9.

104 ibid.; also see the Queen's speeches 1954–1992, MS 9174, National Library of Australia.

105 Grimwade & Meiklejohn, p. 20 and Bev Shay (ed.), *50 Years of Discovery Festival and Re-enactment at Cooktown*, p. 1.

106 Queen Elizabeth's speech in Melbourne, 6 April 1970, in MS9174, National Library of Australia.

107 'Oral History of Cape York', compiled by Duncan Jackson, Cooktown Shire Council, 1989, Cooktown Library.

108 Cooktown Historical Society, permanent exhibition, Cooktown.

109 *The Australian Women's Weekly*, 13 September 1967; also see Bev Shay (ed.), *50 Years of Discovery Festival and Re-enactment at Cooktown*, p. 5.

110 Alberta Hornsby to me, Cooktown, April 2016.

111 Bev Shay (ed.), *50 Years of Discovery Festival and Re-enactment at Cooktown*, pp. 13–14.

112 John McDonald to me, April 2016.

113 Phillip Goad, 'Cultural Endeavours', January 2002, http://architectureau. com/articles/cultural-endeavours/

114 Alberta Hornsby to me, Cooktown, April 2016.

115 Eric Deeral, interviewed by Phillip Connors, 28 September 1999, held at National Library of Australia, TRC 5000/58.

116 Alberta Hornsby & Loretta Sullivan to me, Cooktown, April 2016.

117 On the dictionary, Alberta to me, Cooktown, April 2016; as an 'unlettered historian', 'Cook in Cooktown', Radio National, 'Earshot', 15 September 2015.

118 Eric Deeral's text as it stands today in the James Cook Museum, Cooktown; Alberta Hornsby's text; Alberta Hornsby to me (authorised by Alberta)

2016; Eric Deeral's text is also reproduced in Lisa Chandler (ed.), *East Coast Encounter*, pp. 28–31. I have left spelling discrepancies as they stand in the originals.

119 Cook on the country, 4 August 1770, in Parkin (ed.), p. 386; and claiming possession, 22 August 1770, p. 442.

120 Eric Deeral, text, James Cook Museum, Cooktown.

121 Loretta Sullivan, Radio National, 'Earshot', 15 September 2015.

122 John McDonald to me, April 2016.

123 Alberta Hornsby to me, Cooktown, April 2016.

124 Iain McCalman, email to me, July 2014.

125 Eric Deeral, interviewed by Phillip Connors, 28 September 1999, held at National Library of Australia, TRC 5000/58.

126 ibid.; and Alberta Hornsby to me, Cooktown, April 2016; Noel Pearson on his layered identity, *A Rightful Place*, pp. 29–32; for an inspiring example of the work of one Cooktown resident, painter and botanical collector Vera Scarth-Johnson, see her *National Treasure: Flowering Plants of Cooktown and Northern Australia*, Vera Scarth-Johnson Gallery Association, Cooktown, 2000; where possible, Vera sourced the Aboriginal names for all the plants she collected.

Acknowledgements

From the Edge is the first of two books that explore Australian history through place. Over the last four years, I've travelled to the far corners and centre of the continent in an attempt to write these histories from the ground up. Each place demanded a different angle and approach. The road in was not always easy to find. I had to write both from the inside and the outside. I had to be true to each place. And there was always more to know. The more research I did, the more the history of each place expanded. Without the generous support of friends, colleagues and my family, it would have been impossible to find the necessary time to travel and write.

To my fellow travellers—John Blay, Edwin Ride, Ben Armstrong, Christine Freudenstein, Moya McKenna, John Carrick, Geraldine McKenna, Iain McCalman and my family, Fiona, Siobhan and Claire—thank you! Sally Heath at MUP read chapter drafts as they appeared and supported me from the inception of the project. The close working relationship I've developed with Sally, Louise Adler and MUP over the last six years has made an enormous difference to my work. The same applies to my literary agent, Lyn Tranter, who has supported my work since 2006. Thanks, too, to copyeditor Meaghan Amor.

Every work of history is the product of a community of scholarship that stretches far beyond the author's place and time. I owe a great debt to the work of many historians and writers who have provided me with valuable research, insights and advice. Conversations have mattered as much as words on the page. John Blay, Iain McCalman, Peter Read, Bruce Birch and Ken Mulvaney read chapter drafts and provided valuable feedback. As well as my friends and colleagues mentioned above, I would also like to thank Tom Griffiths, Ann Curthoys, John Docker, Stuart Ward, Jan Bruck, Henry Reynolds, Drusilla Modjeska, James Curran, James Warden, William Mulligan, Frank Bongiorno, Alan Atkinson, Shane White, Sheila Fitzpatrick, Ben Wellings, Shanti Sumartojo and Bain Attwood. John Mulvaney's path-breaking book *Encounters in Place* (1989) has been a constant source of inspiration.

From 2012, an Australian Research Council Future Fellowship gave me valuable research and writing time. I've also been fortunate to work in an extremely supportive and collegial environment—the University of Sydney's History Department. There are a number of people who deserve special thanks. On the 1797 walk: John Blay, Grace Karskens, Kirsten McKenzie, James Luddington and the Queen Victoria Museum, Launceston. In Scotland, Angus Martin and Jean Glen and the National Archives of Scotland in Glasgow. On Port Essington: Bruce Birch, Edwin Ride, Warwick Anderson, Robert Aldrich, Nick Eckstein, Francoise Barr at the Northern Territory Archives, Michael Wells, Peter Gartlan, Ros Coggan, Darwin and the Propaganda Fide Archives, Vatican City, Rome. On the Burrup Peninsula and the Pilbara: Ken Mulvaney, Mark O'Neil, Mandy Leeming, Brad Beaumont and Sally Culver at the Karratha Library. On Cooktown: Alberta Hornsby, Loretta Sullivan, John MacDonald, Iain McCalman, Ray Evans, Catherine McGrath, Russell McGregor, Kate Eastick at the James Cook Museum and Diana Burns at Cooktown Library.

Finally, heartfelt thanks to my friends and extended family who have listened patiently to my stories over the last four years: Ockert and Meiri Meyer, Ross Gengos, Michael Joyce, Martin Dwyer, Catherine McGrath, Sharon Ride, Rory Slater, Lyn Turner, Mark and Ingrid O'Neill, Phil and Kimberley Dodd, Sue Hill, Martin Harris, Louise Hopson, Tim O'Rourke, Brad Tarlington, Robert Morrell, Dirk Neldner, Odette Bereska, Ronald Kruger, Dave Clarke, Jennifer Balint, Peter and Genief Koutsoukis, Alastair McKenna and Clare Branch,

Chris McKenna, Deborah Hoffman, Adrian McKenna, Kieran and Carolyn McKenna, Virginia and Steve Churchill and Kathleen Dowse.

The photographs throughout this book are by Mark McKenna with the following exceptions: Eyeing the Country—Botany Bay, New South Wales 2004, Jesse Allen, Digital Globe. Chapter One— Nadgee River, with permission, John Blay. Chapter Two—Turkey Bush, with permission, Edwin Ride; 'Specimen of the Aboriginal Language or Short Conversation with the Natives of North Australia', Port Essington, 1847, with permission, Propaganda Fide Archives, Vatican City, Rome; Oswald Brierly, *Native Bier, Port Essington* (1853), image extracted from page 526 of *A Visit to the Indian Archipelago, in H.M.S. Meander, with Portions of the Private Journal of Sir James Brooke* by Henry Keppel, original held and digitised by the British Library, see https://commons.wikimedia.org/wiki/Category:A_ visit_to_the_Indian_Archipelago_(1853)_by_KEPPEL#/ media/File:KEPPEL_(1853)_pg526_NATIVE_BIER,_PORT_ ESSINGTON.jpg. Chapter Three—Rio Control Room, Perth, with permission, Rio Tinto; Climbing Men and Karratha Gas Plant, with permission, John Blay; Fred Williams, *Mount Nameless, Afternoon 1979*, with permission, Lyn Williams. Chapter Four—Charlotte Street, Cooktown, Courthouse, Grassy Hill, and Queen Elizabeth on the steps of the James Cook Museum, all three images with permission, James Cook Museum and the National Trust, and Eric Deeral, with permission Nellie Pratt/Newspix.

As I turn to write the second book, I know the conversations with my family, friends and colleagues will continue to sustain me.

April 2016

Index

THE MIEGUNYAH PRESS

This book was designed by Patrick Cannon
The text was typeset by Cannon Typesetting
The text was set in 11½ point Bembo with 15 points of leading
The text is printed on 120gsm woodfree

This book was edited by Meaghan Amor

THE
MIEGUNYAH
PRESS